W9-BEV-420

Education-Based Incarceration and Recidivism

The Ultimate Social Justice Crime-Fighting Tool

A Volume in
Educational Leadership for Social Justice

Series Editor:
Jeffrey S. Brooks
University of Missouri

Educational Leadership for Social Justice

Jeffrey S. Brooks, Series Editor

Leadership for Social Justice:
Promoting Equity and Excellence Through Inquiry and
Reflective Practice (2008)
edited by Anthony H. Normore

Bridge Leadership: Connecting Educational Leadership
and Social Justice to Improve Schools (2009)
edited by Autumn K. Tooms and Christa Boske

The Emperor Has No Clothes: Teaching About Race and Racism
to People Who Don't Want to Know (2010)
by Tema Okun

Educational Leaders Encouraging the Intellectual
and Professional Capacity of Others: A Social Justice Agenda (2011)
edited by Elizabeth Murakami-Ramalho and Anita McCoskey Pankake

Education-Based Incarceration and Recidivism:
The Ultimate Social Justice Crime-Fighting Tool (2012)
edited by Brian D. Fitch and Anthony H. Normore

Education-Based Incarceration and Recidivism

The Ultimate Social Justice Crime-Fighting Tool

Edited by

Brian D. Fitch
Los Angeles County Sheriff's Department
Inmate Services Bureau

and

Anthony H. Normore
California State University Dominguez Hills

Information Age Publishing, Inc.
Charlotte, North Carolina • www.infoagepub.com

Library of Congress Cataloging-in-Publication Data

Education-based incarceration and recidivism : the ultimate social justice
crime-fighting tool / edited by Brian D. Fitch, Los Angeles County Sherriff's Depart-
ment, Inmate Services Bureau, and Anthony H. Normore, California State
University Dominguez Hills.
 pages cm. — (Educational leadership for social justice)
 Includes bibliographical references.
 ISBN 978-1-61735-710-7 (paperback)—ISBN 978-1-61735-711-4 (hardcover)—
ISBN 978-1-61735-712-1 (ebook)
 1. Recidivism—Prevention. 2. Social justice. I. Fitch, Brian D. II.
Normore, Anthony H.
 HV6049.E38 2012
 365'.666—dc23

                                                                        2011045671

Copyright © 2012 IAP–Information Age Publishing, Inc.

All rights reserved. No part of this publication may be reproduced, stored in a retrieval
system, or transmitted in any form or by any electronic or mechanical means, or by
photocopying, microfilming, recording or otherwise without written permission from
the publisher.

Printed in the United States of America

CONTENTS

PART III: PROMISING AND PROVEN
"BEST PRACTICES": GLOBAL PERSPECTIVES

PART IV: IMPLICATIONS FOR THE FUTURE
OF CORRECTIONAL EDUCATION

SERIES EDITOR'S PREFACE

Jeffrey S. Brooks

I am pleased to serve as series editor for this book series, *Educational Leadership for Social Justice*, with Information Age Publishing. The idea for this series grew out of the work of a committed group of leadership for scholars associated with the American Educational Research Association's (AERA) Leadership for Social Justice Special Interest Group (SIG). This group existed for many years before being officially affiliated with AERA, and has benefitted greatly from the ongoing leadership, support, and counsel of Dr. Catherine Marshall (University of North Carolina-Chapel Hill). It is also important to acknowledge the contributions of the SIG's first president, Dr. Ernestine Enomoto (University of Hawaii at Manoa), whose wisdom, stewardship, and guidance helped ease a transition into AERA's more formal organizational structures. This organizational change was at times difficult to reconcile with scholars who largely identified as nontraditional thinkers and push toward innovation rather than accept the status quo. As the second chair of the SIG, I appreciate all of Ernestine's hard work and friendship.

I am particularly indebted to my colleagues on the SIG's first publications committee, which I chaired from 2005-2007: Dr. Denise Armstrong, Brock University; Dr. Ira Bogotch, Florida Atlantic University; Dr. Sandra Harris, Lamar University; Dr. Whitney Sherman, Virginia Commonwealth University, and; Dr. George Theoharis, Syracuse University. This committee was a joy to work with and I am pleased we have found many more ways to collaborate as we seek to provide publication opportunities for scholarship in the area of leadership for social justice.

Education-Based Incarceration and Recidivism:
The Ultimate Social Justice Crime-Fighting Tool, pp. vii–viii
Copyright © 2012 by Information Age Publishing
All rights of reproduction in any form reserved.

This book, by Brian D. Fitch and Anthony H. Normore, the sixth in the series, breaks new ground by connecting many ideas to educational leadership that have traditionally been discussed as part of leaders' context. We are exited to help provide a forum for this important work in the ongoing conversation about equity and excellence in education, and the role(s) that leadership can assume in educational organizations.

Again, welcome to this fourth book in this Information Age Publishing series, *Educational Leadership for Social Justice*. You can learn more about the series at our website: http://www.infoagepub.com/series/Educational-Leadership-for-Social-Justice. I invite you to contribute your own work on equity and influence to the series. We look forward to you joining the conversation.

PROLOGUE

Brian D. Fitch and Anthony H. Normore

Education-Based Incarceration and Recidivism: The Ultimate Social Justice Crime-Fighting Tool takes a penetrating look at the needs and challenges of society's disenfranchised—the denizens of our streets, the emotionally and physically incarcerated, our children in juvenile hall and in unsettled homes. We believe that it is incumbent to encourage public awareness of the causes that underlie the destructive cycles plaguing these populations, including the abuse and neglect that cycle through generations. When effectively addressed through education the economic burden on society is lightened and an advocacy to increase understanding engenders a humane response. In our efforts to connect educational-based incarceration to leadership and social justice, several issues come to mind, beginning with the universal understanding that definitions of social justice are based on a variety of factors, like political orientation, religious background, and political and social philosophy. Consequently, a general definition of social justice is hard to arrive at and even harder to implement. However, an increased body of researchers in educational leadership, ethics law, sociology, criminal justice, and public health agree that social justice is concerned with equal justice, not just in the courts, but in all aspects of society whereby everyone, from the poorest person on the margins of society to the wealthiest deserves an even playing field.

With this in mind, we build on a relatively new and emerging body of research in education—namely interdisciplinary research focused on education-based incarceration programs, corrections education, and its relation to social justice. Of particular interest to the editors and contributors of this volume is the fact that school systems may at times fail to recognize

Education-Based Incarceration and Recidivism:
The Ultimate Social Justice Crime-Fighting Tool, pp. ix–xiii
Copyright © 2012 by Information Age Publishing
All rights of reproduction in any form reserved.

that inmates in county jails and prisons are relatives of our school children. Hence, collaboratively designed education programs among those who serve the needs of both the children and their inmate relatives could lead to safer communities and productive lives. Camp (2007) asserted that researchers, policymakers, and educational program administrators in the field of corrections must remember that the purpose of education is rehabilitation intended to enhance social order and public safety and that "one could surmise that it is necessary that the proper design of prerelease materials be provided to the offenders for the purposes of helping them become law-abiding citizens and preventing them from recidivating" (p. 51). Camp suggested that jails and prisons should increase opportunities for offenders to be released as law-abiding citizens. Hence, it would behoove researchers, policy makers, and educational program administrators to examine curricula for adult offenders to see if they provide information that aid offenders in becoming law-abiding citizens. Such research would provide "opportunities for correctional facilities to learn how to maximize their correctional training or rehabilitative functions" (p. 196) while simultaneously providing educationally sound programs to marginalized populations in support of social and restorative justice.

Because this book provides an evidence-based research foundation for reducing recidivism, enhancing jail security, and increasing public safety, it should be of great interest to anyone interested in equal justice, lowering recidivism and reducing crime, including law enforcement and correctional institutions nationwide, as well as educational institutions interested in programs that promote education for the greater good, public safety, public health, and correctional reform. This collection of chapters is based on the collaborative efforts of a multicultural member taskforce with vested interests in education-based incarceration. The contributors represent a myriad of disciplines including law enforcement, criminal justice, corrections education, and university departments of educational leadership, special education, political science, psychology, assessment and evaluation.

The book is comprised of 11 chapters and organized into four parts. Each part focuses on a specific theme. Part I contains three chapters around "The Culture and Politics of Corrections: A Social Justice Phenomenon." In Chapter 1, Brian D. Fitch and Rakel Delevi examine the case for education-based incarceration. These authors explore why evidence-based incarceration is not only a viable, but highly cost effective method for reducing crime and recidivism. They discuss the social, institutional, and human capital outcomes of investing in correctional education. Chapter 2 focuses on the history and politics of correctional education. Amy Widestrom, David Werner and Sylvester "Bud" Pues document the history of education in jails and prisons, the theories of education that work in the carceral environment, and the politics that drive the debate around providing education to those incarcerated. Chapter 3 is presented by Brian D. Fitch, Jeff Mulhaussen, and Brian Mattson. These authors conceptualize how education-based technologies may be integrated with other technology in the justice system to help agencies determine what educational content and technical approaches work for different inmate populations to achieve a variety of individual and system outcomes. The chapter concludes with a presentation of disruptive technologies that are being explored through the education-based incarceration initiative and the benefits these innovations afford incarcerated individuals.

Part II is comprised of four chapters with focus on the "Human Side of Education-Based Incarceration: Understanding Recidivism." David Werner, Amy Widestrom, and Sylvester Pues extend their work in Chapter 4 by examining the characteristics of the prisoner-student and the environment and influences shaping their educative experience while incarcerated, includes an examination of the specific accommodations that must be made to offer an education program in a jail or prison environment. The authors give special consideration to the educational needs and problems of the jail inmate, where wide variations in length of stay exacerbate the considerable problems of prison education. Raquel Warley confronts the impact of correctional staff attitudes on inmate education in Chapter 5 and asserts that the impact of correctional staff attitudes on inmate education begins with a "top-down" approach, that is, from the department director's attitude and commitment to the positive value of the education program in changing inmates lives—both within the institution and after discharge. Chapter 6 is presented by Brian D. Fitch, Jeff Mulhaussen, and Brian Mattson. These authors conceptualize how education-based technologies may be integrated with other technology in the justice system to help agencies determine what educational content and technical approaches work for different inmate populations to achieve a variety of individual and system outcomes. The chapter concludes with a presentation of disruptive technologies that are being explored through the education-based incarceration initiative and the benefits these innovations afford incarcerated individuals. Chapter 7 takes a in-depth look at the reentry process linking inmates to community services. Presented by Jessica Nolan Daugherty, Laura Abrams, and Gary Greene, this chapter examines the parallels to the transition of youth with disabilities to a quality adult life. Relating reentry to the experience of transitioning youth with disabilities, the authors emphasize the importance of interagency collaboration, wrap-around services, and connection to community-based organizations. The chapter also highlights model transition programs that utilize many of these practices.

Chapters 8, 9, and 10 are presented in Part III which discuss "Promising and Proven 'Best Practices': Global Perspectives." Chapter 8 focuses on teaching strategies and practices for correctional education programs. Sara A. Millman Silva, Kimberly B. Hughes, Selene Kurland, June Kizu, and Sylvester Pues provide an overview of the current tapestry of programs that are endeavoring to modify behavior in order to reduce patterns of repeated incarceration. Chapter 9 examines an international and comparative survey of best practices in correctional education. Arthur Jones, Richard Gordon, and Richard Haesly describe a systematic analysis of the most demonstrably successful correctional education programs presently in use in a number of countries worldwide. The comparative nature of this international survey reveals a high degree of similarity and a number of common features of successful programs, whether pursued in Norway, South Korea, Australia, Switzerland, or elsewhere. Chapter 10 is presented by M. C. Esposito, Anthony H. Normore and Arthur Jones who examine best practices for maximizing benefits of correctional educational programs and synthesizes the types of educational programs currently implemented within the correctional setting (e.g., basic skills, vocational and post secondary), reviews the effectiveness of such programs, identifies key factors increasing the likelihood such programs are effective, and summarizes best practices specific to education-based incarceration.

Part VI concludes the book with Chapter 11. Anthony H. Normore, Brian D. Fitch, and Sarah Camp offer reflections of the collective essays and suggest recommendations that may be validated by documenting and verifying results, thus making education-based incarceration an evidence-based system. With the scientific research assembled, findings are crafted in a way for the continued validation of education-based incarceration guiding principles. In the words of Leroy Baca, "the cycle of refinement will drive future policy formulation and management decisions and eventually anchoring EBI throughout the Los Angeles County Sheriff's Department and the California Department of Corrections and Rehabilitation" (2010, p. 58).

REFERENCES

Baca, L. D. (2010, March/April). Education-based incarceration: Changing the way we incarcerate. *Sheriff Magazine, (62)*1, 54-58.

Camp, S. (2007). *An explanatory mixed methods content analysis of two state level correctional institutions' pre-release handbook curriculum designs, looking through the lenses of two philosophical orientations of education* (Unpublished doctoral dissertation). Florida State University, Tallahassee, FL.

FOREWORD

Leroy D. Baca

Education-based incarceration (EBI) is a component of the criminal justice system focused on deterring and mitigating crime by investing in its offenders through education and rehabilitation. By providing substantive and intellectual education in jails, and being supportive rather than punitive, the likelihood that offenders will recidivate and return to custody is significantly reduced, while increasing community success and stability. Correctional institutions have operated as warehouses for too long, simply locking up offenders without any real effort to rehabilitate or educate. The results have been unacceptably high rates of recidivism throughout the nation, with a national average of more than 68%. This means that for every 10 people released from custody, 7 individuals will be rearrested, reconvicted, and resentenced for a new crime within 3 years.

EBI is not soft on crime. Holding lawbreakers accountable for their actions is the main priority of EBI, and incarceration is still the chief means of imposing accountability for acts that threaten public safety. The investment made through EBI is a legitimate, evidence-based endeavor to enhance public safety. Indeed, studies on correctional education have consistently supported links between education, lower levels of recidivism, and higher levels of employment.

As sheriff of Los Angeles County, I understand firsthand the importance of education and the need for education-based incarceration in our jails and prisons. More than a decade ago, I created the Inmate Services Bureau to oversee the development and implementation of traditional education, vocational training, and life skills programs to the inmates in each of our eight custody facilities. I have witnessed personally the trans-

Education-Based Incarceration and Recidivism:
The Ultimate Social Justice Crime-Fighting Tool, pp. xv–xvi
Copyright © 2012 by Information Age Publishing
All rights of reproduction in any form reserved.

formational power of education and the ways it has changed the lives of numerous inmates over the years. The education-based incarceration unit of the sheriff's department represents the next step in creating, implementing, and assessing evidence-based programs. Changing the ways correctional institutions operate requires us to think differently about the purpose, structures, and values of the current system.

This book *Education-Based Incarceration and Recidivism: The Ultimate Social Justice Crime-Fighting Tool,* edited by Brian D. Fitch and Anthony H. Normore, is groundbreaking in its contribution to the body of theory, research, and practice on inmate incarceration, recidivism, and social justice education. The book is crafted from the professional experiences, intellectual engagements, and moral commitments of the editors and contributing authors. It is based on foundation of equal and social justice concerning a multitude of lenses used to view and attempt to understand the factors that contribute to incarceration, the relationship between crime and education, and the programs and support structures necessary to assist inmates in preparation for reentry into a more just and harmonious society.

Fitch and Normore have presented us with a significant work in the fields of social and criminal justice and educational learning. As readers of this book we embark on a journey that requires us to engage in thinking about the history of EBI programs and how these programs can contribute to the design and implementation of future programs. In the words of Jonathan Sacks (2007), the editors and the contributing authors have demonstrated that, "Difference does not diminish; it enlarges the sphere of human possibilities" (p. 209).

REFERENCES

Sacks, J. (2007). *The dignity of difference.* New York, NY: Continuum

ACKNOWLEDGMENT

This book could not be made possible without the support of Sheriff Leroy D. Baca at the Los Angeles County Sheriff's Department who relentlessly demonstrates his belief that when implemented properly, education taps the unlimited capacity for growth and desire for a productive life shared by all members of society, including those who are incarcerated. Sincere gratitude also goes to each of the authors who contributed to this book. Their time, efforts, and patience to help produce the finished product are most appreciated. We also thank our friend and colleague, Dr. Jeffrey S. Brooks, series editor of the Information Age Publishing series, *Educational Leadership for Social Justice*, and the executive members of the Leadership for Social Justice Special Interest Group of the American Educational Research Association for their support and encouragement throughout the development process. Finally, we offer many thanks to Information Age Publishing for the ongoing diligence throughout the publication process. Our hope is that this book and the chapters therein will serve as catalysts for further discourse about research on education-based incarceration, corrections education, and recidivism within the context of social justice. Please feel free to make contact with any of the authors. Their contact information is provided accordingly. On behalf of all contributors, thank you.

PART I

THE CULTURE AND POLITICS OF CORRECTIONS:
A SOCIAL JUSTICE PHEMONENON

CHAPTER 1

A REVIEW OF EVIDENCE

The Case for Education-Based Incarceration

Brian D. Fitch and Rakel Delevi

Prison and jail populations have grown to more than 2.3 million, despite the fact that violent and property crime rates are at their lowest levels in more than 30 years. Rather than increasing as the outcome of new crimes, evidence suggests that much of the recent rise in prisoner population is the result of new sentencing laws, with prison sentences growing at a faster rate than crime. This phenomenon has been further exacerbated by increasing rates of re-arrest and reconviction among previously incarcerated individuals. While there is no strong and consistent body of evidence linking incarceration with lower crime, many former inmates lack the life skills, education, and opportunity to reintegrate successfully back into society. This chapter explores why evidence-based incarceration is not only a viable, but highly cost effective method for reducing crime and recidivism. The chapter further discusses the social, institutional, and human capital outcomes of investing in correctional education.

According to the U.S. Department of Justice, Bureau of Justice Statistics, there are currently 1,617,478 prisoners under federal and state authority, while the number of inmates housed in county and city jails is estimated at 767,620 (Minton, 2010; West, 2010). This brings the total number of

Education-Based Incarceration and Recidivism:
The Ultimate Social Justice Crime-Fighting Tool, pp. 3–19
Copyright © 2012 by Information Age Publishing
All rights of reproduction in any form reserved.

3

incarcerated persons in federal, state, and local custody to 2,385,098. In one 10-year period alone, the country's population grew an average of 60,779 inmates a year, for a total increase of 607,987 (Beck & Harrison, 2001). Estimates suggest that as much as one in every 132 people are currently in prison or jail, with the United States having the highest per-capita inmate population in the Western world—as much as seven times higher than the median rate for other "rich countries" (Schmitt, Warner, & Gupta, 2010).

The amount of monies the United States spent for police protection, corrections, and judicial and legal activities follows a similar pattern. Between 1982 and 2003, the operating and outlays for the justice system increased by 418%—from about $36 billion dollars in 1982 to more than $185 billion in 2003 (Hughes, 2006). In 2003, the United States spent an estimated $57.8 billion dollars on federal, state, and local corrections alone. When calculated on a per capita basis, in 1982 total spending on corrections cost each U.S. resident $39. By 2001, the figure rose by more than 400%—costing each person about $200 (Bauer & Owens, 2004). In fact, 7.2 cents of every dollar spent by state and local governments in 2001 went to justice activities, compared with about 30 cents of every dollar being spent on education (Hughes, 2006).

Even more surprising is that while prison and jail populations throughout the county continue to grow, crime has fallen steadily since 1994, with violent and property crime rates at their lowest levels in more than 30 years. The number of reported property crimes in 1973 was approximately 51.5 million and three times greater than reports of similar misconduct in 2001, when the number was estimated at 18 million (Rennison & Rand, 2002). Similar trends have emerged with other offenses as well, including simple assaults and other violent crimes. Rather than increasing as the outcome of new crimes, evidence suggests that much of the recent rise in prisoner population is the effect of new sentencing guidelines, with prison sentences growing at a faster rate than crime. This phenomenon has been further exacerbated by the increasing rates of re-arrest and reconviction among previously incarcerated individuals—a phenomenon referred to as recidivism (Fagan, West, & Holland, 2003; Hull, Forrester, Brown, Jobe, & McCullen, 2000; Langan & Levin, 2002).

Clearly, one of the functions of the judicial and correctional systems is to reduce crime (Gehring, 2000)—a goal which has proven increasingly illusive under current "tough-on-crime" policies. Social justice requires that everyone be given equal access to education, resources, and opportunities—especially disenfranchised individuals who lack an appropriate social voice. This chapter explores why education-based incarceration is not only a viable, but highly cost-effective method for reducing crime and recidivism. It includes an examination of "tough on crime legislation," the relationship between incarceration and recidivism, and the debate surrounding society's role in providing correctional education. Finally, the chapter concludes with a discussion of the social, institutional, and human capital outcomes of investing in correctional education.

TOUGH ON CRIME LEGISLATION

Crime is understandably ranked as one of the most distressing issues facing modern society (Gibbs, 1993). Public fears and the high-profile nature of many violent offenses have sparked considerable debate about the best ways to reduce criminal activity, especially crimes committed by recidivist offenders. Nor are these concerns without merit. In 1994, for example, more than two thirds of all released prisoners were rearrested for a new offense, typically a felony or serious misdemeanor, with about half being reconvicted and resentenced for a new crime (Langan & Levin, 2002).

Between 1993 and 1996, the federal government and 25 states responded to growing public safety concerns by adopting what is commonly referred to as "three strikes" legislation (Kovandzic, Sloan, & Vieraitis, 2004). These new regulations were part of a growing "tough on crime" movement in the United States which sought to reduce misconduct by mandating significant sentencing enhancements for offenders with prior convictions, including, in some cases, a compulsory term of at least 25 years to life on conviction of a second or third violent felony (Clark, Austin, & Henry, 1997).

Advocates of three strikes legislation argued that targeting recidivist offenders, mandating longer sentences, and limiting judicial discretion were the best strategies for reducing crime (Stolzenberg & D'Alessio, 1997; Walker, 2001; Zimring, 2001). Yet, despite the commonsense—and not to mention popular—appeal of this approach, studies have failed to uncover evidence of a strong link between three strikes legislation and a homogeneous decrease in any individual category of crime. For virtually every type of offense assessed, the number of states experiencing significant decreases in crime rates is about the same as the number experiencing significant increases in similar offenses (Kovandzic et al., 2004).

In California, one of the few states to apply three strikes laws consistently, comparisons of pre- and postlaw data have failed to support the alleged reduction in crime promised by the legislation—on average finding a reduction in short-term felony crime of between 0% and 2% (Zimring, 2001). Indeed, the California counties which enforced the laws vigorously did not experience a decline in any crime category compared to counties which applied the laws less frequently, while Santa Clara, one of the six counties enforcing the statutes most frequently, actually experienced an increase in violent offenses (Males & Macallair, 1999).

National studies have produced similar results. For example, panel data collected from 188 U.S. cities (110 treatment cities and 78 control cities) with populations of 100,000 or more found that crime rates in three different groupings—cities within states never passing three strikes legislation; cities within states passing three strikes legislation in 1994; and cities passing three strikes legislation in 1995—moved roughly in tandem over the 20-year period between 1980 and 2000. These and similar findings led the authors to conclude that criminality, rather than being affected by local legislation, appears to be influenced by "broad forces" that tend to push crime up and down nationwide (Kovandzic et al., 2004, p. 221).

None of this is meant to suggest that sentencing laws have no effect. Certainly, the threat of punishment is enough to keep some people from committing crimes (Doob & Webster, 2003; Levitt, 2002). Yet, while three strikes legislation has almost certainly incapacitated any number of violent offenders, there is no credible evidence to suggest that three strikes laws reduce crime by deterring new offenses or by reducing recidivism (Akers & Sellers, 2004; Devine, Sheley, & Smith, 1988; Kovandzic, Sloan, & Vieraitis, 2002; Levitt, 1996; Marvell & Moody, 2001). In fact, in cities adopting three strikes sentencing policies, homicide rates increased an average of 10.4%—a phenomenon attributed to the fact that offenders facing the possibility of lengthy prison terms may be more likely to kill witnesses to avoid apprehension (Kovandzic et al., 2004; Marvell & Moody, 2001). Similarly disappointing results have been found with "boot camp" and "scared straight" programs (Aos, Phipps, Barnoski, & Lieb, 2001; Petrosino, Turpin-Petrosino, & Buehler, 2003), and supervisory and management strategies stressing deterrence and retribution (MacKenzie, 2008).

On the other hand, the social and monetary costs associated with get tough on crime legislation are significant—including building and staffing correctional institutions (Austin, 1996; Greenwood et al., 1994), hiring and training law enforcement and corrections officers (Levitt, 1997), jury and court expenditures (Cushman, 1996), and providing medical care for the country's aging prison population (King & Mauer, 2001). Additionally, there have been serious questions raised about racial inequities in the application of three strikes and other "tough on crime" legislation (Crawford, Chiricos, & Kleck, 1998; Fagan et al., 2003; Males & Macallair, 1999), as well as considerable discussion regarding the nation's alarming rise in recidivism.

THE RELATIONSHIP BETWEEN EDUCATION AND INCARCERATION

While there is no strong evidence that imprisonment rates are consistently and significantly related to lower crime rates (DeFina & Arvanities, 2002), the majority of persons housed in correctional institutions around the country tend come from disadvantaged neighborhoods where educational opportunities are limited (Crayton & Neusteter, 2008). Additionally, many convicted inmates tend to be poor, male, young, racial minorities, and suffering from substance or alcohol abuse (Andrews & Bonta, 2003; Fagan et al., 2003; Lipsey & Cullen, 2007; Rose & Clear, 1998).

Recent evidence, for example, suggests that the risks associated with being arrested actually increase over time for those living in poorer, disadvantaged neighborhoods (Rose & Clear, 1998). At least some of this increased risk appears to be the product of stricter police enforcement—often for minor or drug-related offenses—even as crime rates fall (Tonry, 1995). Once in motion, this dynamic creates a self-reinforcing cycle of arrest, re-arrest, and incarceration that continues unabated despite changes in the labor market, population structure, or reduction in crime. In this way, incarceration results in more incarceration, which begets more crime. This, in turn, invites more aggressive reinforcement, which then re-supplies incarceration (Fagan et al., 2003).

There is also support for the hypothesis that convicted offenders are, on average, less educated and have fewer marketable skills than other members of society (Greenberg, Dunleavy, & Kutner, 2007). Whereas approximately 82% of the general population has earned a high school diploma or General Education Development diploma (GED), only about 60% of inmates housed in federal and state prisons have received similar credentials. To further complicate matters, incarcerated adults demonstrate high levels of illiteracy—with some experts estimating the literacy levels of more than half of America's inmates at the sixth-grade level (Ryan, 1991). This disparity in education is even greater at higher levels. While it is reported that more than half the general population has some college schooling, less than one fourth of all state and federal inmates report having any postsecondary education (Harlow, 2003).

Many formers prisoners also lack the life skills necessary to conduct job searches, reason critically, and manage finances (Cecil, Drapkin, MacKenzie, & Hickman, 2000; Ross & Fabiano, 1985). Additionally, simply having a criminal record is often enough to significantly impair one's ability to find and maintain employment that pays a livable wage (Bushway, 1998; Western, Kling, & Weiman, 2001). Finally, spending time behind bars can impair one's ability to cope in society because the values and behaviors needed to succeed in prison are often in direct conflict with societal norms (Bloom, 2006; MacKenzie, 2008). Indeed, approximately one fourth of prisoners initially incarcerated for nonviolent offenses are sentenced a second time for committing a crime of violence—stressing the likelihood that prisons may be transmitting violent habits rather than reducing them (Haney & Zimbardo, 1998).

Considering their deficits in getting along with others, forming social bonds, problem solving, values, and obtaining employment, it is not surprising that many former offenders slip back into criminal activity (Kachnowski, 2005; Tyler & Kling, 2004; Visher, Winterfield, & Weiman, 2004). In spite of these and other obstacles, inmates, on the whole, want to secure and maintain employment upon release (Visher & Lattimore, 2007). More importantly, inmates who are successful are less likely to reoffend (Harer, 1994; Sampson & Laub, 1997; Uggen, 2000). Thus, it appears that if society has any hope of stemming the recent rises in incarceration and recidivism, it must begin to think differently about incarceration—particularly the relationship between education and crime.

SOCIETY'S ROLE IN PROVIDING EDUCATION

While the relationship between crime and incarceration is theoretically and methodologically complex, one factor that has consistently correlated with lower rates of criminality and recidivism is education. Higher levels of education have been linked with lower rates of institutional discipline (Taylor, 1992), more instances of postrelease employment (Jenkins, Steurer, & Pendry, 1995), and fewer occurrences of recidivism upon release (Frolander-Ulf & Yates, 2001). Yet, despite the many benefits promised by education, not everyone agrees on society's role in providing schooling, vocational, and life skills training to offenders. In fact, the extent of society's role has been a subject of contention since the first scholastic program was offered at Philadelphia's Walnut Street jail in 1798 (Coley & Barton, 2006).

Opponents of correctional education argue that a lack of education does not mandate a life of crime. While education can help people pursue their social goals, it does not necessary make someone a good person (Gehring, 2000). Crime results from criminogenic thinking or poor character—thus, offenders should not be entitled to any advantage which exceeds the benefits enjoyed by the lowest members of a free society. Simply put, offenders should be punished for their crimes, not rehabilitated at taxpayer expense.

In contrast, proponents of education contend that crime is the product of environmental factors that promote deviant and antisocial behavior, with many of these pressures beyond a person's control, such as poverty, family violence, and parental alcohol or drug abuse (Christoffersen, Francis, & Soothill, 2001). Advocates of this view portray inmates as victims of circumstance and social justice and social justice—disadvantaged individuals who grew up with little access to education or employment opportunities. And, because incarceration poses a further liability, justice and equality mandate that society do whatever is possible to help those less-advantaged members (Braithwaite, 1980).

While the attitudes and politics of incarceration have vacillated between these contrasting themes for decades, arguments about whether ex-offenders are victims or victimizers overlook an important point. Regardless of which view is correct, one irrefutable fact remains: With the exception of those inmates who are executed or die in custody, all offenders eventually return to society (Travis, 2005). In 2005, more than 690,000 men and women were released from state and federal prisons (Sabol, Minton, & Harrison, 2007)—while an estimated 9 million people rotate through local jails each year (Osborne & Solomon, 2006). The question is what will happen to these former inmates once they return to society? Will they adopt socially responsible behaviors, gain employment, and contribute to their communities? Or, will they simply return to their former lifestyles because they lack the skill, education, and opportunity to do otherwise?

Today, most federal, state, and local correctional facilities offer some form of education, including GED courses, vocational training, life skills programs, cognitive-behavioral therapy, and, in some cases, postsecondary course work (MacKenzie, 2008). Educational programs involve both on-site instruction and distance learning that is used to link students with local community colleges and universities. While the characteristics of offenders differ, evidence suggests that the most successful programs are those aimed at changing criminogenic thinking (Andrews & Bonta, 2003; Illescas, Sánchez-Meca, & Genovés, 2001; Ross & Fabiano, 1985). Cognitive-behavioral programs involve instruction, exercises, reinforcement, modeling, and role-plays designed to alter the dysfunctional thinking patterns characterized by many offenders—that is, the antisocial attitudes, low levels of self-efficacy, and feelings of entitlement that often lead to criminal behavior (Andrews & Bonta, 2003; Walters, 1990).

Life skills programs, on the other hand, are intended to address the ability deficiencies that offenders face when attempting to function successfully in everyday life (Cecil et al., 2000). The actual components of life skills programs often vary, but focus typically on finances, interpersonal relationships, conflict management, job search skills, and anger management. Vocational programs offer classroom-based instruction, apprenticeships, and on-the-job training in a number of trades, such as painting, horticulture, printing, carpentry, and auto body repair. Although both types of programs are common among correctional institutions, neither course of study has been linked with a significant reduction in recidivism, most likely because they fail to address the cognitive deficits associated with criminal activity (MacKenzie, 2008).

Similar to cognitive-behavioral programs, adult basic secondary education, GED, and postsecondary courses have consistently demonstrated positive effects on postrelease employment and recidivism (Aos, Miller, & Drake, 2006; Chappell, 2004; Cho & Tyler, 2008; Hull et al., 2000; Steurer, Smith, & Tracy, 2001). Studies on the relationship between education and crime suggest that time spent in school significantly reduces the risk of criminal activity (Farrington, Gallagher, Morely, St. Ledger, & West, 1986; Gottfredson, 1985; Lochner, 2003; Witte & Tauchen, 1994)—with estimates uncovering a robust and significant effect of high school graduation on arrests for both violent and property crimes. When arrests are further analyzed by crime, the greatest impact of high school graduation is associated with murder, assault, and motor vehicle theft (Lochner & Moretti, 2004).

A study by Lochner and Moretti (2004) found that both years of schooling and high school graduation reduce the annual probability of incarceration among both White and Black male adults. More specifically, their findings suggest that an additional year of schooling reduces the probability of incarceration by about 0.6% for Whites and 2% for Blacks—leading the researchers to conclude that "education significantly reduces the probability that a young man will be incarcerated" (p. 180). Not surprisingly, much of this decrease is believed to be the result of higher earning potential, with high school graduation raising average annual income by around $8,040.

It is important to note that the accumulation of even small effects can have a much greater impact on a large population than the accrual of large effects on a small population (Gaes, 2008). For example, Lochner and Moretti (2004) estimate that nearly 400 fewer murders and 8,000 fewer assaults would have taken place in 1990 if high school graduation rates had been increased by 1%—suggesting that the social benefits of a 1% increase in male U.S. high school graduation rates would have saved as much as $1.4 billion in victim expenses, property losses, and court costs, or an amount approximately equivalent to $2,100 per additional high school graduate.

The link between higher levels of education and increased income holds even among inmates with low cognitive skills. This relationship is also believed to serve as a protective factor against crime because for people who work, crime is usually a less-attractive path (Lochner & Moretti, 2004; Tyler, Murnane, & Willett, 2000). For inmates who receive vocational training during their incarceration, this association should be even stronger as having a marketable vocational skill should make it easier to find employment.

EDUCATIONAL OUTCOMES AND RECIDIVISM

While the majority of research on correctional education has focused on recidivism and economic effects, there are other social outcomes worth noting, many of which may help shed light on the relationship between education and recidivism. For example, many governments and political spokespersons argue formal schooling is a right that each and every member of society is entitled to enjoy (Universal Declaration of Human Rights, 1948). Proponents of this position contend that education is not a means to an end, but an end in itself—an inalienable right with its own intrinsic value. Furthermore, some educators assert that education is a prerequisite to moral thinking, as well as an important component of pro-social behavior (Dewey, 1916; Kohlberg, Kauffman, Scharf, & Hickey, 1975)—and, for these reasons, a necessary component of any legitimate effort to rehabilitate offenders.

A second, often overlooked, focus of correctional education is literacy. A meta-analysis of 23 studies found that literacy leads to various gains, including improved employment, increased income, and continued education among participants (Beder, 1999). Further, the Tennessee Longitudinal Study found that adults who participated in literacy programs demonstrated significant gains in self-esteem, as measured by the Rosenberg Self-Esteem scale (Rosenberg, 1965). More specifically, 70% of the participants agreed that their feelings about themselves changed for the better (Merrifield, Smith, Rea, & Shriver, 1994). Although these studies did employ inmates as participants, it is reasonable to expect these results to translate to inmate populations. Because correction education provides inmates with valid experiences and attainable and self-identified goals, it also has the potential of promoting a greater sense of achievement and enhanced self-esteem (Harer, 1995).

Additionally, there is some evidence that correctional education is linked positively with inmates' adjustment, resilience, happiness and overall psychological well-being (Fordyce, 1997; Lane, 2000). Craft (1996) found that correctional education was associated with inmates' self-esteem, confidence, and overall happiness during incarceration. Similarly, correctional education is associated with promoting motivation, a factor which could be tied to the positive psychological well-being of incarcerated individuals. A study, for instance, found that 56% of inmate students reported that they were self-motivated, while others reported family, friends, and teachers as their motivators to pursue correctional education (Moeller, Day, & Rivera, 2004).

Correctional education also provides inmates an opportunity to separate themselves from the criminal subculture, thereby breaking the isolation that often accompanies incarceration. Harer (1995) examined the effects of prison education program involvement and found that participation rates in educational programs were negatively associated with recidivism rates. He concluded that it's not necessarily a specific diploma or program certificate that reduces recidivism but, rather, what he referred to as "the normalization process." By participating in correctional education, inmates learn the important skills necessary to comply with a system, while gaining the added benefit of specific self-identified outcomes.

Furthermore, taking courses lessens the amount of time that offenders have to engage in troublesome behavior within custody settings, while providing inmates with suitable role models and appropriate behaviors to emulate (MacKenzie, 2006). Interacting with educators can help familiarize inmates with positive societal norms, as well as build pro-social identities after release—effectively allowing them to become better family and community members. Overall, it can be argued that the educational process improves inmates' social skills which make it easier for them to seek employment and, in turn, to reduce recidivism (Harer, 1995).

Lastly, correctional education offers several benefits to the overall functioning of the correctional system. Given that schooling keeps inmate students engaged and active, while minimizing opportunities for misbehavior, correctional education can lead to less violence among inmates, thereby creating a more positive and manageable environment for both staff officers and inmates (Vacca, 2004). As a result, correctional education is not only beneficial to the postincarceration adjustment of inmates, but can also improve the quality of correctional facilities as well.

IMPLICATIONS FOR POLICY AND LEADERSHIP

Several types of correctional education have demonstrated a variety of short- and long-term benefits, including lower recidivism rates, improved earning potential and higher rates of employment (Mitchell, 2002; Steurer et al., 2001; Steurer & Smith, 2006). Yet, despite strong evidence supporting education as a highly cost-effective and economically viable method of reducing crime and lowering recidivism (Lochner & Moretti, 2004), participation rates in correctional educational programs have not kept pace with the exploding prison population (Crayton & Neusteter, 2008). Indeed, recent evidence suggests that only 14% of inmates participate in correctional education, despite overwhelming demand (Freudenberg, 2007). This is especially troubling considering that most incarcerated prisoners do not earn their GED prior being released. In fact, data suggests that between 1997 and 2004, 7 out of 10 state and federal prisoners earned their GED while imprisoned (Harlow, 2003)—further stressing the importance of the role played by correctional institutions in providing inmates with the education, vocational, and life skills necessary to transition successfully back into society.

In Relation to Procedures and Policy Changes

If society has hope of reducing the staggering costs associated with incarceration, as well as lessoning the high rates of recidivism seen throughout the nation, elected officials, law enforcement managers, and other civic leaders must begin defining the problems of crime and recidivism differently. Heifetz (1994) identifies two types of challenges that leaders face—technical challenges and adaptive challenges. The first type, technical challenges, involves situations where the problem is clearly understood and the technology necessary to remedy the difficulty already exists. Thus, solving the problem is simply a matter of applying current technical knowledge, theory, and practice.

In contrast, adaptive challenges are situations where the problem is obvious, but it cannot be resolved with current structures, procedures, or ways of thinking (Heifetz, Grashow, & Linsky, 2009). To successfully remedy an adaptive challenge, leaders must reframe and redefine questions in new and innovative ways. Only when government leaders begin to see recidivism for what it really is—an adaptive challenge that cannot be solved with current theories, procedures, and structures—can they begin to reason differently about the relationship between recidivism and education.

In Relation to Leadership

Reframing the problem of recidivism will require leaders to revisit the questions of value, purpose, and process associated with the current correctional system (Heifetz et al., 2009). Undoubtedly, the failure to do so will result in still greater public expenditures, larger numbers of individuals in custody, and higher rates of recidivism. Rather than seeing monies spent on correctional education as futile attempts to rehabilitate those who have violated societal norms, it is time to begin looking at correctional education as an opportunity to promote positive social change, specifically in the areas of equal education and opportunity. Considering the strong negative correlation between education and crime (Lochner & Moretti, 2004), only by investing in the education of offenders and at-risk youth can we begin to mitigate the current alarming rates of incarceration and recidivism.

In Relation to Social Justice

One of the primary objectives of incarceration is rehabilitation. Thus, social justice requires that political leaders and correctional institutions focus their limited resources on rehabilitating and educating offenders. While there is no strong and consistent evidence to support a relationship between longer sentences and lower crime rates (Defina & Arvanitties, 2002), higher levels of education have been linked with fewer instances of recidivism (Frolanderr-Ulf & Yates, 2001) and more occurrences of postrelease employment (Aos et al., 2006; Jenkins et al, 1995). Ultimately, the goal of education-based incarceration is to empower inmates to work toward a more socially just society—a society where everyone has equal access to education and resources. While those who violate the law must be held accountable for their actions, it is only through education that we can create a safer and more socially just society with equal opportunity for everyone.

REFERENCES

Akers, R. L., & Sellers, C. S. (2004). *Criminological theories: Introduction, evaluation, and application* (4th ed.). Los Angeles, CA: Roxbury.

Andrews, D. A., & Bonta, J. (2003). *The psychology of criminal conduct.* Cincinnati, OH: Anderson.

Aos, S., Miller, M., & Drake, E. (2006). *Evidence-based public policy options to reduce future prison construction, criminal justice costs, and crime rates.* Olympia, WA: Washington Institute for Public Policy.

Aos, S., Phipps, P., Barnoski, R., & Lieb, R. (2001). *The comparative costs and benefits of programs to reduce crime.* Olympia, WA: Washington State Institute of Public Policy.

Austin, J. (1996). Three strikes and you're out: The likely consequences on the courts, prisons, and crime in California and Washington State. *Saint Louis University Public Law Review, 14*(1), 239-261.

Bauer, L., & Owens, S. D. (2004). *Justice expenditures and employment in the United States, 2001.* Washington, DC: U.S. Department of Justice.

Beck, A. J., & Harrison, P. M. (2001). *Prisoners in 2000.* Washington, DC: U.S. Department of Justice.

Beder, H. (1999). *The outcomes and impacts of adult literacy education in the United States*. Cambridge, MA: National Center for the Study of Adult Learning and Literacy.

Bloom, D. (2006). *Employment focused programs for ex-prisoners: What we have learned, what we are learning, and where we should go from here?* New York, NY: National Poverty Center.

Braithwaite, J. (1980). *Prisons, education, and work: Towards a national employment strategy for prisoners*. Queensland, Australia: University of Queensland Press.

Bushway, S. D. (1998). The impact of arrest on the job stability of young White American men. *Journal of Research in Crime and Delinquency, 35*(4), 454-479.

Cecil, D. K., Drapkin, D. A., MacKenzie, D. L., & Hickman, L. J. (2000). The effectiveness of adult basic education and life-skills programs in reducing recidivism: A review and assessment of research. *Journal of Correctional Education, 51*(2), 207-226.

Chappell, C. A. (2004). Post-secondary correctional education and recidivism: A meta-analysis of research conducted 1990-1999. *The Journal of Correctional Education, 55*(2), 148-169.

Cho, R., & Tyler, J. H. (2008, March-April). *Prison-based adult basic education (ABE) and post-release labor market outcomes*. Paper presented at the Reentry Roundtable on Education, John Jay College of Criminal Justice, City University of New York, New York, NY.

Craft, M. (1996). *Long-term benefits of higher education programs in maximum-security prisons* (Unpublished doctoral dissertation). State University of New York at Albany.

Christoffersen, M. N., Francis, B., & Soothill, K. (2001). An upbringing to violence? Identifying the likelihood of violent crime among the 1966 birth cohort in Denmark. *Journal of Forensic Psychiatry and Psychology, 1*(2), 367-387.

Clark, J., Austin, J., & Henry, D.A. (1997, September). *Three strikes and you're out: A review of state legislation*. Washington, DC: National Institute of Justice.

Coley, R. J., & Barton, P. E. (2006): *Locked up and locked out: An educational perspective on the U.S. prison population*. Princeton, NJ: Educational Testing Service.

Crawford, R., Chiricos, T., & Kleck, G. (1998). Race, racial threat, and sentencing of habitual offenders. *Criminology, 36*(3), 481-511.

Crayton, A., & Neusteter, S. R. (2008). *The current landscape of correctional education:* Paper presented at the annual meeting of the ASC Annual Meeting, St. Louis Adam's Mark, St. Louis, Missouri.

Cushman, R. C. (1996). Effect on a local criminal justice system. In D. Schichor & D. K. Sechrest (Eds.), *Three strikes and you're out: Vengeance as public policy* (pp. 90-113). Thousand Oaks, CA: SAGE.

Defina, R. H., & Arvanites, T. M. (2002). The weak effect of imprisonment on crime: 1971-1998. *Social Science Quarterly, 83*(3), 635-653.

Devine, J. A., Sheley, J. F., & Smith, M. D. (1988). Macroeconomic and social-control policy influences on crime and crime rate changes, 1948-1985. *American Sociological Review, 53*(3), 407-420.

Dewey, J. (1916). *Democracy and education*. New York, NY: Macmillan.

Doob, A. N., & Webster, C. M. (2003). Sentence severity and crime: Accepting the null hypothesis. In M. Tonry (Ed.), *Crime and justice: A review of research* (Vol. 30, pp. 143-195). Chicago, IL: University of Chicago Press.

Fagan, J., West, V., & Holland, J. (2003). The reciprocal effects of crime and incarceration in New York City neighborhoods. *Fordham Urban Law Journal, 30*, 1551-1602.

Farrington, D., Gallagher, B., Morely, L., St. Ledger, R., & West, D. (1986). Unemployment, school leaving, and crime. *British Journal of Criminology, 26*(4), 335-356.

Fordyce, M. W. (1997). Educating for happiness. *Quebec Review of Psychology, 18*(2). Retrieved from http://gethappy.net/quebec

Freudenberg, N. (2007, March-April). *Coming home from jail: A review of health and social problems facing US jail populations and of opportunities for reentry interventions.* Paper presented at the Reentry Roundtable on Education, John Jay College of Criminal Justice, City University of New York, New York, NY.

Frolander-Ulf, M., & Yates, M. (2001, July/August). Teaching in prisons. *Monthly Review,* 114-127.

Gaes, G. G. (2008, March-April). *The impact of prison education programs on post-release outcomes.* Paper presented at the Reentry Roundtable on Education, John Jay College of Criminal Justice, City University of New York, New York, NY.

Gehring, T. (2000). Recidivism as a measure of correctional education program success. *Journal of Correctional Education, 51*(2), 197-205.

Gibbs, N. (1993). Up in arms: Anger over violence. *Time, 142*(6), 18.

Gottfredson, M. (1985). Youth employment, crime, and schooling. *Developmental Psychology, 21*(3), 419-432.

Greenberg, E., Dunleavy, E., & Kutner, M. (2007). *Literacy behind bars: Results from the 2003 National Assessment of Adult Literacy Prison Surveys.* Washington, DC: U.S. Department of Education, Institute of Education Series, National Center for Education Statistics.

Greenwood, P. C., Rydell, P., Abrahamse, A. F., Caulkins, J. P., Chiesa, J., Model, K. E., & Klein, S. P. (1994). *Three strikes and you're out: Estimated benefits and costs of California's new mandatory sentencing law.* Santa Monica, CA: RAND.

Haney, C., & Zimbardo, P. (1998). The past and future of U.S. prison policy: Twenty-five years after the Stanford prison experiment. *American Psychologist, 53*(7), 709-727.

Harer, M. D. (1995). *Prison education program participation and recidivism: A test of the normalization hypothesis.* Washington, DC: Federal Bureau of Prisons, Office of Research and Evaluation.

Harer, M.D. (1994). *Recidivism among federal prisoners released in 1987.* Washington, DC: National Center for Education Statistics, U.S. Department of Education.

Harlow, C. W. (2003). *Education and correctional populations.* Washington, DC: Bureau of Justice Special Report, Office of Justice Programs, U.S. Department of Justice.

Heifetz, R. A. (1994). *Leadership without easy answers.* Cambridge, MA: The Belknap Press of Harvard University Press.

Heifetz, R. A., Grashow, A., & Linsky, M. (2009). *The practice of adaptive leadership: Tools and tactics for changing your organization and the world.* Boston, MA: Harvard Business Press.

Hughes, K. A. (2006). *Justice expenditures and employment in the United States, 2003.* U.S. Department of Justice, Bureau of Justice Statistics, Washington, DC: U.S. Department of Justice.

Hull, K. A., Forrester, S., Brown, J., Jobe, D., & McCullen, C. (2000). Analysis of recidivism rates for participants of the academic/vocational/transition education programs offered by the Virginia department of correctional education. *Journal or Correctional Education, 51*(2), 256-261.

Illescas, S. R., Sánchez-Meca, J., & Genovés, V. G. (2001). Treatment of offenders and recidivism: Assessment of the effectiveness of programs applied in Europe. *Psychology in Spain, 5*(1), 47-62.

Jenkins, H., Steurer, S., & Pendry, J. (1995). A post-release follow-up of correctional education program completers released in 1990-1991. *Journal of Correctional Education, 46*(1), 20-24.

Kachnowski, V. (2005). *Returning home Illinois policy brief: Employment and prisoner reentry.* Washington, DC: Urban Institute.

King, R. S., & Mauer, M. (2001). *Aging behind bars: Three strikes seven year later.* Washington, DC: The Sentencing Project.

Kohlberg, L., Kauffman, K., Scharf, P., & Hickey, J. (1975). The just community approach to corrections: A theory. *Journal of Moral Education, 4*(3), 243-260.

Kovandzic, T. V., Sloan, J. J., & Vieraitis, L. M. (2002). Unintended consequences of politically popular sentencing policy: The homicide promoting effects of "three strikes" laws in U.S. cities (1980-1999). *Criminology and Public Policy, 1*(3), 399-424.

Kovandzic, T. V., Sloan, J. J., & Vieraitis, L. M. (2004). "Striking out" as crime reduction policy: The impact of "three strikes" law on crime rates in U.S. Cities. *Justice Quarterly, 21*(2), 207-239.

Lane, R. E. (2000). *The loss of happiness in market economies.* New Haven, CT: Yale University Press.

Langan, P. A., & Levin, D. J. (2002). *Recidivism of prisoners released in 1994.* Washington, DC: U.S. Department of Justice.

Levitt, S. D. (1996). The effects of prison population size on crime rates: Evidence from prison overcrowding litigation. *Quarterly Journal of Economics, 111*(2), 319-351.

Levitt, S. D. (1997). Using electronic cycles in police hiring to estimate the effects of police on crime. *American Economic Review, 87*(3), 270-290.

Levitt, S. D. (2002). Deterrence. In J. Q. Wilson & J. Petersilia (Eds.), *Crime: Public policies for crime control* (pp. 435-450). Oakland, CA: ICS Press.

Lipsey, M. W., & Cullen, F. T. (2007). The effectiveness of correctional rehabilitation: A review of systematic reviews. *Annual Review of Law and Social Science, 3*, 297-320.

Lochner, L. (2003). Education , work, and crime: A human capital approach. *International Economic Review, 45*(3), 811-843.

Lochner, L., & Moretti, E. (2004). The effect of education on crime: Evidence from prison inmates, arrests, and self-reports. *The American Economic Review, 94*(1), 155-189.

MacKenzie, D. L. (2006). *What works in corrections: Reducing the criminal activities of offenders and delinquents.* New York, NY: Cambridge University Press.

MacKenzie, D. L. (2008, March-April). *Structures and components of successful educational programs.* Paper presented at the Reentry Roundtable on Education, John Jay College of Criminal Justice, City University of New York, New York, NY.

Males, M., & Macallair, D. (1999). Striking out: The failure of California's three strikes and you're out law. *Stanford Law and Policy Review, 11*(1), 65-74.

Marvell, T. B., & Moody, C. E. (2001). The lethal effects of three strikes laws. *The Journal of Legal Studies, 30*(1), 89-106.

Merrifield, J., Smith, M., Rea, K., & Shriver, T. (1994). *Longitudinal study of adult literacy participants in Tennessee: Year two report.* Knoxville, TN: Center for Literacy Studies, University of Tennessee.

Minton, T.D. (2010). *Jail inmates at midyear, 2009.* Washington, DC: U.S. Department of Justice.

Mitchell, O. (2002). *Statistical analysis of three-state CEA data,* College Park. MD: University of Maryland.

Moeller, M., Day, S., & Rivera, B. (2004). How is education perceived on the inside? A preliminary study of adult males in a correctional setting. *Journal of Correction Education, 55,* 40-59.

Osborne, J., & Solomon, A. (2006). *Jail reentry roundtable meeting summary.* Washington, DC: The Urban Institute.

Petrosino, A., Turpin-Petrosino, C., & Buehler, J. (2003). Scared straight and other juvenile awareness programs for preventing juvenile delinquency: A systematic review of randomized experimental evidence. *The Annals of the American Academy of Political and Social Science, 589,* 41-62.

Rennison, C. M., & Rand, M. R. (2002). *Victimization 2002.* Washington, DC: U.S. Department of Justice.

Rose, D. R., & Clear, T. R. (1998). Incarceration, social capital and crime: Examining the unintended consequences of incarceration. *Criminology, 36*(3), 441-445.

Rosenberg, M. (1965). *Society and the adolescent self-image.* Princeton, NJ: Princeton University Press.

Ross, R. R., & Fabiano, E. A. (1985). *Time to think: A cognitive model of delinquency prevention and offender rehabilitation.* Johnson City, TN: Institute of Social Sciences and Arts.

Ryan, T. A. (1991). Literacy training and reintegration of offenders. *Journal of Correctional Education, 3*(1), 1-13.

Sabol, W. J., Minton, T. D., & Harrison, P. M. (2007). *Prison and jail inmates at midyear, 2006.* Washington, DC: Bureau of Justice Statistics.

Sampson, R., & Laub, J. (1997). A life-course theory of cumulative disadvantage and the stability of delinquency. In T. P. Thornberry (Ed.), *Developmental theories of crime and delinquency: Advances in criminology theory* (Vol. 7, 133-161). New Brunswick, NJ: Transaction.

Schmitt, J., Warner, K., & Gupta, S. (2010). *The high budgetary cost of incarceration*. Washington, DC: Center for Economic and Policy Research.

Stolzenberg, L., & D'Alessio, S.J. (1997). Three strikes and you're out: The impact of California's new mandatory sentencing law on serious crime rates. *Crime and Delinquency, 43*(4), 457-469.

Steurer, S. J., Smith, L., & Tracy, A. (2001). *Three state recidivism study*. Landham, MD: Correctional Education Association.

Steurer, S. J., & Smith, L. J. (2006) *Education reduces crime: Three states recidivism study, executive summary*. Lanham, MD: Correctional Education Association; and Centerville, UT: Management and Training Corporation.

Taylor, J. M. (1992). Post-secondary correctional education: An evaluation of effectiveness and efficiency. *Journal of Correctional Education, 43*(3), 132-141.

Tonry, M. (1995). *Malign neglect: Race, crime, and punishment in America*. New York, NY: Oxford University Press.

Travis, J. (2005). *But they all come back: Facing the challenges of prisoner reentry*. New York, NY: Urban Institute.

Tyler, J. H., & Kling, J. R. (2004). Prison-based education and re-entry into the mainstream labor market. In S. D. Bushway, M. Stoll, & D. Weisman (Eds.), *Barriers to reentry: The labor market for released prisoners in post-industrial America* (pp. 227-256). New York, NY: Russell Sage Foundation Press.

Tyler, J. H., Murnane, R. J., & Willett, J. B. (2000). Estimating the labor market signaling value of GED. *Quarterly Journal of Economics, 115*(2), 431-468.

Uggen, C. (2000). Work as a turning point in the life course of criminals: A duration model of age, employment, and recidivism. *American Sociological Review, 65*, 529-546.

Universal Declaration of Human Rights. (1948, December 10). *United Nations, General Assembly Resolution 217A (III)*. New York, NY: United Nations.

Vacca, J. S. (2004). Educated prisoners are less likely to return to prison. *Journal of Correctional Education, 55*(4), 297-305.

Visher, C. A., & Lattimore, P. K. (2007). Major study examines prisoners and their reentry needs. *NIJ Journal, 258*, 30-33.

Visher, C., Winterfield, L., & Weiman, D. (2004). *Baltimore prisoners' experiences returning home*. Washington, DC: The Urban Institute.

Walker, S (2001). *Sense and nonsense about crime and drugs: A policy guide* (5th ed.). Belmont, CA: Wadsworth.

Walters, G. D. (1990). *The criminal lifestyle: Patterns of serious criminal conduct*. Thousand Oaks, CA: SAGE.

West, H. C. (2010). *Prison inmates at midyear, 2009*. Washington, DC: U.S. Department of Justice, Bureau of Justice Statistics.

Western, B., Kling, J. R., & Weiman, D. (2001). The labor market consequences of incarceration. *Criminal Justice and Behavior, 30*(4), 399-421.

Witte, A. D., & Tauchen, H. (1994). Work and crime: An exploration using panel data. *Public Finance, 49*(Supplement), 155-167.

Zimring, F. E. (2001). The new politics of criminal justice: Of three strikes, truth-in-sentencing, and Megan's laws. In National Institute of Justice (Ed.), *Perspectives on crime and justice: 1999-2000 lecture series* (pp. 1-22). Washington, DC: National Institute of Justice.

CHAPTER 2

HISTORY AND POLITICS OF CORRECTIONAL EDUCATION

David R. Werner, Amy Widestrom, and Sylvester "Bud" Pues

In the early U.S. penitentiary system, prison education consisted simply of providing prisoners with Bibles and letting them contemplate their sins for the duration of their sentence. Beginning with prison reforms in the 1870s and 1880s, education in prisons evolved so that correctional facilities began to offer some educational or vocational programs. However, the short time an inmate stays in jail rather than prison has made it difficult to develop educational programming that is effective in the jail environment, making the provision of jail education more difficult and less consistent than prison education. Moreover, providing education to the incarcerated—in either prisons or jails—has always been subject to the changing public perception of the purpose and expense of incarceration. With the dramatic rise in recent decades of both the cost of incarceration and the number of people incarcerated, there may be an emerging sense that educating inmates might be a cost-effective way of slowing both the escalating expense of incarceration and the swelling prison population; however, recent economic realities may counter this trend. If education is to take on more importance with the incarcerated population, jail education, because it is the point of entry into the incarceration system, is poised to become increasingly important. This chapter will explore the history of education in jails and prisons, the theories of education that work in the carceral environment, and the politics that drive the debate around providing education to those incarcerated.

Education-Based Incarceration and Recidivism:
The Ultimate Social Justice Crime-Fighting Tool, pp. 21–40
Copyright © 2012 by Information Age Publishing
All rights of reproduction in any form reserved.

Why do people commit crimes, and if they commit crimes what do we, as a society, do about it? If society considers crime to be inevitable and without hope of eradication, then it is reasonable to believe that those who commit crimes will be treated differently than if society believes that criminals can be rehabilitated or reintegrated into society. To understand the development of the system of incarceration in western society is to first understand the theories of criminal activity that preceded it.

This chapter proceeds as follows. In the first section, we examine the evolution of the conception of criminal activity and the nature of criminals, as well as the history and growth of the penal system and of programs, including education, within correctional institutions. Over time, the ideas of punishment and rehabilitation have evolved. By the end of the twentieth-century, educational and work programs were seen as rehabilitative and offered in many facilities. Next, we outline the theories of education that apply to the carceral environment. Unlike a traditional educational setting, offering educational programs within prisons and jails presents a unique set of challenges, outlined here, but elaborated on in subsequent chapters of this book. Finally, the idea of offering educational programs within correctional facilities is often controversial, and the fourth section of this chapter outlines some of the political battles that have defined and continue to shape the provision of education to the incarcerated.

THE HISTORY OF PUNISHMENT
AND PRISONS IN THE UNITED STATES

As originally conceived, prison was a place for a monarch or dictator to retain political offenders or those who had been captured in battle. Caesar had his dungeons, France its Bastille, and England, the Tower of London or one of the other of the Monarch's castles. This type of incarceration was defined by external politics rather than by crime. The individual was often held until the political regime changed, at which point he or she was released and, often, those formerly in power become the incarcerated. The concept of housing offenders for nonpolitical causes came as a result of new laws that were passed in response to the changing economy as the monarchy faded from view. Even America had prisons during the Revolutionary War to house wartime prisoners. When these wartime prisons were no longer needed they were converted to house offenders of new colonial laws (American Correctional Association [ACA], 1983, pp. 1-9).

Prior to the seventeenth century, punishment in both Europe and America tended to be used as a method of holding those awaiting corporal or, more likely, capital punishment. If imprisonment was employed for purposes other than corporal punishment, it was only for very specific purposes. For example, debtors' prison, which is familiar to most people, was not intended to keep the individual debtors incarcerated but rather served as a sort of state-sanctioned kidnapping. Its only end was to raise money. Upon raising the required money, the debtor was set free. If the debt could not be paid, the debtor was subject to indentured or forcible service. Other punishments included being conscripted as sailors or galley slaves, or even sent to "the colonies" as was done with England sending its prisoners to Australia to start a new colony (ACA, 1983, pp. 8-9).

Crime and Punishment in the American Colonies and the New Republic

Judicial practice and response to crime in colonial America followed closely the principles of Christian monarchy. Colonists tended to depend on noninstitutional means of handling problems, and jails were not the ordinary mechanism for correction. David J. Rothman, in *The Discovery of the Asylum,* notes that colonial jails held those "in the process of judgment, not those who had completed it" (1971, p. 48). As in Medieval society, an offense was most often punished severely. Colonial society defined a wide range of behavior as sinful and deviant, and capital punishment was prescribed for diverse crimes such as murder, arson, horse stealing, and disrespect of one's parents (Rothman, 1971). The heavy dependence on the gallows for juridical response in colonial America indicates the connection that the colonists saw between sin and crime. With a world view that saw sin as endemic to nature, punishment served three specific purposes: (1) it intimidated the offender; (2) it was essential to public safety; and (3) it was the vehicle by which "society carried out God's law.... To allow the criminal to escape was to implicate everyone in his crime" (Rothman, 1971, p. 18).

Among the first penal facilities in the newly independent nation was a jail on Walnut Street in Philadelphia, which opened in January of 1776. The jail had an inglorious debut as a military prison during the Revolutionary War, used by whichever side happened to be occupying the city (McKelvey, 1977). It was by any description a vile place: the keeper ran a taproom on the first floor, and any new inmate was required either to stand the house to a round of drinks or to surrender his or her clothes; and, notably, the sexes were not separated (Werner, 1990). In response to these horrors, and following the work of the Quaker Richard Wistar, in 1776 Philadelphians formed the Society for Assisting Distressed Prisoners, the origin of modern prison reform movements. While the society disbanded the following year due to the war, the 15 years following the end of the war saw a remarkable transformation in the response to crime, and the prison was to become a uniquely American invention. Negley K. Teeters, a penologist whose life and career spanned the end of the nineteenth and much of the twentieth centuries, was the first to describe the Walnut Street Jail as "the cradle of the Penitentiary" (quoted in McKelvey, 1977, p. 8).

At the end of the war the Walnut Street jail was turned into a prison. But by 1788, the Philadelphia Society for Alleviating the Miseries of Public Prisons had issued a declaration stating that solitary confinement and abstinence from hard drink would prove the most useful in the reformation of the convicted (Rothman, 1971); jails needed to be modified to reflect this new thinking. The Walnut Street Jail reopened in 1790 with a small block of 16 individual cells erected within the yard of the facility. This reopening is generally regarded as the beginning of the modern prison system, and the jail's operating system reflected significant changes: the facility's operating procedures advocated enforced solitary confinement, and the prisoner would only have personal contact with the chaplain or religious instructor. The only reading material allowed to the prisoner was the Bible (Gehring, 2007, p.8).

The Pennsylvania and Auburn Systems

In 1818, construction was begun on the Western State Penitentiary near Pittsburgh. Its design was based on the Walnut Street model, with cells that allowed for individual isolation, arranged in a semicircular block, with individual exercise yards. It was opened in 1826, and is still in operation (Pennsylvania Historical and Museum Commission, n.d.). Authorized by the Pennsylvania State Legislature, the Cherry Hill Penitentiary opened in 1829 to serve the eastern part of the state (McKelvey, 1977). This penitentiary was replaced by the New Eastern Penitentiary that included a maximum-security facility at Graterford, which is the only remaining operational facility of the Eastern Penitentiary and houses approximately 3,600 inmates (Pennsylvania Historical and Museum Commission, n.d.).

Together, in the mid-1800s, these institutions and the methods used within them became known as the Pennsylvania System, which entailed total isolation of the inmate from other inmates. While work tasks were minimal, any work was to be done in the individual cells, and each cell had an attached exercise facility and in-cell toilet and washing facilities. With this design, there was no reason for an inmate to ever leave the confines of his or her cell. While isolation was thought ideal at the time, abso-lute isolation proved "harmful" to the individual prisoners. In fact, many cases of mental breakdown were reported (de Beaumont & de Tocqueville, 1964, p.82).

Auburn Prison in New York was opened in December of 1821, based also on the principle of isolation without labor. Even though the cells had no toilet facilities, prisoners were not permitted to leave their cells. By 1824, Captain Elam Lynds introduced the system of prison discipline that would become known as the Auburn System—isolation at night with communal work during the day. Complete silence was always to be observed, and discipline was strict in all other respects: inmates were to keep their eyes downcast. The "lock-step" was used, and flogging was the punishment of choice. Lynds had no illusions about the ability to reform the individual. He believed that there was little hope of transforming older inmates. The young, he thought, could possibly be taught to be "good craftsmen" (Rothman, 1971, p. 103).

By 1825, the growing inmate population of New York necessitated the construction of another prison and a new prison known as Sing Sing was built, based on the Auburn system. Lynds' instructions to new inmates, in 1826, gave little doubt that complete silence and isolation was to be maintained: "It is true that while being confined here you can have no intelligence concerning relatives or friends...You are to be literally buried from the world" (Rothman, 1971, p 104).

The Prison of the Late 1800s

The period from 1840 to 1900 was characterized by an increasing conflict between the ideal of the prison as imagined by scholars and penologists and the reality of the prison as an institution dictated by practice. Practitioners in the latter half of the nineteenth century were engaged in a debate about the merits of the Pennsylvania System versus the Auburn System, with the gradual emergence of the Auburn System as dominant despite that the Pennsylvania System was widely recognized as superior (Rothman, 1971, p. 14-14). This was in large part because of the failure of the Pennsylvania System, which occurred for two reasons: cost and the fact that isolation as an ideal did not work in practice (ACA, 1983, p. 51; McKelvey, 1977, p. 11).

Isolation was rarely completely achievable in any one institution for very long. Moreover, in the Pennsylvania System, inmates who had been subjected to isolation and then released from prison were found to be unfit to resume life in society; the general feeling was that isolation had served to derange and embitter (McKelvey, 1977). Complicating matters for the Pennsylvania System was that both Walnut Street and Cherry Hill were soon so overcrowded with new admissions that true isolation was not sustainable. Finally, and perhaps due to evolving ideas about the merits of isolation, the most lasting contribution of the late 1800s to subsequent penology was the emerging notion that work, specifically communal work, was essential to the imprisonment process. In some places, the lease, or contract, system was developed, leasing prison labor to outside contractors. The contract system was especially popular in the South following the Civil War, but it was also responsible for the growing corruption of the southern prison system during this period (Werner, 1990). This practice continued until the development of resistance by free labor in the 1900s.

As institutions became overcrowded in the late 1800s, disciplinary methods used in prisons became increasingly harsh as wardens attempted to control growing prisoner populations. Prison management manuals of the time make frequent allusion to the use of severe punishment. Administrators in the 1800s "were judged by the prison's production record and number of escapes, not by the number of inmates rehabilitated" (ACA, 1983, p. 55). Because of this prevailing spirit, rules were designed to keep prisoners under total control. The use of the rod was not uncommon (McKelvey, 1977).

What is remarkable about the evolution of carceral institutions in the United States, particularly the reliance on the Auburn System and its methods of work and discipline, is the speed with which incarceration as punishment came to dominate thinking about what to do with individual criminal offenders. Within less than 100 years the entire way in which the Western World punished criminals changed from a reliance on public, corporal punishment to complete dependence on discipline and incarceration (Foucault, 1979). Within a comparatively short time, a major shift in thinking occurred; the colonists tended to see crime as a product of an imperfect but perfectible social system, not as the result of inevitable sin that required castigation.

Prison as punishment continued throughout the latter half of the nineteenth century to take on the self-evident character it has today. In a society that values liberty, perhaps imprisonment is simply the obvious form of punishment (Foucault, 1979), and the commitment to prison as punishment is even more evident today. Despite that overcrowding continues to be a problem and institutions are increasingly less than effective, it is still difficult to find other solutions to criminality. Perhaps the primary effect of the development of the prison system in the 1800s has been the creation of a deeply entrenched institutional system and a philosophy of punishment that continues to pervade society to this day.

The Roots of Rehabilitation and the Modern Penal System

During the late 1800s, U.S. prisons experienced phenomenal growth—right in step with the growing population of the country—mostly due to immigration. Between 1860 and 1870 alone, the prison population in the United States rose from 19,000 to 33,000, an increase of 72% in 10 years (ACA, 1983, p. 63)! While some of this increase is explained by post-Civil War incarceration, many of those being admitted to prison were recidivists. French and U.S. prisons during this period reported recidivism rates of upwards of 30%, laying the groundwork for a persistent problem in the U.S. prison and jail systems.

In 1847, Samuel Gridley Howe, a member of the Boston Prison Discipline Society, expressed hope in the new U.S. method of incarceration, which set the tone for the next 150 years of penological reformist thinking:

> The doctrine of retributive justice is rapidly passing away, and with it will pass away, I hope, every kind of punishment that has not the reformation of the Criminal in view. One of the first effects of this will be, I am sure, the decrease in the length of sentence and the adoption of some means by which the duration and severity of imprisonment may in all cases be modified by the conduct and character of the prisoners. What we want now—what no system that I know offers—is the means of training the prisoner's moral sentiments and his power of self-government by actual exercise. I believe that there are many who might be so trained as to be left upon their parole during the last period of their imprisonment. (McKelvey, 1977, p. 42).

At this specific time Howe was trifle optimistic. It was to be 100 years before his words would even be given a general hearing among penologists in the United States. The first concern of prisons for many years was profit.

Penology in the latter half of the nineteenth century was dominated by the concern for profit. The primary reason the Auburn System finally won over the Pennsylvania System was that it promised to be cost-efficient (ACA 1983, p. 51). Early wardens were primarily concerned with making the prison a self-supporting institution and with creating a prosperous prison industry. It must be remembered that almost all of the ablest wardens of the 1800s—namely Zebulon Brockway, as well as Amos, Moses, and Louis Pilsbury, those who later were to earn fame as significant personalities in the movement for prison reform and redefinition—first won distinction as managers of efficient and profitable prisons (McKelvey, 1977). Retribution, it was discovered, costs money. Yet, in 1867, Enoch Wines and Theodore Dwight surveyed nearly all of the prisons then existing and issued their landmark *Report on the Prisons and Reformatories of the United States and Canada*. They concluded that "there is not a state prison in America in which the reformation of the convict is the supreme object of the discipline" (1867/1976, p. 26). While Wines and Dwight praised efforts of wardens toward reform that might achieve these ends, they recognized that profit was still sovereign.

After Enoch Wines' tour of U.S. prisons in 1865, he and a few companions sent invitations for delegates to meet in Cincinnati in 1870. Attending were 130 men and women interested in prison reform from 24 states who were welcomed by Governor Rutherford B. Hayes, later president of the National Prison Association, as well as president of the United States. The congress met as the National Congress on Penitentiary and Reformatory Discipline (ACA, 1983). Wines spent most of the conference in an unsuccessful attempt to persuade the attendees that states should make the reformation of inmates the sole goal of incarceration and should agree to support their own prison systems. The participants of the congress drafted a declaration of principles. Of particular importance, Principle 10 supported prison education, reading: "Education is a vital force in the reformation of fallen men and women.... Education is therefore, a matter of primary importance in prisons, and should be carried out to the utmost extent consistent with the other purposes of such institutions" (Wines, 1895, p. 542). Among the presentations was Zebulon Brockway's address, "Ideal for a True Prison System for a State."

While many of the changes discussed at the Cincinnati congress did not bear fruit until well into the next century, the spirit of reform was clearly evident in some penal institutions. For example, inmates were sentenced traditionally for set terms, with all inmates serving time thrown together in whatever prison happened to be available. Nothing an inmate did had an affect on his or her sentence or on the ease or difficulty of the time he or she spent incarcerated. In fact, the concept of the "indeterminate sentence"—that it should be the progress an inmate made while incarcerated and not a judicial order that determined the length of imprisonment—did not appear on the congress' agenda until 1870. However, one emerging trend in penology was the possibility of furthering the use of the "Mark System."

In 1840, Captain Alexander Machonochie was appointed commander of the Norfolk Island penal colony in Australia. Machonochie's philosophy of incarceration had, for some time previously, centered on the idea of reformation rather than punishment. He noted that when one considers the effects of physical pain, one's concern is with the individual, but when an individual is "morally dislocated" so that he or she commits crimes, one thinks only of the consequences to society (Gehring, 2007).

Accordingly, Maconochie, in common with most wardens of the middle and late 1800s, believed work to be essential to the reformation process. He went further, however, in stating that a prison sentence should combine "specific punishment for the past" with "specific training for the future" (McKelvey, 1977, p. 36). As part of this training for the future, Maconochie saw the importance of giving inmates some responsibility for their behavior while they were incarcerated. He developed what became known as the Mark System, whereby an inmate could earn credits or marks toward early release. Maconochie was one of the first to conceptualize incarceration by task rather than by time, the principle that lies at the heart of most modern-day indeterminate sentencing laws (cf. Hughes, 1986). But it was the reformatory enthusiasm of Zebulon Brockway that was finally able to combine these elements into a cohesive program of prison organization and procedure.

There is also evidence of early correctional education, mirroring the recommendations in Principle 10, drafted by the Cincinnati congress in 1870. In 1861, Zebulon Brockway, who had earned his reputation as warden of New York's Monroe County Penitentiary, was appointed as the first organizing attendant of the Detroit House of Correction. Brockway had recently undergone a significant religious conversion, and came to Detroit with the zeal of a true reformer. Brockway developed educational and industrial programs, granted wages for extra production, arranged for employment for those released, and eventually put into place a grading or classification system when a women's adjunct to the House of Corrections was opened (McKelvey, 1977).

In 1876, Brockway assumed the post of warden at New York's newly opened Elmira prison. Elmira was designed to be the first New York prison to implement actively the reforms called for in the Declaration of Principles adopted at the American Prison Association Congress in Cincinnati. Brockway was the ideal warden for such an innovative endeavor. Elmira soon became a showcase for Brockway's principles and the current thinking on prison in the United States (ACA, 1983).

It is perhaps a mistake to term any process going on in prisons before the 1870s as "correctional education" or "corrections education." The early prisoners of the Walnut Street Jail were supplied only with Bibles and received occasional visits from the prison chaplain; however, these activities were not intended to reform inmates. Instead, they were intended to provide inmates with opportunities to reflect on their sins. While, Louis Dwight and the Boston Prison Discipline Society organized Sabbath Schools in certain prisons, the effort was occasional and sporadic. Nonetheless, it is worth noting that in 1847, New York provided the first instance of public support for education in prison with the passage of a state law that provided two instructors for every state prison. Still, it was

Brockway's educational reforms at Elmira that outlined the first true education and training program for prison inmates (Gehring, 2007).

The Elmira facility contained both academic and vocational sections. The academic area contained 28 classrooms, while the vocational section, or "trade school," eventually grew to offer as many as 36 trades. In addition, the prison boosted a 600-seat lecture hall, where Brockway instituted a series of Sunday lectures on current cultural topics, a military drill hall, and a large gymnasium (Gehring, 2007, pp. 31-35).

Moral and vocational education formed the heart of the program at Elmira. Brockway also started education programs for disabled learners, referred to at the time as "dullards"—earning him credit for beginning the first special education programs in prison. Additionally, he started an inmate newspaper, used Maconochie's Mark System to give inmates some control over their release time, and began a prerelease program that allowed inmates to gain some experience with budgeting money and with personal nutrition (Gehring, 1982).

The academic environment that Brockway established at Elmira was quite extensive, even by today's standards. Courses were offered in geometry, psychology, natural history, nature studies, physical geography, political economy, and natural science. Brockway even went so far as to make completion of English literature a requirement for parole, effectively increasing enrollment in 1 week from 50 to 600 (Gehring, 1982, 2007). The offerings at Elmira still stand as uniquely well-rounded. In fact, it would be another 40 years before another prison education program of this caliber would be seen anywhere.

Brockway, who eventually became president of the American Prison Association, continued to push for reform. But public reaction to Brockway's program at Elmira was often harsh, with the now-familiar cries of providing the inmates with too many creature comforts and opportunities among the most frequent complaints. In spite of the program's success and because of general belief in discipline and punishment as the carceral goal, public pressure for more rigorous discipline continued to mount, significantly affecting the policies, structures, and procedures of future correctional institutions.

U.S. Prisons in the Twentieth Century

When the majority of the prisons in the North, Midwest, and California were built, the large factory or industrial prison was in vogue. The prisons in the Northwest and mountain states developed out of what had been primarily territorial prisons under the control of the military. Deer Lodge in Montana, Walla Walla in Washington, and Calgary in Alberta,

Canada, are all examples of prisons based on early territorial models (ACA, 1983). In the Deep South, before the Civil War, plantations were essentially private prisons for slaves, so it had been necessary to develop small holding institutions for the handful of urban White miscreants who required incarceration. It only seemed natural for Southern states to turn prisoners over to private contractors for work. The great prison farms of the Deep South, reaching as far as Texas, are, in effect, modern-day extensions of this era. Florida's first prison at Raiford was not even constructed until 1913. Unfortunately, the plantation system also inherited much of the violence and abuse associated with slavery. It was not until after World War II that reform began to have an appreciable effect on Southern penology (ACA, 1983).

It can easily be argued that the United States still suffers from its chaotic penal heritage. While there have been significant developments in penology since the early 1900s, six of the 120 maximum-security institutions in operation in 2000 were built before 1900 and 25% of the prisons operating in 2000 were built before 1920. The prevalence of antiquated, outdated institutions hampers state departments of correction in any attempts at modernization. San Quentin, for example, the oldest prison in California, begun in 1850 by a lessee with convict labor, was largely built in the late 1800s and early 1900s. Today, San Quentin stands as a prime example of America's gothic, large-scale industrial prisons still common to many states. The antiquated architecture, the size of the prison and the number of inmates it holds (6,000 in 2000) makes the construction of newer facilities a major financial undertaking, a fact that is particularly important in light of today's tight state budgets. Not surprisingly, the prison has been the subject of several court orders claiming obsolete and inhumane conditions. Most northern states have at least one similar institution (ACA, 1983).

The concept and nature of work in these institutions has also changed in important ways that shape the day-to-day operations of penal institutions. While the early 1900s is often referred to as the "industrial period" of U.S. penology, prison industrialization during this period changed dramatically. Growing labor unions combined with powerful industrial magnates to pressure prisons to stop competing with private corporations on the free-market with their labor services and goods. Prison reformers had for some time objected to the contract system, or the practice of states "loaning" prisoners to private contractors for work, and joined in pressuring state legislatures to abandon the system (ACA, 1983). In 1888, New York passed the Yates Law, ordering the cessation of all prison industries. The industries at Brockway's beloved Elmira facility ground to a halt. It should be noted, however, that within a few days Brockway had all the inmates formerly involved in industry doing close-order drills in the recreation yard. He also expanded the institution's fife-and-drum corps to a full-scale brass band (Gehring, 1982).

The types of goods produced by prison industries also changed over the course of the century, from for-profit manufacturing to public-sector products (i.e., products that would only be used by state agencies). Gradually, the notion that prisons would be supported by inmate labor and goods production gave way to prisoners working to learn trades but avoiding public markets. These changes marked a shift in the psychological concept of labor and its use in correctional facilities. In the early prisons, while labor was believed to be beneficial to the individual, prisoner labor more importantly provided financial support for the prison (Platt, 1980). With the decline of for-profit industries, prison labor evolved to produce materials solely for the purposes of governmental consumption. Where there was no need for this, the idea of meaningless work, or work for the sake of work, developed, and inmates found themselves moving rocks from one side of the prison yard to the other or, in an echo of today, cleaning and recleaning floors and equipment (Platt, 1980; Werner 1990).

The major casualty that emerged from the decline of for-profit prison industry was the number of employed prisoners. Following the Civil War, the population of U.S. prisons had risen dramatically (ACA, 1983). Wars tend to "employ" people otherwise on the fringe of society, and the ending of wars has traditionally been echoed in a rise in the prison population as the numbers of those in the underclass increase. Prison administrators were faced with two new problems: an increasing minority population and an increasing idle population (Platt, 1980).

With the end of World War I, prison populations again swelled as returning soldiers found an economy that could not absorb them. The prisons into which these exsoldiers settled were mostly idle. By 1923, anti-contract legislation had produced a 20% decrease in the number of employed prisoners, compared to 1895 figures, when 72% were employed (Werner, 1990). These and other factors contributed to two series of harsh prison riots: the first between 1918 and 1921, and the second from 1929 to 1930.

In response to these dramatic institutional changes, the period from 1918 to 1940 saw the beginning of a series of long-needed changes in penology. Although most of the elements that came into place during this period had earlier roots, the rise of the U.S. prison population following World War I provided new impetus to reform, as well as to revising the structure of penology. For the first time, there was a real attempt to understand what caused offenders to commit crimes. This period also saw the first attempts to classify prisoners using statistically sound algorithms. By this time, indeterminate sentencing and parole were in wide use, affecting prisoner distribution across facilities. Finally, the period saw the development of a modern corrections philosophy based on determining the cause and nature of an individual's crime. This shift in philosophy resulted in the first attempts to classify offenders based on the nature of their offenses, establishing a system that determined security risk as well as access to education, work, and other programs. This new focus on causation and classification opened the door for access to educational and vocational programs for the incarcerated in ways that were previously unheard of.

This has not meant a flourishing of educational and vocational programming in all correctional facilities in the United States. It has meant, however, that some institutions provide a wide range of educational programming for the incarcerated. More importantly, the changes that occurred over the course of the twentieth century in correctional facilities, and among the population of the United States and its carceral institutions, have provided an opening for institutions and experts to consider the possibility of educational programming in these facilities, including what theories of correctional education could operate in such institutions and whether educational programming would be political and economically viable in jails and prisons.

THEORIES OF CORRECTIONAL EDUCATION

Because the overriding concern among those who manage jails and prisons is safety and security, any theory of correctional education is, to some extent, formed by the theory that guides the prison itself. Thus, one way to understanding correctional education is to first consider the theories and purpose of incarceration itself and then place educational programming within the environment implied by these theories. In other words, any theory of correctional education depends on the approach taken to developing educational programming in an institution, which is in turn based on the theory guiding a particular correctional institution (Werner, 1990). It is also important to note different correctional facilities might be structured differently, depending on the politics and policies of the state in which they are located and the nature of the leadership of the facilities.

Drawing on our examination of the evolution of incarceration and carceral institutions, we propose that there are five ways one could understand the purpose and intent of imprisonment (cf. ACA, 1983; McKelvey, 1977; Werner, 1990). The first is incarceration purely for punishment. Under this concept, individuals possess free-will, but some individuals make bad decisions; any person who makes a bad decision must then be a bad person, and that bad person should be punished. The second concept, closely related to the first, is the idea that prison is for the correction of behavior. This perspective suggests not only that individuals possess free will but that they are also rational. Because they are rational, the threat of prison will deter or "correct" behavior. If it does not, prison or jail is the punishment, and presumably the threat of future imprisonment will alter future action. Thus, incarceration under this concept is viewed as a deterrent. The third concept is the understanding of prisons and jails as institutions of reform. This theory posits that individuals are actors with free will. Those who make bad decisions are not inherently bad people; therefore, they can be reshaped or reformed into good people. This theory suggests that there is a desired ideal and that imprisonment can reshape individuals to match that ideal.

The fourth theory poses the idea that incapacitation is unconcerned with whether people who make bad decisions are inherently good or bad, but posits that they should be kept off the streets because they engaged in bad behavior and may do so again. This is based, in part, on Martinson's classic and often-quoted, though largely discredited, assertion that after-the-fact rehabilitation or punishment of crime does not work and that the only effective strategy for preventing crime is incarcerating offenders (1974). This is also based, in part, on a fear of what a person *might* do, rather than what a person *has done*. It represents a major shift in thinking about incarceration because it punishes not only what has been done, but what an individual might do in the future.

Finally, the fifth theory is a theory of rehabilitation. It is fundamentally different from the others. The theories of punishment and correction rest on the assumption that an individual is inherently bad by virtue of engaging in bad behavior, while theories of reform and incapacitation are silent about the inherent nature of the "goodness" or "badness" of an individual, but they do assume that individuals can become bad, and therefore must be punished. The theory of rehabilitation, though, rests on the idea that people are inherently good and that while they may have engaged in bad behavior, it is in part not their fault and they can and should be returned to a state of goodness.

If one is guided by theories of punishment, correction, or incapacitation, there would be little use for prison or jail education because educational programming does not fit into the punishment-model, corrections-model, or incapacitation-model of incarceration: the ideas of punishment or corrections would view any provision of education as a "perk" and therefore contrary to the goal of punishment, while the theory of incapacitation would view the provision of education as "too-little-too-late." Conversely, both the notion of reform and the notion of rehabilitation suggest that education could play a role in a correctional environment, though the role of education would be different if it were based on ideas of reform or ideas of rehabilitation. Both would place an emphasis on developing values, but rehabilitation would also emphasize developing skills and knowledge that a particular individual lacked.

If the purpose of reform is guiding the structure and day-to-day operations of a correctional facility, education could play a key role. However, it could only do so if the theory of education guiding the development of educational programming is one that views education as a tool to mold and reshape students. In this conception, educational programs would need to be targeted at specific goals, and aimed at developing specific attributes of incarcerated individuals. If, however, a theory of rehabilitation is structuring the day-to-day workings of the correctional institution, then education could play a much different role. In this model of incarceration, individuals are inherently good, but simply have not had access to many positive aspects of civil society and, therefore, educational programming should be targeted at providing that access.

We suggest that the flaw in the theory of *re*habilitation is that most incarcerated individuals were never *habilitated* to begin with because of their lack of access to positive socializing and educational institutions in society. In fact, it can be argued that the real problem with "rehabilitation" as a philosophy for prison or jail education is in the name itself. Rehabilitation may fail because it tries to replace or renew something that never existed. Real prison or jail education is more in the way of "habilitation," of exposing inmates to a life that most are not aware of. Why such individuals never were habilitated is often the subject of furious debate, with the most extreme arguments describing the conscious social exclusion of under- and lower-class individuals.

Education operating under such a theory must play an usual role, given that for many in the lower and under classes prison or jail education may be the last chance to receive any formal education. Education operating under this assumption would be an expansive enterprise, opening avenues of thought and allowing students to explore a new world through new perspectives. Once habilitated, students could use the education they received while incarcerated to finally flourish as productive members of society, once released

To conclude, it seems clear that the development of educational programming within a correctional facility depends greatly on two elements: first, why one thinks people are incarcerated, and second, what one thinks education can actually accomplish. Nearly all current research on adult education suggests that any education must be relevant to the adult and tailored to the student's strengths. If the purpose of imprisonment is to either habilitate or reform, then correctional facilities will need a variety of educational strategies to help them accomplish this goal. These educational programs will need to be designed to use and develop the individual's strengths and be made relevant to the individual so that upon release the individual has new values, knowledge, and skills or a trade that will allow him/her to either remain reformed or have real access to social systems on the outside. In most cases, this would describe a new theory of correctional education guiding the provision of educational programs in correctional settings in the United States, unlikely to be implemented give the history of political and economic barriers to robust educational programming in correctional facilities throughout the country.

THE POLITICS OF EDUCATION IN CORRECTIONAL INSTITUTIONS

The politics of providing educational opportunities to jail or prison inmates must be placed in the broader political debate about the American criminal justice system. It is generally understood that Americans tend to be punitive in their approach to criminal justice, and that this has found expression in a variety of laws governing crime and punishment, including the three-strikes laws and mandatory minimum sentencing requirements (Frost, 2010). However, public opinion and attitudes of criminal justice practitioners have begun to change over the last decade and are more nuanced than the punitive understanding allows. This is in part because public opinion on issues of crime and punishment is largely uninformed and based on incomplete information, particularly with respect to trends in crime, and because of this, is highly determined by the survey instrument used to measure public opinion on this topic (Davis, 1997; Frost, 2010; The Sentencing Project, n.d.).

Research, however, does show that attitudes toward punishment have changed in recent decades, particularly as it pertains to the punitiveness of the criminal justice system, and that policymakers do not accurately understand public attitudes about crime and punishment (The Sentencing Project, n.d.). This last point is important; in a representative democracy elected officials are to assess and respond to the needs and demands of citizens. However, if public attitudes shift while official policies do not, public policy will not accurately reflect the will of the people (Stimson, 2004). This is particularly important in the arena of criminal justice because the policies made have a direct effect on the lives of criminals and the nature of punishment in the criminal justice system.

Despite a pervasive belief that Americans are punitive in their approach to crime, a 1994 Gallup poll found that 48% of respondents agreed with the following statement: "We need a tougher approach to dealing with the causes of crime with an emphasis on improving job and vocational training, providing family counseling, and increasing the number of neighborhood activity centers for young people" (Peter D. Hart Research Associations, 2002, p. 2). In 1995, a survey conducted by the National Opinion Survey on Crime and Justice showed significant support for rehabilitative measures: 21% of U.S. adults indicated rehabilitation should be the *principal* goal in sentencing offenders, and 50% of respondents said it should be the *most* important factor in sentencing juveniles (The Sentencing Project, n.d.). These surveys show how the wording of questions matter for capturing public opinion, but they also reveal a commitment to habilitation or rehabilitation not reflected in the national debate about criminal justice or criminal justice policies considered by law makers.

Importantly, the public's commitment to alternative ways to address crime, including the causes of crime as well as program provision to the incarcerated, has increased over time. A 2001 Gallup poll found that the number of respondents agreeing to the statement that 'causes of crime need to be better addressed' increased from 48% in 1994 to 65% in 2001. Moreover, in a 2002 national study, Hart Research Associates found that "A failure to rehabilitate prisoners is seen as a major shortcoming of the U.S. prison system" by the American public (p. 13). This study further showed that 70% of respondents strongly favored and 21% of respondents somewhat favored "Requiring prisoners to take classes and get an education so that they can find a job when they are released from prison" (Peter D. Hart Research Associates, 2002, p. 14). A key source of this turn from punishment to (re)habilitation is that "there is widespread agreement that the nation's existing approach to criminal justice is off-target," and "that the political conventional wisdom misjudges the mood of the voters, who now see the "lock 'em up" strategy as having failed in crucial respects" (Peter D. Hart Research Associates, 2002, p. 6). This suggests that there may be emerging support for educational programming.

SUMMARY, CONCLUSIONS AND IMPLICATIONS

The history of correctional institutions in the United States is in many ways the history of individual state systems shaped occasionally by national themes; Northern and East Coast facilities tended to follow the early models of the Pennsylvania and Auburn systems, Midwestern correctional facilities tended to be of the larger, fortress, or industrial models, Western jails and prisons tended to exhibit their territorial roots, while Southern institutions developed a farm- or plantation-like structure. A common aspect of early correctional facilities in the United States was that they were self-supporting institutions, and early wardens and managers were judged primarily on their success as fiscal servants of the state.

While a number of wardens managed to use this system to the benefit of reform, the profit motive limited reform to a peripheral role in prison organizations prior to 1900.

As the profit motive became less relevant, due to attacks on the contract system, the growing labor unions, and the Great Depression, the belief emerged that the inmate might not bear total responsibility for his or her incarceration; the responsibility for crime might also lie somewhere else in the social fabric of society. This shifted attitudes about corrections from incarceration as punishment to incarceration for correction or rehabilitation. Along with this change in penal philosophy came an interest in other aspects of incarceration which might prove beneficial to the correctional program. Following Brockway's success at the Elmira facility, education gradually came, for a time, to play a central role in the correctional process, culminating in the establishment of the Correctional Education Association in 1945, an off-shoot of the newly renamed American Correctional Association.

Complicating the issue of prison or jail education is the fact that as public attitudes seem to be shifting toward a more habilitative or rehabilitative model of incarceration, which would allow for the increased provision of education to the incarcerated, the economy of the United States fell into a deep recession in the fall of 2008. This, in effect, means that any proposal for prison or jail education now exists in an era of extraordinarily limited resources. Proposals for any education for the incarcerated do not fare well if forced to compete for limited dollars with public education, healthcare, parks, or a host of other items on the social agenda. Historically, prison and jail education programs have only been well-funded in times of surplus. Whatever social good prison or jail education may promise, it is still a low funding priority for most Americans.

All of this presents a unique challenge to lawmakers who first must realize this shift in public opinion and then must attempt to change correctional institutions to meet the new goal of (re)habilitation, and do all of this with extremely limited resources. This will be difficult for two reasons. First, as the history of correctional institutions makes clear, we have built a system that is in many ways self-perpetuating, making institutional reform very costly, both fiscally and in terms of the culture and operation of these institutions. Second, addressing the causes of crime and providing programs to the incarcerated costs money and since most states and localities do not have the budget to develop the types of comprehensive programs habilitation or rehabilitation would require, redirecting funds from other services, such as from traditional education to *correctional* education, may be politically unfeasible. What is more, Hart Associates found that survey respondents placed the reduction of prison spending at the top of their list for ways to reduce public spending in general, tied only with spending on transportation (Peter D. Hart Research Associates, 2002). While shifting resources to address the sources of crime and to reduce recidivism by providing programs to the incarcerated would lead to long term spending reductions, this would require an initial monetary investment the public may not have the stomach for. Thus, a shift toward habilitation or rehabilitation and toward the provision of education in correctional institutions, while ideologically supported by much of the public, may be difficult to achieve, particularly in a time of resource scarcity.

The evolution of correctional facilities in the United States and the politics surrounding these institutions are important to understand if we are to understand educational programs and the possibility for effective education in correctional institutions. The subsequent chapters in this book explore various contemporary challenges for, and aspects of, providing education in a carceral environment, but it is important to understand these challenges in their appropriate historical context. With the dramatic rise in recent decades of both the cost of incarceration and the number of people incarcerated, there is an emerging sense that educating inmates might be a cost-effective way of slowing both the escalating cost of incarceration and the swelling prison population. If this notion takes hold, then jail education at the point of entry into the carceral environment will play an important role. Even public opinion suggests that Americans would be open to greater service provision to inmates, yet the unwieldy nature of correctional institutions and the lack of budgetary resources may make the type of reform necessary to promote real and effective prison or jail education or "habilitation" difficult to achieve.

REFERENCES

American Correctional Association. (1983). *The American prison from the beginning— Pictorial history.* College Park, MD: American Correctional Association.

Davis, D. W. (1997). *State of the state survey: Attitudes toward crime and criminal justice: What you find depends on what you ask* (Briefing paper No. 97-20). Retrieved from http://www.ippsr.msu.edu/publications/bp9720.pdf

de Beaumont, G., & de Tocqueville, A. (1964/1833). *On the penitentiary system in the United States and its application to France.* Carbondale, IL: Southern Illinois University Press.

Foucault, M. (1975). *Discipline and punish.* New York, NY: Pantheon Books.

Frost, N. (2010). Beyond public opinion polls: Punitive public sentiment & criminal justice policy. *Sociology Compass 4*(3), 156-168.

Gehring, T. (1982). Zebulon Brockway of Elmira: 19th Century CE hero. *The Journal of Correctional Education, 33*(1), 7-9.

Gehring, T. (2007). *Teaching within prison walls.* San Bernardino, CA: California State University at San Bernadino.

Hughes, R. (1986). *The fatal shore: The epic of Australia's founding*. New York, NY: Vintage Books.

Martinson, R. (1974). What works: Questions and answers about prison reform. *National Affairs, 35*, 22-54.

McKelvey, B. (1976). *American prisons: A history of good intentions*. Montclair, NJ: Patterson Smith.

Pennsylvania Historical and Museum Commission. (n.d.). Bureau of Archives and History, Pennsylvania State Archives, Records of the Department of Justice, #RG15.

Peter D. Hart Research Associates, Inc. (2002). *Changing public attitudes toward the criminal justice system: Summary of findings*. Retrieved from http://www.soros.org/initiatives/usprograms/focus/justice/articles_publications/publications/hartpoll_20020201/Hart-Poll.pdf

Platt, T. (1980). *Prison management: A critique of current practices*. Keynote address presented at the Correctional Management Conference—"Prisons in Crisis," The University of La Verne, La Verne, California.

Rothman, D. J. (1969). *The discovery of the asylum*. Boston, MA: Little Brown.

The Sentencing Project. (n.d.). *Crime, punishment and public opinion: A summary of recent students and their implications for sentencing policies*. Retrieved from http://lobby.la.psu.edu/049_Criminal_Justice_Reform/Organizational_Statements/Sentencing%20Project/SP_Crime_Pub_Opinion.pdf

Stimson, J. A. (2004). *Tides of consent: How public opinion shapes American politics*. New York, NY: Cambridge University Press.

Werner, D. R. (1990). *Correctional education: Theory and practice*. Danville, Il: The Interstate.

Wines, E., & Dwight, T. (1976). *Report on the prisons and reformatories of the United States and Canada*. Montclair, NJ: Patterson Smith. (Original work published 1867)

Wines, F. H. (1895). *Punishment and reformation*. New York, NY: Thomas Y. Crowell.

CHAPTER 3

ASSESSING EDUCATIONAL NEEDS IN CORRECTIONAL SETTINGS

Brian Mattson, M. C. Esposito, and Carolyn Eggleston

Education-based incarceration strives to provide educational opportunity, in some form, to all inmates. There are a range of possible offerings that may be considered. In its most developed form, education-based incarceration involves an accurate assessment foundation that identifies inmates learning needs and informs a tailored educational approach. The chapter reviews current educational assessment literature specific to the relevant educational domains (e.g., academic achievement, learning efficacy, motivation, learning ability, and style) and then identifies current assessment techniques specific to these domains. The chapter examines how criminogenic risk and need help inform an understanding of educational need. In addition, the chapter examines how assessment is used to link inmates with appropriate educational programming. The chapter concludes with consideration for a variety of implementation challenges involved in assessing educational need and applying it to practice.

Surprisingly, the benefits of education for incarcerated individuals are an area of unresolved debate. There are more than 200 years of research on the role education has played in the lives of individuals in corrections (see Gehring & Eggleston, 2007; Gehring & Rennie, 2008). These efforts have

Education-Based Incarceration and Recidivism:
The Ultimate Social Justice Crime-Fighting Tool, pp. 41–58
Copyright © 2012 by Information Age Publishing
All rights of reproduction in any form reserved.

substantially informed the debate about the effectiveness of correctional education, with more or less attention paid to the lessons of the past, and with far too little of this knowledge having harnessed enough support in present day political circles to impact choices about making education broadly available to all people. The causal questions connecting education and crime appear unresolved or are not compelling enough to drive political action to explore definitively the role that a missed education experience has on the emergence of a criminal lifestyle. In these circumstances, the role education may play redirecting lives caught in stories of addiction and limited opportunity also goes unexplored. In a recent review commissioned by the Urban Institute, Layton-Mackenzie (2008) concluded that research on correctional education programs fails to untangle the issues of what works for whom, when, why and in what circumstances.

Despite these findings, there are efforts that help productively frame the challenges ahead. According to Erisman and Contardo (2005),

> Prisoners nationwide are far less educated than the general U.S. population and, before incarceration, were significantly more impoverished. Young minority men are particularly overrepresented in American prisons. Overall, the people who make up the incarcerated population are, in fact, those who have had the least opportunity prior to imprisonment ... higher education can improve conditions within correctional facilities, enhance prisoner self-esteem and prospects for employment after release, and function as a cost effective approach to reducing recidivism. Educating prisoners also allows them access to the many economic and social benefits associated with higher education ... correctional education offers a chance to break the cycle of inequality and benefit both the formerly incarcerated person and the society in which he or she lives. (p. v)

Collectively, these impressions reinforce the need to look at people in context and to explore the importance of educational need and opportunity in light of the life histories that have lead to crime (Elliott, 2006). Education and opportunity will lead people to a path away from the experiences of crime, focused on the future and the opportunities that remain in the lives of the adults in our corrections system and on the children for whom they model the often difficult path to a more holistic and fulfilling life.

NATURE OF THE PROBLEM

According to the Bureau of Justice Statistics (Glaze, 2010), at year-end 2009, there were 7,225,800 people under correctional supervision (includes community or incarcerated individuals). The figure represents a

48,800-person reduction from 2008, representing the first decline since the Bureau of Justice Statistics began reporting in 1980. The total number of offenders under correctional supervision at year-end 2009 represented about 3.1% of adults in the U.S. resident population or 1 in every 32 adults. The majority (70%) were supervised in the community although men under correctional supervision were more likely to be incarcerated. In 2000, 30% more African American men were in prison than were enrolled in college (Schiraldi & Ziedenberg, 2002). In fact, an African American man in his thirties is twice as likely to experience prison as to earn a college degree (Western, Schiraldi, & Ziedenberg, 2003).

The educational needs of individuals in corrections are staggering. About 75% of state prison inmates, almost 59% of federal inmates, and 69% of jail inmates did not complete high school; 35% of the jail population reported they dropped out of school because they were having academic or behavioral problems or they generally lost interest in school (Harlow, 2003). Correctional populations report lower educational attainment than do those in the general population. An estimated 40% of state prison inmates, 27% of federal inmates, 47% of inmates in local jails, and 31% of people on probation had not completed high school or its equivalent compared with 18% in the general population (Harlow, 2003). Sixty-six percent of state prison inmates with a learning disability had not completed high school or a General Equivalency Diploma (GED) (Harlow, 2003). Approximately 38% of inmates who completed 11 years or less of school were not working before entry to prison and the unemployment rate for State prison inmates at admission was 22% for those with less than a high school diploma (Harlow, 2003).

According to findings from the National Assessment of Adult Literacy (Greenberg, Dunleavy, & Kutner, 2007), approximately 17% of adult prisoners have been diagnosed with some type of learning disability compared to 6% of the general adult population (Greenberg et al., 2007). Approximately 39% of adult prisoners have below basic quantitative literacy compared to only 21% in the adult general population (Greenberg et al., 2007). Female adults in the general population were much more likely to score at a proficient level on all literacy scales than the female prison population; 47% of the female prison population scored below basic quantitative literacy compared to 22% in the general population. These same kinds of differences exist for men in prison (Greenberg et al., 2007). In general, prison inmates, both men and women, had lower average prose, document, and quantitative literacy than adults living in the general population. Among adults whose parents were high school graduates or attained postsecondary education, prison inmates had lower average literacy than those adults who lived in households whose parents had the same level of educational attainment.

There are several studies exploring the empirical relationship between education and crime. Steurer and his colleagues (2001) concluded that participation in correctional programming reduced the probability of incarceration by 29%. Lochner and Moretti (2003) estimate that a 1% increase in the U.S. male high school graduation rates would save as much as $1.4 billion, or about $2,100 per additional male high school graduate. A 1-year increase in average years of schooling reduces murder and assault by almost 30% (Moretti, 2005). These estimates are stable using aggregate state estimates, individual data, and data from longitudinal studies (Moretti, 2005).

There is a compelling need in present correctional discussions to understand these data in the context of the individual and the life experiences that have lead to their involvement in crime. These individual level assessments and commensurate move toward interpreting and working with individuals have promising potential for revealing the answers to what kinds of programs work with what kinds of people under what kinds of circumstances. As early as 1931, systemic educational approaches have been recommended to prescribe separate diagnostic and treatment plans for all inmates so each received that which they require for academic and vocational enhancement (Koski, 2002). Assessment tools coupled with the provision of appropriately matched services could lead to more high-need, high-risk offenders being referred to treatment and, ultimately, to improved treatment and public safety outcomes (Taxman, Cropsey, Young, & Wexler, 2007).

UNDERSTANDING EDUCATIONAL NEED

In order to answer the question about what educational programming works for whom and under what circumstances, it is important to first consider the realities of the individual learner. These students are not blank slates. In the corrections setting, it is necessary (i.e., risk management) to understand a person's educational need in the context of the other features that create risk in an individual across various settings including jails, prisons, and the community. These risks are assessed by understanding the features that lead to or cause crime and the persons history of offending. Based on an assessment of the individual's needs, a case plan is produced that prioritizes how services will be delivered. These assessed risks and needs are used by corrections agencies to inform decisions about who will be prioritized for educational programs using triage systems that assign limited program resources. In the end, the corrections agency uses these systems to improve outcomes for individuals and to increase the likelihood that a person will live a life free of crime.

As this work has evolved, a series of evidence-based principles has emerged to guide the practice of correctional agencies (Scott, 2008). More and more, these principles are informing the design and decision-making practices of an agency. It is within this context that educational-based programming effectiveness and priority is determined. Moreover, it is within this context that an appreciation for what programs work for whom and under what circumstances will emerge. The criminal justice profession has defined principles of evidence-based practices and the programs/strategies aligned with these principles that have an impact on public safety. These principles have been promulgated in the Unites States to help frame the practices of corrections agencies (Andrews & Bonta, 2010; Bogue, Campbell, & Clawson, 2004; Gaes, Flanagan, Motuik, & Stewart, 1999; Serin, 2005). These principles—risk, need, and responsivity—are briefly summarized below (Andrews & Bonta, 2010).

Risk Principle

First, corrections agencies should use risk assessment tools to measure an inmate's risk of reoffending, as well as to better understand the individual's criminogenic needs. This principle is based on research demonstrating that actuarial assessments more accurately predict misconduct in custody and reoffending in the community than professional judgments alone (for example, see Andrews, Bonta, & Wormith, 2006; Grove & Meehl, 1996; Meehl, 1995). The *risk principle* describes who should receive services. Risk levels are the result of an assessment and may be used to triage correctional populations. The higher risk individuals are in turn prioritized for educational programming (assuming a need is established) and prioritized on waitlists to receive these services when access is limited. Services are delivered to individuals prioritizing those who pose the greatest risk with an appreciation for the needs that underlie the risk and mindful of the individual responsivity considerations that will ensure services are effective (Andrews et al., 2006).

The principle draws from Andrews et al. (1990) meta-analytic research that shows a 30% reduction in recidivism when higher risk individuals receive services (Andrews et al., 1990). These reductions accrue, in part, because these individuals are more likely to reoffend. They account for a greater proportion of all offenses, therefore, reducing the criminal propensity of these individuals will have a greater impact on crime overall. In addition, research shows that mixing low-risk individuals with their high-risk peers will lead to more criminal behavior in the low-risk offenders (Andrews & Bonta, 2010). Thus, identifying risk and separating individuals to receive educational programming mitigates the antisocial learning opportunities and ensures higher risk offenders receive programming priority.

Need Principle

The *need principle* defines what should be treated (Andrews & Bonta, 2010). An offender's underlying deficits are commonly referred to as criminogenic needs and they are measured through assessment of people in corrections environments. Examples of criminogenic needs are criminal personality; antisocial attitudes, values, and beliefs; criminal peers; substance abuse; vocation and education; and dysfunctional family (see Andrews & Bonta, 2010). Criminogenic needs have an empirical relationship with past and future crime. They are targeted in programming in an attempt to mitigate the future risk of reoffending. Criminogenic needs are dynamic risk factors and serve as intermediate targets of change in rehabilitation programming (Andrews & Bonta, 2010). Seen through this lens, correctional education is a means to an end, an intermediate outcome on the path to a more meaningful identity often through acquiring a meaningful employment.

Responsivity Principle

The responsivity principle asserts that services should be responsive to the temperament, learning style, motivation, gender, and culture of the individual (Andrews & Bonta, 2010). The principle has prominence when addressing educational needs. Learning styles and learning disabilities are at the root of criminal onset trajectories. Following this principle, an inmate's unmet educational needs should be addressed with services that accommodate the variety of ways people learn and making these available to individuals based on their learning strengths.

There is considerable evidence to support the use of cognitive-behavioral strategies that focus on how thinking affects an individual's behavior (Allen, MacKenzie, & Hickman, 2001; Polaschek, Wilson, Townsend, & Daly 2005). These approaches establish that individuals should be trained in skills that help them manage risks in their lives (e.g., addiction) and provide the requisite ability to succeed in future endeavors. Additionally, cognitive-based approaches have relevance in education and may serve as thematic components to be assessed, prioritized, and addressed in all interactions, both operational and programmatic.

Motivation is a primary responsivity consideration. Research strongly suggests that motivational techniques, rather than persuasion tactics, more effectively enhance motivation for initiating and maintaining behavior changes (Miller & Rollnick, 2002). Serin (2005) describes behavioral change as an *inside job* and asserts that a certain level of intrinsic motivation is necessary for lasting change to occur. Presuming access to an educational opportunity, intrinsic motivation acts as a catalyst to help individuals see themselves in a new light and apply new knowledge and skills in shaping their identity (Burke & Stets, 2009; Maruna, 2001). If the redefined identity is attractive (e.g., mother over addict; carpenter over thief), it appears to ignite an intrinsic motivation driving toward the crime free alternative.

Finally, measuring relevant processes and practices is the foundation of evidence-based practice (Martin, Mattson, & Lynn, 2005). Corrections interventions must integrate into a known case management approach that is linked to outcome objectives of the individual and the agency. The case management practice should ensure that practitioners understand and align the outcomes of the agency, the practices that are used to produce the outcomes, the rationale that underscores why the approach will work and matches approaches to a differentiated understanding of which individuals are receiving services (Martin et al., 2005).

With this in hand, corrections practitioners are able to identify meaningful data metrics that address the completion and quality of the practice, the dosage of intervention and the performance measures that demonstrate new knowledge, skills, behaviors and attitudes have been learned. These data metrics are used to evaluate the process and inform what parts of the system are working to improve outcomes for individuals (Martin et al., 2005). Moreover, when this alignment exists, it produces data that can be used to understand what services work for particular groups of individuals and what impacts these services have on outcomes (i.e., educational attainment, institutional safety, recidivism) (Martin et al., 2005).

ASSESSING EDUCATIONAL NEED IN ADULTS

The discussion now shifts to understanding how educational need is assessed in correctional populations. Steurer (2001) recalls a history of correctional education culminating in an appreciation for the cooccurring need to understand the individuals' learning needs in the context of their criminogenic history. The evolved model of correctional education includes basic and secondary education, career/technical education, cognitive education, postsecondary education, transitional education, and specialized instruction for special education and learning disabilities (Steurer, 2001). The model goes on to include training for the student as a family member, parent, and community member in need of the relationships that will sustain them in their new relationships, roles, and identity. The preceding discussion describes how criminogenic assessments help define the context of the learner. The subsequent discussion considers how the individuals' educational needs are evaluated and used to inform action.

There have been significant developments in the assessment of educational need over the last 40 years (Gehring, 2007). These developments have emerged across human services sectors including education, social services, workforce development, and criminal justice. The more progressive work has explored how educational assessment links with functional competencies of adults. In fact, the work has produced a repository of standards that are used to match individual learners with primary skills and competency requirements including life skills and vocational skills (Comprehensive Adult Student Assessment System, 2009). The discussion begins with a review of the primary educational assessment technologies and then considers how the knowledge developed from these assessments refines our understanding of individuals in the criminal justice system.

Educational decisions within correctional setting are often based on standardized assessments (Foley & Gao, 2004). Within educational contexts standardized assessments are used for a variety of reasons—such as program evaluation, compliance with legal mandates, measure of student progress and educational placement decisions (Overton, 2010).

There are numerous standardized instruments to choose form. As such the subsequent sections will review some of the more common assessments used for educational programming decisions, including the identification of specific learning disabilities (SLD). The authors of this chapter hold that these instruments are psychometrically adequate and, thus, useful in making educational decisions. There are four primary assessments discussed below: (1) the Comprehensive Adult Student Assessment System (CASAS); (2) the Test of Adult Basic Education (TABE); (3) the Wide Range Achievement Test (WRAT); and (4) the Woodcock-Johnson Test of Achievement. The discussion begins with the CASAS assessment overview.

Comprehensive Adult Student Assessment System

The CASAS is widely used method of assessing adult basic skills and English language abilities (Tewksbury & Vito, 1994). CASAS measures skills that range from beginning literacy to GED and high school preparation and transition to postsecondary education training and employment. It is designed for individuals who function at or below a high school level.

The CASAS was developed out of a statewide assessment of the Adult Basic Education program in California (CASAS, 1993). In 1978, following a review of adult basic education programs in the state, the California Department of Education agreed to adopt a competency based approach for the delivery of adult basic education. The performance requirements for the assessment system included:

- accountability to the individual student and also to report group achievement of skill levels and competency development across levels of adult basic education;
- assessment of students and accurately place them in appropriate programs and levels;
- monitoring progress toward educational goals and certifying competency attainment;
- producing accountability data to ensure students were progressing to meet specified goals; and
- providing program impact reports to state and federal oversight agencies.

In 1980, the California Department of Education was funded by the Federal Adult Basic Education Act and established the CASAS Consortium (CASAS, 2009). The CASAS Consortium included adult schools, community colleges, community-based organizations, and correctional institutions. The consortium was productive in achieving the performance requirements outlined above. In 1984, the CASAS system was validated by the U.S. Department of Education, Joint Dissemination Review Panel. In 1985, the name was changed to the Comprehensive Adult Student Assessment System (CASAS, 1993).

CASAS assessment data are used to place learners at appropriate levels of instruction, to diagnose learner strengths and weaknesses, to monitor progress, and to certify learner mastery at specific levels of instruction or readiness to exit adult education (CASAS, 2009). CASAS created adult basic education (ABE) skill level descriptors (reading, writing, and math skills) to show a continuum of skills from beginning ABE through advanced adult secondary levels; CASAS also created English as a second language (ESL) skill level descriptors (listening, reading, writing and speaking skills) for ESL from beginning literacy/pre-beginning ESL through proficient skills. The descriptors provide a score indicating how a specific skill area corresponds to a job-related and life skill a person can generally accomplish (CASAS, 2009).

The CASAS assessments were developed using item response theory (IRT). IRT uses mathematical models that determine student ability as a function of test item difficulty, the discriminating power of the items, and the probability of the students getting items correct by chance (CASAS, 1993). In the end, test results relate to what a student knows and can apply in the "adult functional context" (CASAS, 1993).

Test of Adult Basic Education

TABE is designed to assess reading, mathematics, language, and spelling skills (McGraw-Hill, 2000). It also includes a version in Spanish and independent tests that assess basic skills in work-related contexts. TABE is available in paper-and-pencil and computer-based formats. The TABE are norm-referenced tests designed to measure achievement of basic skills commonly found in adult basic education curricula and taught in instructional programs. The test content stresses the integration and application of specific skills in a context meaningful to adults. The assessment levels include introductory reading skills and more advanced areas including the content areas that are measured in the GED tests and in high school (McGraw-Hill, 2000).

When creating TABE, the developers conducted a comprehensive review of adult curricula and met with experts to determine common educational goals, plus the knowledge and skills emphasized in these curricula (McGraw-Hill, 2000). TABE items were then designed to measure this instructional content. TABE has been statistically correlated to the GED tests, and its content has been mapped to the National Adult Literacy Survey literacy categories (McGraw-Hill, 2000).

TABE was designed for a range of audiences (high school equivalency or GED programs, vocational programs, community college programs, welfare-to-work programs, occupational or military advancement programs, alternative educational programs, and ESL programs). The TABE yields a reliable estimate of an individual's overall achievement (McGraw-Hill, 2000).

The automated TABE ties individual student performance to prescriptive reports. The reports provide learning objectives, suggested activities, and a directory of resources for mathematics, reading, and language expression for each student based on their present academic performance level (Winters, Mathew, Booker, & Fleeger, 1993).

Wide Range Achievement Test

The WRAT-Fourth Edition (WRAT-4) is designed to assess children and adults aged 5 through 94 on basic academic skills. This assessment provides both standard scores; age and grade equivalencies; percentiles on four basic subtests—word reading, sentence comprehension, spelling, and math computation. The WRAT-4 is quick and easy to administer (Wilkinson & Roberson, 2006). The subtests of spelling and math computation can be administered individually or in a small-group setting. The WRAT-4 takes between 20 and 45 minutes to administer. The WRAT-4 provides a basic picture of academic skill levels (Dell, Harrold, & Dell, 2008); however, it is not intended to be used as the sole indicator in the identification of cognitive and learning disabilities (Wilkinson & Roberts, 2006). These authors concur with Wilkinson and Roberts and recommend using the WRAT-4 for placement decisions only.

Woodcock Johnson

The Woodcock-Johnson III (WJ III) is an individually administered battery of tests that provide a comprehensive measure of abilities and achievement across a wide age range (Blackwell, 2001). The WWJ Battery (Woodcock, McGrew, & Mather, 2001) is comprised of both an academic and cognitive tests. This assessment system is widely used to make educational decisions specific to placement and diagnosis of cognitive and learning disabilities (Overton, 2010). The tests yield both standardized and derived scores. The academic batteries may be used individually to determine specific academic functioning within domain specific areas such as reading, writing, mathematics, and oral language. The WJ 111 Cognitive assessment is designed to assess general intellectual ability. These two batteries, the achievement and cognitive, provide a comprehensive assessment of cognitive abilities and academic skills (Overton, 2010). When seeking to demonstrate an aptitude achievement discrepancy, both batteries are administered. Suggested time frames for administering each battery range from 60-120 minutes. Trained educational professionals administer the test. Graduate-level training in cognitive assessment, academic assessment and interpretation are recommended (Mather & Woodcock, 2001).

LEARNING DISABILITIES DEFINITION AND PREVALENCE

As noted above, there is a growing appreciation that individuals with learning disabilities are overrepresented in the corrections system. Generally speaking individuals with disabilities struggle academically. Given the high rates of disabilities within the prison population, the fact that many inmates have not experienced success academically is not surprising. As Vacca (2004) notes, "many prisoners lack self-confidence and have a negative attitude toward school" (p. 302). As a result, assessment systems designed to appropriately match programming with individual need must also appreciate how people learn and how best to match their learning abilities and disabilities to services. As Jensen and Reed (2006) conclude a critical step in providing effective programs is matching offenders with suitable programs—that is, responsivity.

A specific learning disability (SLD) is defined under the Federal Individuals with Disabilities Education Improvement Act (IDEIA) of 2004 as a "disorder in one or more of the basic psychological processes involved in understanding or using language, spoken or written, that may manifest itself in the imperfect ability to listen, think, speak, read, write, spell or to do mathematical calculations (10)(1)." IDEIA further stipulates that SLDs do not result from vision loss, hearing deficits, cognitive disabilities, emotional disturbances, or disadvantages stemming from cultural differences or socioeconomic status. Research evidences strong agreement that SLDs persists throughout an individuals' life and affect functioning within and outside of educational settings.

The literature examining rates of SLDs within inmate populations vary with general agreement among researchers that incarcerated youth and adults have significantly higher rates than does the general population. Greenberg et al. (2007) estimated that 17% of adult prisoners have been diagnosed with a SLD compared to 6% of the population at large. The interest among correctional educators regarding the effective practices specific to adults with SLDs has grown (Taymans & Corley, 2001). The primary impetus for improving correctional educational programs results from the empirical relationship between educational program participation and reduced recidivism rates (Jensen & Reed, 2006; Solomon et. al, 2008). Individuals with disabilities comprise a large percentage of the prison population (Harlow, Jenkins, & Steurer, 2010) reinforcing the need to understand the factors that lead to successful educational outcomes for these individuals.

IDEIA's mandate that school districts identify, locate, and evaluate all children with disabilities to ensure that effective interventions can be implemented. Trained personnel currently evaluate most students within the preschool through Grade 12 setting. Because these assessments are timely and costly, they are not administered widely to adults within correctional settings (Taymans & Corley, 2001).

Learning disabilities under IDEIA are determined by demonstrating a severe discrepancy between cognitive abilities and achievement or a students' inability to respond to scientific research based intervention. The most applicable model for assessing SLD within prison populations is to demonstrate that an attitude and achievement discrepancy exists.

CHALLENGES IN IMPLEMENTING ASSESSMENT
IN CORRECTIONAL EDUCATION

Implementing assessment in correctional education presents a variety of challenges that include program access, record sharing and reentry planning. The most significant challenge is program access. Education is not available to all inmates. In most states, there is a substantial waiting list for entry into most programs (Klein & Tolbert, 2007). Greenberg and colleagues (2007) found that 29% of prison inmates participated in vocational training. However, more inmates reported being on waiting lists for these programs than were enrolled. Similarly, Maryland reported having a correctional education waiting list of over 2,000 prisoners and cited insufficient capacity as the primary explanation for the gap between eligibility and program enrollment (Maryland General Assembly, 2003).

Vocational education has been found by some to be available in all states, with an average availability rate of 69% (Foley & Gao, 2004). A national study of access to academic education suggested that 40 of the 41 responding states had a 91% availability rate of ABE and GED (Foley & Gao, 2004). Postsecondary and social skills education is reported to be available less frequently (Foley & Gao, 2004). The average availability of special education was identified as 39%, largely in institutions for juveniles (Foley & Gao, 2004). In a California survey of released parolees from state prison, only 19% reported access to academic education while incarcerated (Rennie, Eggleston, & Riggs, 2008).

The transfer of educational records is also a challenge for both adult and juvenile offenders. Educational considerations are rarely a factor during sentencing, unless there is an identified special education problem. The shared awareness of assessment information is largely dependent upon skills and training among court staff (Ruddell & Thomas, 2009).

Program participation is also affected by educational assessment (Klein & Tolbert, 2007). A number of systems require that completion of a high school diploma or GED be obtained prior to admission into educational programs. The requirement limits access to vocational programming in particular (Klein & Tolbert, 2007). Educational programming may be instrumental in facilitating the successful transition from institution to the community. If offenders are to return to the communities and maintain law-abiding lifestyles, they must be provided with a variety of readily accessible tools—critical among these tools are formal educational skills (Tewksbury & Vito, 1994).

There also appears to be a problem with a testing effect from repeated administrations of assessment tools. When records are transferred between prison schools, assessment data is of limited value due to the frequency of test administrations. Many teachers in correctional classrooms depend heavily on standardized measures such as TABE or CASAS. These may have been over administered to the point that they are not useful indicators for instruction. In addition, assessment often occurs in large crowded and noisy rooms with many distractions and calls into question the value of the results (Eggleston, 2003, cited in Hoge, Guerra, & Boxer, 2008).

Educational programs in prisons tend to be designed to be for acquisition of basic and marketable skills. There is an emphasis on basic and beginning academic skill development. Unlike European counterparts, education in America's prisons avoids instruction in the humanities, arts, or developmental areas (Gehring, 2008). This can lead to a continuation of a dull educational experience, as well as a lack of the kind of education that can lead to transformation (Gehring & Rennie, 2008).

The prison classroom varies substantially between states, from strict allegiance to a standardized curriculum, to state correctional system developed curricula, to a maximally unregulated teacher directed curriculum (Eggleston, 2003). This leads to difficulty in continuity across prisons, as well as comparison of results. In part because state requirements for teacher licensure vary from state to state, while the skill level among teachers can also vary dramatically (Eggleston, 2003). While some teachers have excellent skills for developing informal or qualitative assessments for students, as a way of evaluating instruction, other teachers struggle using assessment data

Many educational programs use assessments such as TABE or CASAS, and use the results to tailor instructional efforts. In some cases however, the link between assessment and instruction is limited. Educational programs in many prisons are predetermined by the correctional system and may not account for the varied skill levels of the inmate students.

CONCLUSIONS AND IMPLICATIONS

In the end, there are considerable challenges to be overcome in the conceptualization, implementation, and use of assessment systems that inform correctional education practice. These challenges are met by efforts to appreciate and understand the life course of an individual, their needs, how they learn, and what they aspire to become (see, for example, Brennan, Breitenbach, & Dieterich, 2010; Gehring, 1992). The truly transformative change needed for individuals caught in a life involving crime will be facilitated using the aforementioned kinds of information to match individuals with effective and appropriate services.

There is general agreement in the extant correctional literature that a positive relationship exists between education based incarceration and recidivism rates (Jensen & Reed, 2006; Przybylski, 2008). In fact, this positive relationship provides the greatest incentive for implementing education-based incarceration programs, and the impetus for ensuring that such programs are effective. However, not all programs are equally as effective for all individuals. One factor contributing to successful educational programs within the correctional setting is ensuring that inmates receive an appropriate education (Vacca, 2004)—one that meets students' individual needs. Meeting individual need requires an assessment system designed to understand how individuals learn best and which programs are most suited for their particular need—academic, vocational, or social. Moreover, the educational experience for inmate learners happens at the midstream of a life course often marked by trauma, failure, and isolation. These features have shaped the individual's identity, affecting not only what and how they learn but what their aspirations are for learning in the future. Thus, educational assessments are best understood when situated in how the individual became involved in crime and how likely he or she is to move away from crime in the future. With this larger context clearly appreciated, the commensurate work may be thoughtfully determined leading to an educational experience that establishes path away from crime and toward a means for achieving educational and life success.

REFERENCES

Allen, L. C., MacKenzie, D. L., & Hickman, L. J. (2001). The effectiveness of cognitive behavioral treatment for adult offenders: A methodological, quality-based review. *International Journal of Offender Therapy and Comparative Criminology, 45*(5), 498-514.

Andrews, D. A., & Bonta, J. (2010). Rehabilitating criminal justice policy and practice. *Psychology, Public Policy and Law, 16*(1), 39-55.

Andrews, D. A., Bonta, J., & Wormith, S. J. (2006). The recent past and near future of risk/need assessment. *Crime and Delinquency, 52*, 7-27.

Andrews, D. A., Zinger, I., Hoge, R. D., Bonta, J., Gendreau, P., & Cullen, F. T. (1990). Does correctional treatment work? A psychologically informed meta-analysis. *Criminology, 28*, 369–404.

Blackwell, T. L. (2001). Woodcock-Johnson 111 Test. *Rehabilitation Counseling Bulletin, 44*(4), 232-235.

Bogue, B., Campbell, N., & Clawson, E. (2004). *Implementing evidence based practice in community corrections.* Washington, DC: National Institute of Corrections.

Brennan, T., Breitenbach, M., & Dieterich, W. (2010). Unraveling women's pathways to serious crime: new findings and links to prior feminist pathways. *Perspectives, 34*(2), 34-46.

Burke, P. J., & Stets, J. E. (2009). *Identity theory.* Oxford, England: Oxford University Press.

Comprehensive Adult Student Assessment System. (1993). *An application submitted to the program effectiveness panel of the national diffusion network* (U.S. Department of Education: Summary document).

Comprehensive Adult Student Assessment System. (2009). *Assessment policy guidelines* (Internal report). San Diego, CA: Author.

Dell, C. A., Harrold, B., & Dell, T. (2008). Test review. *Rehabilitation Counseling Bulletin 52,* 57-60.

Eggleston, C. (2003, November). *The need and value of correctional education: Why it is important.* Paper presented at the Australian Correctional Education Conference, Brisbane, Australia.

Erisman, W., & Contardo, J. B. (2005). *Learning to reduce recidivism: A 50-state analysis of postsecondary correctional education policy.* Washington, DC: The Institute for Higher Education Policy.

Elliott, D. S. (2006). *Good kids from bad neighborhoods: successful development in social context.* New York, NY: Cambridge University Press.

Foley, R., & Gao, J. (2004, March). Correctional education: Characteristics of academic programs serving incarcerated adults. *Journal of Correctional Education* 55(1), 6-21.

Gaes, G., Flanagan, T., Motiuk, L., & Stewart, L. 1999. Adult correctional treatment. In M. Tonry & J. Petersilia (Eds.), *Prisons* (pp. 361-426). Chicago, IL: University of Chicago Press.

Gehring, T. (1992). Correctional teacher skills, characteristics, and performance indicators. *Issues in Teacher Education, 1*(2), 26-42.

Gehring, T. (2007). *Handbook for correctional education leaders.* San Bernardino, CA: California State University, San Bernardino.

Gehring, T., & Eggleston, C. (2007). *Teaching within prison walls.* San Bernardino, CA: California State University, San Bernardino.

Gehring, T., & Rennie, S. (2008). *Correctional education history from A to Z.* San Bernardino, CA: California State University, San Bernardino.

Glaze, L. E. (2010). *Correctional populations in the United States, 2009.* Washington, DC: U.S. Department of Justice.

Greenberg, E., Dunleavy, E., & Kutner, M. (2007). *Literacy behind bars: Results from the 2003 National Assessment of Adult Literacy Prison Survey.* Retrieved from http://nces.ed.gov/pubs2007/2007473_1.pdf

Grove, W. M., & Meehl, P. E. (1996) Comparative efficiency of informal (subjective, impressionistic) and formal (mechanical, algorithmic) prediction procedures: The clinical–statistical controversy. *Psychology, Public Policy and Law, 2,* 293-323.

Harlow, C. W. (2003). *Education and correctional populations.* Washington, DC: U.S. Department of Justice.

Harlow, C. W., Jenkins, H. D., & Steurer, S. (2010). GED holders in prison read better than in the household population: Why? *Journal of Corrections Education, 61*(1), 68-92.

Hoge, R., Guerra, N., & Boxer, P. (Eds.). (2008). *Treating the juvenile offender.* New York, NY: The Guilford Press.

Individuals with Disabilities Education Improvement Act of 2004, P.L.108-446, 20U.S.C. § 1400 et seq. Retrieved from http://nces.ed.gov/pubs2007/2007473 .pdf

Jensen, E. L., & Reed, G. E. (2006). Adult correctional education programs: An update on current status based on recent studies. *Journal of Offender Rehabilitation, 44*(1), 81-98.

Klein, S., & Tolbert, M. (2007, September). Correctional education: Getting the data we need. *Journal of Correctional Education, 58*(3), 284-292.

Koski, D. D. (2002, February 1). *Barriers to inmate education: Factors affecting the learning dynamics of a prison education program.* Retrieved from http://www.all-business.com/human-resources/careers-job-training/1049424-1.html

Layton-MacKenzie, D. (2008). *Structure and components of successful educational programs.* Proceedings of the John Jay College of criminal justice reentry roundtable on education (pp. 1-17). New York, NY: University of Maryland.

Lochner, L., & Moretti, E. (2003). The effect of education on crime: evidence from prison inmates, arrests, and self-reports. *The American Economic Review, 94*(1), 155-189.

Martin, J.A., Mattson, B., & Lynn, J. (2005). *A guidebook to system innovation: Lessons and tools from the youth service improvement initiative* (Report to the Office of Juvenile Justice and Delinquency Prevention). Washington, DC: U.S. Department of Justice.

Maruna, S. (2001). *Making good.* Washington, DC: American Psychological Association.

Maryland General Assembly. (2003). *Correctional education—Waiting list reduction initiative, HB 545.* Annapolis, MD: Author

Mather, N., & Woodcock, R. W. (2001). *Woodcock-Johnson® III tests of cognitive abilities: Examiner's manual standard and extended batteries.* Itasca, IL: Riverside.

McGraw-Hill. (2000). *Frequently asked questions about TABE: Tests of adult basic education.* Monterey, CA: CTB/McGraw-Hill.

Meehl, P. E. (1995). Extension of the MAXCOV-HITMAX taxometric procedure to situations of sizeable nuisance covariance. In D Lubinski & R. V. Dawis (Eds.), *Assessing individual differences in human behavior: New concepts, methods, and findings* (pp. 81-92). Palo Alto, CA: Consulting Psychologists Press.

Miller, W., & Rollnick, S. (2002). *Motivational interviewing: preparing people for change.* New York, NY: The Guilford Press.

Moretti, E. (2005). *Does education reduce participation in criminal activities?* Berkeley, CA: UC Berkeley Department of Economics.

Overton, T. (2010). *Assessing learners with special needs: An applied approach* (7th ed). Upper Saddle River, NJ: Pearson Education.

Polaschek, D. L. L., Wilson, N. J., Townsend, M. R., & Daly, L. R. (2005). Cognitive-behavioral rehabilitation for high-risk offenders: an outcome evaluation of the violence prevention unit. *Journal of Interpersonal Violence, 20*(12), 1611-1627.

Przybylski, R. (2008). *What works: Effective recidivism reduction and risk-focused prevention programs-a compendium of evidence-based options for preventing new and persistent criminal behavior.* Lakewood, CO: RKC Group

Rennie, S., Eggleston, C., & Riggs, M. (2008). *Parolee statistics, best practices, and needs assessment*. San Bernardino, CA: California State University, San Bernardino, Center for the Study of Correctional Education.

Ruddell, R., & Thomas, M. (Eds.) (2009). *Juvenile corrections*. Richland: KY, Newgate Press.

Schiraldi, V., & Ziedenberg, J. (2002). *Education and incarceration*. Washington, DC: The Justice Policy Institute.

Schiradli, V., & Ziedenberg, J. (2003). *Cellblocks or classrooms: The funding of higher education and corrections and its impact on African-American men*. Washington, DC: The Justice Policy Institute.

Scott, W. (2008) *Effective clinical practices in treating clients in the criminal justice system*. Washington, DC: U.S. Department of Justice.

Serin, R. (2005). *Evidence-based practice: Principles for enhancing correctional results in prisons*. Washington, DC: U.S. Department of Justice.

Solomon, A. L, Osborne, J. W. L., Stefan, F., LoBuglio, S. F., Mellow, J., & Mukamal, D. A. (2008). *Life after lock up: Improving re-entry from jail to community*. Washington, DC: Urban Institute, Justice Policy Center.

Streurer, S. J., Smith, L., & Tracy, A. (2001). *OCE/CEA three state recidivism study*. Landham, MD: Correctional Education Association.

Taxman, F. S., Cropsey, K. L., Young, D., & Wexler, H. (2007). Screening, assessment, and referral practices in adult correctional settings: a national perspective. *Criminal Justice and Behavior, 34*(9): 1216-1234.

Taymans, J. M., & Corley, M. A. (2001). Enhancing services to inmates with learning disabilities: Systemic reform of prison literacy programs. *Journal of Correctional Education, 52*(2),74-78.

Tewksbury, R. A., & Vito, G. F. (1994). Improving the educational skills of jail inmates preliminary program findings. *Federal Probation, 58*(2), 55-59.

Vacca, J. S. (2004). Educated prisoners are less likely to return to prison. *Journal of Correctional Education, 55*(4), 297-305.

Wilkinson, G. S., & Robertson, G. J. (2006). *Wide range achievement test* (4th ed.). Lutz, FL: Psychological Assessment Resources.

Winters, C. W., Mathew, M., Booker, F., & Fleeger, F. (1993). The role of a computer-managed instructional system's prescriptive curriculum in the basic skill areas of math and reading scores for correctional pre-trial detainees (inmates). *Journal of Correctional Education, 44*(1), 10-17.

Woodcock R. W., McGrew, K. S., & Mather, N. (2001). *Woodcock-Johnson® III Test*. Itasca, IL: Riverside.

PART II

THE HUMAN SIDE OF EDUCATION-BASED INCARCERATION: UNDERSTANDING RECIDIVISM

CHAPTER 4

PRISON EDUCATION

The Inmate as Student

David R. Werner, Amy Widestrom, and Sylvester "Bud" Pues

The character and psyche of the inmate as student presents particular problems when it comes to designing an education program that can operate efficiently inside the walls of a jail or prison institution. The prison, as a confining space, seems, in addition, inherently in theory in opposition to the philosophical goals of an education program. An education program seeks to expand knowledge of the world and grant insight into different perspectives on various subjects, but the physical environment of the prison shapes any program that takes place within it. Moreover, the experience of incarceration affects those who go through it and falls most heavily on certain segments of the population who share similar characteristics, complicating the educative process. An examination of the characteristics of the prisoner-student and the environment and influences shaping their educative experience while incarcerated includes an examination of the specific accommodations that must be made to offer an education program in a jail or prison environment. This chapter gives special consideration to the educational needs and problems of the jail inmate, where wide variations in length of stay exacerbate the considerable problems of education in a correctional facility.

Education-Based Incarceration and Recidivism:
The Ultimate Social Justice Crime-Fighting Tool, pp. 61–79
Copyright © 2012 by Information Age Publishing
All rights of reproduction in any form reserved.

The concept of the inmate as a "student" is relatively new. As discussed in Chapter 2, early approaches to incarceration were intended to encourage "rehabilitation" through "work." Under the direction of Brockway at Elmira, the first real prison education program was established at New York prison in the 1870s. Brockway used the prison's organizational structure to emphasize the educational aspects of the institution. Elmira's architecture, staffing pattern, and organizational structure provided strong evidence of the institution's focus on education. Reformatories in the United States during this period were modeled primarily after Elmira with classrooms, lecture halls, and vocational programs (Gehring, 2007). Education in the Elmira facility focused on traditional academic studies, as well as vocational training and physical fitness. The comprehensive nature of these programs suggests something important about the students being educated and the concept of inmates as students at Elmira, a view that would take several decades to reemerge.

When considering inmates as students, there are several factors which appear to influence the types of educational opportunities inmates are afforded: what is the nature of the infraction that caused incarceration; what might be the individual's relevant psychological and social factors (such as locus of control, personality, values, self-esteem); what is the individual's previous educational experience and level of educational attainment, and; what is the inmate's term of incarceration—short-term, long-term, or life. The ways correctional institutions answer these questions can have a profound effect on educational programming and the carceral environment in general (Werner, 1990).

For purposes of better understanding inmate as students, are there useful generalizations that can help better us better meet their educational needs? While the answer seems fairly clear, there are, nonetheless, a number of qualifications. In this chapter we first review the relevant literature on incarcerated populations. Second, we take up the notion of "student"—more specifically, we examine the profile of both "traditional" students and inmate-students. Next, we examine correctional institutions as an educational settings and how this environment can affect our understanding or conception of what a student is. The fourth section considers briefly postsecondary education in the carceral environment. Finally, we conclude with a discussion about treating the inmate-student as inherently different from the "traditional" student, and the negative implications this can have for the effective provision of correctional education. Before proceeding any further, it is important to note that most postsecondary education in correctional institutions occurs in prisons, not jails. Nonetheless, it is important to understand the characteristics of the students who participate in correctional education, particularly inmates

housed in local jails, prior to examining any specific educational program.

THE PROFILE OF A "TYPICAL" PRISONER INMATE

To begin, most prisoners in the United States are male (Glaze, 2009).
More than likely, he is a member of a minority group, between the ages of
21 and 33, and from a lower socioeconomic class (Glaze, 2009). Either the
inmate or some family member has received government assistance, perhaps in the form of welfare, at some time in their life. He most likely
comes from a single- or divorced-parent household, with the high probability that other members of his family are incarcerated. As a result, he
probably knows others who are currently in prison or have served time at
a correctional institution. He may well know people who are prison
guards as well. He may also face a host of other personal challenges, such
as substance use and abuse, child and/or spousal abuse, a record of previous incarceration, and early trouble with the law. Finally, it is also very
likely that he is functionally illiterate (Montrose & Montrose, 1997).

Despite that this sketch of the average inmate is largely accurate, two
important factors have come into play over the last 20 years that have
contributed to the changing makeup of jail and prison populations. The
first is the increasing number of ethnic minorities entering the U.S. population. This also includes increasing numbers of illegal immigrants, especially Hispanic and Asian. Although this reflects a general trend, it has,
nonetheless, affected the demographic composition of most jails and prisons (Snell, 1995; Glaze, 2009). The second factor is the changing structure of American families. The crisis facing today's U.S. African American
families has been well documented, with the decline of two-parent families and the rising dominance of single, female-headed households. This
trend appears to be growing in Hispanic and Asian communities as well
(Cartwright, 1996; Hymowitz, 2005).

Much has been written about the importance of positive role models,
particularly male role models for young boys during critical stages of
early development. Yet, the vast majority of inmates have been raised in
communities of women because so many lower- and underclass males no
longer have a significant place in their families. Without positive, family
role models, many young males turn to gangs for identification and
acceptance. The gang becomes the new family with its attendant role
models (Hymowitz, 2005). Combined, this suggests a changing demographic population in jails and prisons, and additional issues that inmates
bring with them to the carceral and educational environment.

While none of this is intended to excuse criminal conduct, many of these aspects have been linked consistently with high rates of crime and incarceration. While it is certainly true that not everyone with similar experiences turns to crime, several of these factors appear to increase the likelihood that a person will spend some time in a correctional institution (Harer, 1995; Montrose & Montrose, 1997). This evidence does not suggest that the inmate is not at fault for his or her incarceration experience, but it does imply that he or she has had a better opportunity than many for gaining such experiences that might lead to incarceration. This is important to keep in mind when considering the inmate as student.

PROFILE OF THE INMATE-STUDENT

Perhaps the greatest concern to teachers, however, is the students' educational background (Werner, 1990). Thus, it is helpful to consider the role of previous experience among inmates with remedial and special education, high school, and postsecondary education programs, in correctional settings. Such a discussion may be noteworthy because students who have little, if any, prior schooling can present a different set of problems than inmates who have already completed part or all of their formal education.

Most people would imagine that the "average" inmate would be a remedial or special education student, especially in facilities catering to younger inmates. A 2007 survey conducted at a California Youth Authority facility concluded that 50% of the institution's young men (ages 16-25) read at less than a third grade level. Kozol (1985) estimates that 60% of those who are incarcerated in the United States are functionally illiterate, meaning that they lack the skills necessary to read and understand a newspaper, balance a checkbook, or fill out a job application. Indeed, results from a survey of three prisons in Ohio and New York indicated that approximately 75% of the inmates surveyed qualified for special education.

The adult remedial student also carries with him or her, the embarrassment and lack of self-worth that so often accompanies poorly developed education skills (Montrose & Montrose, 1997; Werner, 1990). The job of the jail or prison teacher is as much about redeveloping feelings of self-worth as it is about teaching basic educational skills such as reading and writing. The student profile changes again with high school or postsecondary correctional education. This student tends to have undertaken most of his or her previous educational work in a youth or adult correctional facility of one sort or another, and this can significantly affect the assumptions a teacher can make about prior knowledge and general classroom behavior (Duguid, 2006; Gehring & Eggleston, 2007; Muth, 2006; Werner, 2006).

Students in jail or prison classrooms usually lack the breadth of knowledge possessed by nonincarcerated students. While there are certainly a number of well-educated inmates, this appears to be the exception, not the rule. The knowledge base of many inmate-students tends to be specific rather than general; a student may know, for example, something about history, but will likely be unable to integrate that experience into a broader continuum, or a student in a postsecondary jail or prison class may know a great deal about the history of medieval European warfare but may lack the commensurate ability to express this knowledge (Gehring & Eggleston, 2007; Werner, 2006).

Inmate-students also tend to be unfamiliar with classroom discussion techniques. When teachers lecture in jail or prison classrooms, students generally pay attention. However, when a student asks a question or makes a comment, others rarely listen (Duguid, 2006; Werner, 1990). As a result, students often ask the same question repeatedly. At least part of this phenomenon seems to be influenced by the fact that the majority of inmate-students have completed most of their previous education in "institution classrooms" (Penwell, 2006). Unlike more traditional schools, correctional education classes tend to be open-end/open-exit and, therefore, depend heavily on individualized instruction and programmed learning. In such classrooms, a student will come into class, pick up a packet of material, do his or her individual lesson, and then proceed to the next. Because of this self-directed approach, students fail to have opportunity to discuss ideas or information with the larger class and, thus, fail to recognize discussion as an integral part of the learning process.

Complicating the educational environment in correctional facilities is the authoritarian nature of many prisons, which tends to reinforce preexisting beliefs about the teacher as the sole source of information. The combination of these factors—no prior experience in group discussion and authoritarian expectations—may contribute to an atmosphere where students fail to see the importance of their contributions and that they can learn from one another through discussion. As a result, teachers who value the exchange of ideas may find it difficult to establish an environment that promotes discussion in a jail or prison classroom (Muth, 2006; Wright, 2006).

In additional to these institutional complications, inmate-students in both jail and prison may also have to overcome "peer pressure" from other inmates and staff, which often seems designed to keep inmates from bettering themselves. A former inmate writes that, while in jail, "education was never an option." He notes that:

Being involved in prison politics directly affected my ability to do anything other than what was expected. For many of us the primary goal was racial prominence and racial respect. Consequently, the rules of conduct were strictly enforced and adhered to. This was a full time job. There were no exceptions for the uninitiated. It wasn't until my later years in prison, having risen in the ranks, that I had positioned myself so that I could make decisions beneficial to my future, ironic as that may sound.

While participation in education "on the streets" is generally thought to be positive, quite the opposite is often true in jail and prison.

There are other reasons for inmate-students to be confused about the value of education. Incarcerated students are often unfamiliar with the inherent value of education—that is, as an end in itself. There are at least two factors which appear to contribute to this lack of understanding. First, incarcerated individuals tend to be more deeply concerned with how to "make it" and are more aware of their past failures. Most inmate-students, to the degree they have thought about the value of education, see it as some vague means to an immediate end, that is, bettering oneself to secure a job upon discharge, or developing some specific skill in the hopes of convincing a parole board that they are suitable for release. Often, pursuing education in prison means that an inmate has to sacrifice a paying job, so participating in education can effectively mean making no money (Tewksbury & Stengel, 2006)

Second, incarceration tends to emphasize the immediate present while decreasing the importance of the future, making education a future-oriented endeavor. Jails and prisons are inherently chaotic and unpredictable, promoting instant gratification—a finding that should come as no real surprise considering the ways the popular media often promotes such behaviors. Many incarcerated individuals appear to have a greater interest in the values of immediate satisfaction than people living outside of custody (Irwin, 1970; Sykes, 1958). It can further be argued that many people pursue crime as a means of attaining what they perceive as the "good life," be it one of wealth or drugs or pleasure otherwise defined. This is often accomplished, with little, if any, consideration for consequences associated with those actions. Thus, success as a teacher may well rest on one's ability to translate abstract educational value into the realities of day-to-day living (Muth, 2006).

Women as Inmates and Inmate-Students

While incarcerated women share many of the same characteristics as their male counterparts, women make up only about 5 to 10% of the jail and prison population in the United States. It is, however, worth noting that the percentage of incarcerated women has risen steadily over the past

20 years (Prison Activist Resource Center 2008; West Virginia Division of Corrections, 2000). As women have increasingly become independent actors in many traditionally male-dominated fields, including business and finance, they have also increasingly become principal participants in criminal activity as well (Prison Activist Resource Center, 2008). Nonetheless, many female offenders seem to be the products of "addicted parents, neglect, juvenile homes, sexual abuse, [and] heavy drug use" (Lyke, 2003).

Like men, women share certain socially imbued mores that both contribute to their incarceration and affect their experiences of jail and prison. According to the American Correctional Association (1990), adult female inmates are typically women of color, between the ages of 25 and 29, and single parents who have never been married. She has between one to three children who are currently being cared for by her mother or a grandparent. She, herself, is likely to have been reared in a single parent home. Between the ages of 5 and 14, the typical female prisoner was a victim of sexual abuse, more than likely by a male member of her immediate family, usually her father or stepfather. If she reported the incident, it resulted in no change in the abuser's behavior or it made matters worse. By the time she was 13 or 14 years old, she started using drugs and/or alcohol. Also, before her present incarceration, she used alcohol no less than one or two times a month and she used either cocaine, amphetamines, or marijuana on a daily basis (American Correctional Association, 1990).

The female prisoner has most likely been arrested between two and nine times, usually beginning around age 15. She is usually serving a sentence of 2 to 8 years, and will, on average, serve approximately one fourth of that sentence. Crimes are often committed to relieve economic pressures, to pay for drugs, or because of poor judgment. She probably reacted to her first incarceration with fear, disbelief, or resignation (American Correctional Association, 1990). She is in all likelihood a high school dropout, with one third (34%) of all female inmates failing to complete secondary education because of pregnancy. One out of two (49%) attended vocational school as adults studying to be secretaries, medical assistants, dental assistants, or cosmetologists. She is likely to have previous job experience in clerical, sales, or service occupations. Finally, most female inmates report that they would participate in drug and alcohol treatment or job training programs if available (American Correctional Association, 1990).

There are, however, two characteristics that appear to distinguish female inmates from males: relationships with their significant others, and relationships with their children (Davis, 2001). Many women who are incarcerated have a long history of association with strong male personalities. Most incarcerated women do not have a strong sense of self-esteem or self-worth. While imprisonment tends to cause many inmates to see life as a series of failures, women are especially prone to such self-defeating attitudes (Davis, 2001). Although this pattern appears to be changing, most women who commit crimes still do so at the insistence of a crime partner who is most likely male. Women are, hence, more marginally responsible for their criminality than their average male counterpart. For example, while many women join gangs, they often do so at the behest of a boyfriend or lover who is already a gang member (Lyke, 2003).

Feelings of being provoked into a life of crime and incarceration can cause women to reflect deeply on the dominant influence of men in their lives. As a result, they may begin to define their own lives and wishes as different from those of a male-dominated society. Many women in jail or prison find that their first opportunities to make independent decisions occur while incarcerated. The politically conservative nature of many female inmates can make this a difficult transition. In fact, female inmates may initially reject feminism as contrary to traditional "American" values of home and family. Once incarcerated, however, the philosophical independence associated with many forms of feminism often becomes a subject of great interest (Davis, 2001; Griffith, Pennington-Averett, & Brian, 1981).

Moreover, in spite of recent social changes, mainstream thinking in the United States still defines child rearing as a woman's responsibility. Women are still much more likely than men to stay home with young children. Statistically, women are awarded custody of children in 72% of divorces, as opposed to 9% for men (Divorce Lawyer Statistics, 2008). As a result of their identity and responsibilities, incarcerated women face more social condemnation than males. Not only have women violated the social contract, they have abandoned their children (Davis, 2001). Incarcerated male parents may feel guilt about their inability to care for their children, but the guilt females often feel about abandoning their children can be much more powerful.

THE ENVIRONMENT OF THE CORRECTIONAL INSTITUTION AND ITS EFFECTS ON INMATES

This general profile of the inmate is important to bear in mind when considering how the environment and experience of incarceration can affect incarcerated individuals, which in turn is important when considering correctional education programs. It is popular in prison circles to refer to the incarcerated as products of "institutionalization" or as subjects of what the sociologist Gresham Sykes termed "prisonization" (Sykes, 1958). Certainly, incarceration has an effect on the individual who experiences it.

And indeed, incarceration, for its entire history as a response to crime in the United States, has been *intended* to have transformative effects on inmates (Gehring & Muth, 1985). While the desired transformation—that from criminal to good citizen—most often does not take place, incarceration does produce significant and sometimes unintended effects on inmates and therefore inmate-students. There are several ways in which the carceral environment affects individuals within correctional institutions, which has subsequent effects on the operation of correctional education in these facilities.

The "Convict Identity"

The single most defining characteristic of the incarceration experience for those in jail or prison is their sharing of what John Irwin has termed the "convict identity." Irwin defines this as

> the obligation to tolerate the behavior of others unless it is directly affecting your physical self or your possessions. If another's behavior surpasses those limits, then the problem must be solved by the person himself, that is, *not* by calling for help from the officials. (Irwin, 1970, p. 83)

The most common phrase a jail or prison educator will encounter from their students is that they are "doing their own time" (Wright, 2006). This phrase and the adherence to the code it represents are crucial to defining inmate-students' relationships with each other.

For the educator, this means two things: first, students will avoid interaction with each other when not in class; and second, students will most likely not turn to a staff member or instructor if they have problems with other students. A former inmate writes that

> the stigma that is associated with inmate-staff interaction; always a dicey proposition. Generally speaking, anytime an inmate has contact with staff, it's going to be questioned … any type of ongoing fraternization and the inmate is at risk of consequences.

The additional disinclination on the part of inmates to have contact with each other can and will shape student behavior in class; the classroom is one of the few places in the jail or prison where inmates must have contact and share information with those they do not know, and, because they do not know their classmates, they do not trust their classmates (Irwin, 1970).

Given these two attitudinal factors, instructors should not think it possible to try to get inmates to break their adherence to this code of behavior when attempting to engage the inmate-students in class. Even if it possible to do so, Sykes and Messinger (1960) and later Irwin (1970) argued that such an intense code of individual separation is crucial to survival in the overcrowded, communal conditions of most jails and prisons. People who are forced on a daily basis to be in proximity with others must ignore or tune out much of that contact in order to maintain any trace of individuality and privacy.

Another possible effect of an external locus of control is a diminished sense of self-esteem or self-worth. While it is true that many students on the outside do not exhibit a great deal of self-confidence, this problem is more acute in a jail or prison setting. Both the fear of failure and the willingness to fail are common character traits in jail and prison classrooms. In jail and prison classrooms it is not unusual to have students who have an excellent command of course material yet who will fail to take examinations or who, if given examinations, will perform poorly (Muth, 2006; Werner, 1990; Wright, 2006).

Inmates' Concept of Self and of Authority

A number of researchers have noted that incarceration affects an inmate's conceptualization of self and authority (Griffith et al., 1981). Griffith, Pennington-Averett and Brian's study indicated that while incarcerated, inmates experience a definite shift in what psychologists call "locus of control," from internal to external. Internal locus of control refers to the perception that one controls one's own behavior, whereas external locus of control refers to the perception that "powerful others, chance, and fate" determine outcomes. Researchers have found that the longer inmates are incarcerated, the more they lose internal locus of control (Griffith et al., 1981).

One noticeable effect of this shift in locus of control is in the inmate's view of authority figures, which affects the carceral classroom. The longer an inmate is incarcerated, the more he or she tends to accept an authoritarian world-view (Griffith et al., 1981). Most inmates generally associate instructors with authority and will, because of this, show the instructor considerable courtesy. While this will no doubt contribute to the instructor's own feeling of well-being, it will create considerable difficulty when it comes to having class discussions; instructors will find it necessary to teach students that their own contribution to class can be as important as their instructor's and that the inmate-student should be given attention when speaking or contributing to class. Eventually the instructor will find it possible to teach students that insofar as they recognize the importance of their classmates' contributions, they are recognizing the importance of their own contributions (Wright, 2006).

The Perception and Passage of Time

Even an inmate's perception of time can be affected by incarceration, creating an unusual dynamic for jail or prison classrooms. There is evidence that a period of incarceration of even 6 months can change how some inmates view both the passage of time and future events. While a linear view of time and a grasp of a fairly well-defined future are common among those who live outside correctional facilities, the monotony of a daily routine and the distance of an inmate's release date can influence the way inmates view the passage of time—in many cases, as a sort of an eternal present, or a day which happens over and over again. As a result, many inmates begin to see time as unchanging and lose track of the future (Werner & Davis, 1987).

Among inmates there is generally considered to be a "proper" way to deal with time, which is "easy time," or taking things "one day at a time." In contrast, the "improper" way to deal with time, commonly referred to as "hard time," occurs when an inmate spends time thinking about the future or a prospective release date. Irwin (1970) describes the development of this distinction and adherence to a conception of "easy time" as a "middle stage" of incarceration, lasting from about 6 months after incarceration until a few months before release, where "the outside world fades ... [and] the streets becomes a less and less important reference world" (Irwin, p. 102).

Unless a correctional educator understands how inmates perceive time, he or she may have difficulty understanding why inmates seem to have such a hard time planning for and fulfilling future classroom-related activities. Even though many inmates have the ability to complete their assignments, they may still fail to meet important deadlines or obligations. The instructor must realize that for many inmates the future is effectively of little consequence (except in the vague sense of a release date, which may be months or years away). Assignments, structured with regular due dates, often require follow-up meetings and other warnings of approaching deadlines. By following up on due dates and other important obligations, instructors may begin to notice dramatic student successes. To help keep the future in perspective, correctional instructors might consider scheduling long-term events (graduations, awards presentations, parties) as a way of breaking the general monotony of institutional life (Werner, 1990).

There is an important distinction to be made between the ways inmates' perceive time, which often seeks to ignore the length of stay in a facility, and the way staff in correctional institutions understand time. The institutional perception is based on the institution's legal obligation to house inmates for specific terms of incarceration, that is, days, months, or years. The institution must accommodate inmates with various sentence lengths, as well as manage the daily intake and discharge of inmates, all while maintaining institutional safety (Gehring, 2007).

It is because of this, however, that "institutional time" can complicate the institution's ability to provide educational programs, and it does so in two primary ways. First, the length of sentence varies considerably among inmates, making it difficult to develop programs, especially educational curriculum that requires and assumes steady progress. Second, jail sentences typically require a much shorter length of stay than prison terms. This presents a challenge to jail educators whose programs must be tailored to shorter lengths of stay. Combine short length of stays in jails with fluctuating program participants due to individual differences in sentencing, and the provision of education in jails becomes much more complicated than educational provision in prison, where inmates typically are sentenced for longer periods of time and therefore come and go less frequently from programs.

Race and Ethnicity

Racial or ethnic identity is among the most important elements of personal identity for most inmates, dictating both how he or she will be treated and with whom he or she will associate. People in prisons and jails walk, eat, and recreate, as well as sit in church and school by race. Inmates in many prisons and jails who associate with members of other races run the risk of physical harm. When they are not in class or in a situation where they are forced to interact, inmates may talk with members of different races only on rare occasions. In the classroom, this manifests itself in self-segregation by the students, with Black inmate-students sitting in one section of the room, White inmate-students in another, and Hispanic inmate-students in a third area. As a result, correctional educators can teach for some time without ever having a class that chooses to integrate racially (Muth 2006).

Racial and ethnic identity forms a significant part of jail and prison administration and functioning, as well. Indeed, many correctional facilities take race into account when determining where to house an inmate, though this is often an unwritten rule (*Johnson v. California*, 2000). This institutional segregation coupled with attitudes among inmates regarding racial integration and segregation creates an environment of racial segregation and often racism. Yet given the enormous complexity of managing a jail or a prison, racial separation or racism might be too prevalent and too much a part of institutional life to change (Platt & Takagi, 1980).

An educator might be at first surprised and later discouraged by racial separation and segregation within the institution (Muth 2006; Werner, 1990). One must, however, be careful in choosing tactics to deal with this issue. Some teachers may attempt to establish a nonsegregated classroom environment by assigning seats. While this may have a superficial effect, and in some cases may even look like integration, educators who attempt to use such tactics run the risk of increasing hostilities among students. The teacher has a better chance of fostering change by creating situations where students interact with one another, thereby effectively allowing students to make changes on their own terms (Muth & Kiser 2009; Wright 2006).

Gang Activity

Many prison and jail inmates are or were gang members. Indeed, a 2008 National Institute of Justice study found that two thirds of all inmates were or had been in a gang (Hamm, 2008). Youthful inmates are especially prone to gang membership, which often continues within the confines of jails and prisons. While there little research that focuses specifically on prison gangs (Coughlin & Venkatesh, 2003; Spergal 1995), it is important to recognize that gang membership and activity can shape the jail and prison environment and that members may perceive a number of benefits from this affiliation, including protection and a sense of community or belonging (Coughlin & Venkatesh, 2003).

As a teacher in a jail or prison, one's exposure to, and understanding of, gangs may range from peripheral to moderate. Educators should be aware of the profound influence gangs may have on inmates, both positive—protection—and negative—threats of violence (Coughlin & Venkatesh, 2003). Indeed, understanding gangs can help explain much of the seemingly unexplainable behavior of students. Educators should also recognize the code of behavior required of gang members, with violations for noncompliance strictly enforced and, in some instances, punishable by physical assault or even death. Those who teach at either youth or adult correctional facilities should become familiar with the defining characteristics of gang activity, especially those peculiar to the institution in which they work.

POSTSECONDARY INMATE-STUDENTS

It is useful to distinguish between college inmate-students from the other students in the correctional facilities. A defining characteristic of people incarcerated in the United States is their illiteracy, and this characteristic is obviously not shared by those who pursue college education in jail or prison (Glaze, 2009). Students involved in jail or prison college programs comprise the top few percent of the total inmate population in terms of educational achievement. In addition, those who teach postsecondary courses in jails or prisons are most often contract instructors who face particular difficulties in a situation where they are often viewed by both inmates and staff as outsiders (Muth 2006; Yantz 2006). However, a brief consideration of jail and prison postsecondary instruction provides a useful perspective on the problems inherent in jail and prison education.

The least the instructor can expect from a college inmate-student is that he or she has completed either a high school education or a General Education Diploma before entering the class or program. However, chances are that this high school diploma or General Education Diploma certificate was obtained while incarcerated. The postsecondary inmate-student will vary from being significantly behind to about equal to college students on the outside in terms of writing ability and vocabulary (Werner, 1990). One will find however, that the inmate-student will progress quite rapidly in both writing and discourse if he or she stays involved with the jail or prison postsecondary program. Once they develop a writing ability, inmate-students have more experiences from which to draw and more to say than their student counterparts on the outside. Their initial unfamiliarity with the forms of academic discourse and their experience with a prior educational system that stressed individual work, quickly give way under pressure in a rigorous academic discipline.

Many jail and prison staff members who have not achieved a postsecondary education may see inmates enrolled in college programs as competition and often do not look favorably on the social advancement of inmates (Hackman, 1997). The default attitude of custodial staff in most correctional environments is to provide blue collar training and job preparation for inmates and to be suspicious of and reluctant to offer college-level programming. Many jail and prison staff members will tell you quite forthrightly that they do not think that prisoners should be allowed to pursue "free education." This is not unlike a common public attitude toward postsecondary education for the incarcerated, and the educator will probably find him/herself in the position of defending his/her occupation (Muth, 2006; Werner, 2006; Yantz, 2006). Noting that prisoners who pursue college education have a noticeably lower recidivism rate may or may not be a persuasive argument here.

In addition, inmates often look unfavorably on other inmates whom they perceive as trying to advance themselves. Anyone who is seen as doing something out of the norm is confronted with considerable pressure to conform to general expectations (Hackman, 1997). Educators should be aware that their students face this sort of peer-pressure even though there is little the educator can do about it. Educators can only respond by making the classroom experience as positive as possible for their students.

The values and career goals of inmate-students tend to gain them affinity with students in colleges and universities on the streets, at least insofar as both groups express values. Many of those incarcerated, like their counterparts on the streets, pursue degrees in business upon release. The director of the largest postsecondary correspondence program for inmates states that 35% of prison program majors pursue degrees in business (Armstrong, 1997). While this is similar to the degree pursuit on college campuses, it should be noted that this trend in prison postsecondary education predated the trend on the streets. It could be argued that crime is essentially an entrepreneurial occupation that logically culminates in legitimate enterprise; thus, inmate-students anticipated the trend toward the more vocational career choice (Armstrong).

SUMMARY, CONCLUSIONS, AND IMPLICATIONS

To summarize, in this chapter we sought to recognize that, as in any situation, a student, whether in a traditional school or in prison or jail, is a product of his or her economic and social background. We attempted to describe that background in order to illuminate the type of student that an educator is likely to encounter in prison or jail. This chapter examined a profile of a typical prisoner, including the differences between male and female inmates, the values held by typical prisoners, and the level of immediate gratification to which such a prisoner is accustomed. We also proposed a definition of "institutionalization," an often-heard but rarely-understood term used to describe the complex effects on an individual's psyche produced by incarceration. We defined "institutionalization" to include an inmate's adoption of the "convict identity," perceptions of time by the inmate and the institution, the adoption of institutionally produced attitudes toward self and authority, the adherence to the racially motivated social structure of the institution, and the acceptance of gang activity in the jail or prison environment. All these factors not only affect an inmate's daily life while incarcerated but also serve to shape the atmosphere of any jail or prison classroom.

It is important, also, to keep in mind the history and purpose of incarceration when considering the possibilities of educational programming within correctional institutions. Throughout history, incarceration has been used to punish and only secondarily to reform, habilitate, or rehabilitate. This reform, habilitation or rehabilitation has, from time to time, included traditional academic studies, vocational training and overall fitness, but it has most often been secondary to the incapacitation or punishment goals of the prison (Gehring & Muth, 1985). In 1977 California, for example, struck rehabilitation from its prison enabling legislation: "The Legislature finds and declares that the purpose of imprisonment for crime is punishment" (quoted in Zimring, Hawkins, & Kamlin, 2001, p. 112). The result of this has been an expensive and failing system of incarceration that returns 70% of exinmates to prison. Recently, many states, including California, have reintroduced "rehabilitation" into the titles of their systems of correction, which may be an encouraging sign.

There are several lessons to learn from the information provided in this chapter. In order to create a reform-based, (re)habilitative program with a real chance of success, "Education Based Incarceration" must seek to situate education at the heart of the incarceration experience. In addition to giving inmates a chance at a life they never had, "education based incarceration" must also implement curriculum and protocols that help the inmate learn to *think of him or herself differently*, and to trade his axioms of existence for some new and better ones. Further, to be effective "Education Based Incarceration" needs to fit the needs of its target population by providing real world knowledge and skills, while also developing a positive, affirming concept of the self and the individual inmate's potential and possibilities.

Even though inmates are called students if they participate in educational programs they are still offenders—people who have broken the laws of society and are being punished for their behavior. What assumptions the educator might make about his or her students, including their history, past actions, their present situation, and their future potential, will determine in large part what sort of educational experience is provided in the jail or prison classroom. To some degree, all people live up or down to other's expectations of them. If we expect negative behavior, we often receive it. Conversely, if we expect good behavior, we are often surprised by its occurrence. What the educator expects of his/her students in the jail or prison classroom will in many ways determine the quality of the education provided to them. While the inmate-student presents unique challenges to the educator, the students in any teaching environment of the carceral setting also provide unique opportunities to teachers. Rather than expecting negative learning outcomes and negative classroom behavior, the educator has the opportunity in this environment to treat the inmate-student as simply "student." In doing so, the educator can work toward his or her stated learning goals and outcomes, but also work to improve the inmates' conceptions of self, authority, and self-esteem.

This chapter has examined the challenges faced by teachers in a carceral setting, specifically examining the inmate as student. If the educator is to understand his/her role as a teacher, then it is necessary to first understand his/her students. To claim that a jail or prison calls for particular understanding is not counter to our call to treat the inmate-student as simply "student." Rather it is to recognize that all teaching situations are unique and that all call for awareness and understanding on the part of those who teach in them. If the instructor can avoid negative assumptions and stress positive action, he/she will be a successful jail or prison educator, and therefore offer a sound educational experience.

REFERENCES

American Correctional Association. (1990). *The female offender: What does the future hold?* Washington, DC: Author.

Armstrong, K. (1997). Ohio University: A journey through post-secondary correctional education. *Fire and Ice: The Tumultuous Course of Post-Secondary Prison Education, Journal of Correctional Education, 48*(2), 82-83.

Cartwright, D.T. (1996). *Violent land.* Cambridge, MA: Harvard University Press.

Coughlin, B. C., & Vanketesh, S. A. (2003. The urban street gang after 1960. *Annual Review of Sociology, 29,* 41-64.

Davis, H. C., (2001) Educating the incarcerated female: A holistic approach. *Journal of Correctional Education, 52*(2), 79-83.

Divorce Lawyer Statistics. (2008). *Divorce statistics.* Retrieved from www .divorce-lawyer-source.com/html/law/statistics.html

Duguid, S. (2006). The professor in prison: reflections. In R. Wright (Ed.), *In the borderlands: Learning to teach in prisons and alternative settings.* Fredericksburg, VA: Digital Impressions.

Gehring, T. (2007). *Teaching within prison walls.* San Bernardino, CA: California State University at San Bernadino.

Gehring, T., & Muth, W. R. (1985). The correctional education/prison reform link: Part I,1840-1900. *Journal of Correctional Education, 36,* 140-146.

Gehring, T., & Eggleston, C. (2007). *Teaching within prison walls.* San Bernadino, CA: California State University, San Bernadino.

Glaze, L. (2009). *Correctional populations in the United States, 2009.* Washington, DC: United States Department of Justice.

Griffith, J. E., Pennington-Averett, A., & Bryan, I. (1981). Women prisoners' multidimensional locus of control. *Criminal Justice and Behavior 8*(3), 375-389.

Hackman, K. (1997). Correctional education—Challenges and changes [Special Issue]. *The Journal of Correctional Education Special Issue, 48*(2).

Hamm, M. S. (2008). Prisoner radicalization: Assessing the threat to U.S. correctional institutions. *National Institute of Justice Journal, 261,* 14-19.

Harer, M. D. (1995, September). Recidivism among federal prisoners released in 1987. *Journal of Correctional Education, 46*(3), 98-128.

Hymowitz, K. S. (2005). The Black family: 40 years of lies. *The City Journal.* Retrieved from http://www.city-journal.org/html/15_3_black_family.html

Irwin, J. (1970). *The felon.* Englewood Cliffs, NJ: Prentice-Hall.

Johnson v. California, 207 F.3d 650 (9th Cir. 2000).

Kozol, J. (1985). *Illiterate America.* New York, NY: Plume.

Lyke, M. L. (2003, March 5). Number of female inmates soars. *The Seattle Post-Intelligencer.* Retrieved from http://www.seattlepi.com/local/111040_1women05.shtml

Montrose, K. J., & Montrose, J. F. (1997, December) Characteristics of adult incarcerated students: Effects on instruction. *Journal of Correctional Education, 48*(4), 179-186.

Muth, W. R. (2006). The first two years of prison work: A personal narrative. In R. Wright (Ed.), *In the borderlands: Learning to teach in prisons and alternative settings* (pp. 82-130). Fredericksburg, VA: Digital Impressions.

Muth, W. R., & Kiser, M. (2009). Radical conversations: Part two—Cultivating socialconstructivist learning methods in ABE classrooms. *The Journal of Correctional Education, 59,* 370-397.

Prison Activist Resource Center. (2004). *Women in prison.* Retrieved from www .prisonactivist.org/articles/women-prison

Penwell, J. (2006). How I learned to teach in a women's prison: A tale of growth, understanding, and humor. In R. Wright (Ed.), *In the borderlands: Learning to teach in prisons and alternative settings* (pp. 50-58). Fredericksburg, VA: Digital Impressions.

Platt, T., & Takagi, P. (1980). *Punishment and penal discipline.* Berkeley, CA: Crime and Social Justice Associates.

Snell, T. L. (1995). *Correctional population in the United Stated, 1995.* Washington, DC: United Stated Department of Justice.

Spergel, I. A. (1995). *The youth gang problem: A community approach.* New York, NY: Oxford University Press.

Sykes, G. M. (1958). *The society of captives: A study of maximum security prison.* Princeton, NJ: Princeton University Press.

Sykes, G. M., & Messinger, S. (1960). The inmate social system. In R. A. Cloward, D. R. Cressey, G. H. Grosser, R. McCleary, L. E. Ohlin, G. Sykes, & S. Messinger (Eds.), *Theoretical studies in the social organization of prison* (pp. 1-19). New York, NY: Social Science Research Council.

Tewksbury, R., & Stengel, K. M. (2006). Assessing correctional education programs: The students' perspective. *The Journal of Correctional ,57*(1), 13-25.

Werner, D. R. (1990). *Correctional education: Theory and practice.* Danville, Il: The Interstate.

Werner, D. R. (2006). What I learned in prison. In R. Wright (Ed.), *In the borderlands: Learning to teach in prisons and alternative settings* (pp. 7-16). Fredericksburg, VA: Digital Impressions.

Werner, D. R., & Davis, S. (1987, July). *Inmates' perception of time.* Paper presented at the 42nd Correctional Association International Conference, San Francisco, CA.

West Virginia Division of Corrections. (2000). *Adult female inmate—Crime & demographics.* Retrieved from http://www.wvdoc.com/wvdoc/Portals/0/documents/female.pdf

Wright, R. (2006). Metaphors of experience—The prison teacher as stranger. In R. Wright (Ed.), *In the borderlands: Learning to teach in prisons and alternative settings* (pp. 180-189). Fredericksburg, VA: Digital Impressions.

Yants, S. (2006). Borderland negotiations: Representation of identity as a prison educator. In R. Wright (Ed.), *In the borderlands: Learning to teach in prisons and alternative settings* (pp. 147-156). Fredericksburg, Virginia: Digital Impressions.

Zimring, F. E, Hawkins, G., & Kamlin, S. (2001). *Punishment and democracy: Three strikes and you're out in California.* Oxford, England: Oxford University Press.

CHAPTER 5

IMPACT OF CORRECTIONAL STAFF ATTITUDES ON INMATE EDUCATION

Raquel Warley

The impact of correctional staff attitudes on inmate education begins with a "top-down" approach; that is, from the department director's attitude and commitment to the positive value of the education program in changing inmates' lives, both within the institution and after discharge. This is evidenced in the initial training program and local site orientations for both custodial staff and instructional personnel. A 2006 study conducted by Pennsylvania's Department of Corrections indicated the importance of staff's understanding of how their behavior impacts inmates and also about their responsibility for reinforcing treatment and rehabilitation concepts (Antonio & Young, 2011). This type of commitment and practice, stemming from the philosophy and intent of the administrator as well as the local governing board, has moved the focus of those institutions from "pay for their crime" to "training and rehabilitation." There are many examples of this throughout the United States as well as excellent examples in California. The goal, sometimes stated and sometimes assumed, of these programs is to prove that *through education there is a better way.*

"Get tough on crime" legislation is an aggressive campaign against crime that began in the 1990s. Policies that involve "getting tough" include

Education-Based Incarceration and Recidivism:
The Ultimate Social Justice Crime-Fighting Tool, pp. 81–102
Copyright © 2012 by Information Age Publishing
All rights of reproduction in any form reserved.

mandatory sentencing, three strikes, and truth-in-sentencing. These plans of action apply obligatory and longer incarceration terms for a larger variety of offenses and offenders. Meanwhile, the cost to operate the penal system has skyrocketed. The United States spends $35 billion annually on the various agencies that administer criminal penalties (Bureau of Justice Statistics, 2004; Lambert et al., 2009). Purchases of goods and services for state and federal systems have increased 145% and 150%, respectively, since 1986.

Education programs within correctional institutions have long been promoted as a major reentry tool. Reviews of the research literature indicate that inmates who participate in education programs while they are in prison are less likely to be reincarcerated (Adams et al., 1994; Vacca, 2004; Wilson, Gallagher, & MacKenzie, 2000; Zgoba, Haugebrook, & Jenkins, 2008). Nevertheless, there are doubts about the effectiveness of these programs in view of the negligible impact that they appear to have on postrelease recidivism. When ex-offenders do not return to prison, the nation saves millions of dollars each year; hence, it is worthwhile to increase the efficacy of corrections-based education programs.

In spite of the curriculum, educational programming may be most effective when consideration is focused on the prison environment. This chapter reviews relevant findings on corrections officers' attitudes toward education-based incarceration (EBI), with respect to sociodempographic characteristics such as race, sex, education level, and age, as well as career variables, such as position and military background. The chapter also includes a discussion of public attitudes toward inmate education, and the impact of institutional attributes, that is, hiring, staffing, and training of correctional officers. Ultimately, the success or failure of any incarceration-based education program depends on the acquiescence and skill of these stakeholders.

REVIEW OF LITERATURE

The Bureau of Justice Statistics (BJS, 2010) and the Sourcebook of Criminal Justice Statistics Online (2009a) estimate that there are 7.2 million individuals under adult correctional supervision in the United States. In other words, one in 32 adults are being monitored in the community by means of probation (4,203,961) or parole (819,300), or are confined to federal (208, 118), state (1,405,622), or local (760,400) correctional institutions. The rates of sentenced prisoners under the jurisdiction of state and federal authorities have steadily increased over the last 3 decades. The rate of incarcerated citizens went from 139 per 100,000 in 1980 to

502 per 100,000 in 2009 (Sourcebook of Criminal Justice Statistics Online, 2009b).

Growth in the prison population and the rising cost of corrections are largely the consequences of the "tough on crime" movement. Notwithstanding these policies, 97% of all prisoners will eventually be released from correctional institutions (National Institute of Justice [NIJ], 2010). More alarming, however, is the fact that two thirds of those released will be rearrested, reconvicted, and reincarcerated within 3 years of discharge (NIJ, 2010). Miller (1978) warned of this circumstance 35 years ago. He admonished:

> Although ... [we] cater to a societal philosophy of "out of sight, out of mind," few people consider the fact that with an extreme paucity of exceptions, the inmates of these modern day asylums will eventually return to the community either less or better prepared to cope with the realities and pressures of life in a dynamic environment. (p. xiii)

Miller went on to say:

> If for whatever reason [inmates] have found it either desirable or mistakenly necessary steps are taken between the time of sentence and eventual release to affect a positive change in attitude and behavior, these same people will again revert to crime when back among us. (p. 63)

Although prisons primarily exist to enhance public safety by maintaining secure custody of individuals who pose a threat to society (Miller, 1978; Muraskin, 2005; Peak, 2004), the long-term purpose of correctional sanctions should be to effect positive behavioral changes. By that very fact, criminal rehabilitation is integral to the get tough regime. Certainly, rehabilitation initiatives are focused on inmates and partially motivated by humane considerations in the prison setting. Ultimately, however, the communities into which offenders will be released benefit from these efforts. Transforming lawbreakers into law-abiding citizens has implicit significance for the next potential victim.

The ideology of rehabilitation has been in and out of fashion throughout the development of the penal system. The thought of criminal behavior as a form of pathology that can be treated and cured is the basis of this doctrine (Carlson, Hess, & Orthmann, 1999; Gillespie, 2003; Peak, 2004; Siegel, 2007; Siegel, Welsh, & Senna, 2003). The oldest and most predominant restoration project in the prison setting is religious programming. However, treatment efforts have evolved overtime to include mental health care services; personal hygiene and grooming regimens; inmate visits, as well as mail and telephone services; structured and unstructured exercise and recreational activities; work programs; and educational and personal developmental curricula. The contention is that the correctional system has failed to reduce the recidivism rate in any significant way inasmuch as prison education has not been given an adequate chance (Miller, 1978; Peak, 2004).

Education-Based Incarceration as a Goal of Corrections

As much of the literature on the development of corrections has already been catalogued in earlier chapters, we will briefly examine a few of the major evolutionary trends in the United States. When the first house of detention was founded in Boston, Massachusetts in 1632 (Carlson et al., 1999), imprisonment was a revolutionary idea for the reason that it was more humane than customary penalties for wrongdoing at the time. On the whole, from then until now, the primary goals of corrections have included and vacillated between retribution, deterrence, incapacitation, rehabilitation, and reintegration.

Retribution is the oldest function of imprisonment (Carlson et al., 1999). Some experts believe that the purpose of the penal system is to punish individuals for wrongdoing. It is the eye for an eye ethos from the Old Testament of the Bible (Deuteronomy, 19:21). The supposition is that interment for a commensurable amount of time is an acceptable response to unlawful activity.

Whereas retribution involves the idea of deserved punishment for prior misconduct, deterrence is founded on a more proactive philosophy. In the realm of penology, deterrence theory postulates that if the terms and conditions of incarceration are deliberately forbidding individuals will be discouraged from committing crime in the future. Moreover, this view of corrections assumes that punishment of offenders serve as an example and means of deterring potential criminality in others.

Incapacitation as a correctional objective overlaps the ideas of punishment of offenders and protection of society. Advocates of this ideology presume that the primary purpose of the penal system is to confine individuals in return for breaking the law. In addition, they argue that imprisonment restrains offenders from committing crimes against the public throughout the course of their sentence.

At the same time, penologists maintain that correctional institutions should operate to effect positive change and development in offenders (Carlson et al., 1999; Kifer, Hemmens, & Stohr, 2003; Miller, 1978). Although prisons and jails are intended to enhance public safety by keeping secure custody of individuals whose actions and attitudes cause harm and injury to others, confinement is essentially a provisional measure since the vast majority of all prisoners will eventually be released back into society (NIJ, 2011). Ipso facto, rehabilitation is considered a major focus of prison management and treatment of offenders. Supporters of restorative philosophy concentrate on involving offenders in educational services, vocational development, psychotherapy, and life skills training before their correctional release.

Akin to the goal of rehabilitation is the intention of reintegrating offenders into society as productive, law-abiding members. While rehabilitative initiatives are centered on prerelease remedial services and supports, reentry principles and prescriptions are concerned with helping releasees adjust to responsibilities and vicissitudes after returning to their communities. Reintegration ideology is directly concerned with reducing recidivism and is established around a number of pre- (i.e., assessment and planning) and postrelease (i.e., linkages to educational and mental health services in the community; assistance with obtaining housing, employment, and welfare benefits) services.

Related to theory and practice of prison management is a body of ideas that explains criminality and justifies the goals of corrections. Everything considered there have been two competing ideologies of deviant behavior. The classical view of deviance postulates that people have free will and are consequently responsible for their actions. Therefore, the goals of the penal system include retribution, deterrence, and incapacitation (Carlson et al., 1999; Peak, 2004). On the other hand, the positivist view of wrongdoing presumes that human behavior is shaped by society. For this reason, the goals of criminal justice are incapacitation, rehabilitation, and reintegration (Carlson et al., 1999; Peak, 2004).

Ultimately, an all-important element of both ideologies is education. Imprisonment is inherently a form of punishment as well as an indispensable mechanism for deterring criminal behavior and enhancing public safety. Still, the purpose of education-based incarceration is to reduce recidivism by helping inmates make transformative behavioral changes by the time they are reintegrated into society.

The Enigma of Education-Based Incarceration

Since the 1970s, public discourse concerning crime and criminals has vacillated between punishment and rehabilitation. Still, prison education has evolved and endured. Data indicates that correctional managers support education-based incarceration. The United States Department of Justice (BJS, 2008) reports that nine in 10 public correctional facilities, and six in 10 private institutions, offer academic or vocational training. Secondary education is the most predominant offering. General Equivalence Diploma instruction is provided at 77% of correctional facilities in the union. Basic adult education (i.e., literacy) is a course of study at 66% of the institutions. More than one half (52%) of public and private houses of detention offer vocational training to inmates. Approximately one third (37%) provide special education for adult inmates with learning disabilities. Although Pell grant awards to inmate-students have been rescinded, one third (35%) of public and private prisons allow inmates an opportunity to take correspondence college courses. When life skills and personal development curricula are considered, 70% of the facilities in the penal system offer courses in conflict resolution, drug and alcohol awareness, domestic violence, parenting, or job seeking skills and employment (BJS, 2008).

The preponderance of prison education in the American penal system raises questions about the merits of these programs in reducing recidivism. The most pressing question, perhaps, has to do with factors within the prison environment that influence the effectiveness of education-based incarceration. Generally, prison superintendents and jailers are supportive of reformative educational strategies (BJS, 2008; Cullen, Lutze, Link, & Wolfe, 1989). Theoretically, the orientation toward prison education is top-down. In reality, however, front-line staff are charged with implementing the rehabilitative mission of the correctional system (Antonio & Young, 2011; Farkas, 1999; Kifer et al., 2003). Ipso facto, the effectiveness of prison education is determined by their attitudes toward rehabilitative ideals, as well as their interaction with inmate-students (Crewe, Bennette, & Wahidin, 2008; Warr, 2008). Certainly, these factors can create barriers to full implementation of education-based incarceration.

The Total Institution Effect

Inmate rehabilitation efforts are surely affected by the prison environment. The scope, nature, and extent of that influence, however, is a complex matter. Incarceration is intrinsically a major form of punishment. Prison is a total institution (Gillespie, 2003). It is a place where similarly situated individuals are divested of liberty for a considerable period of time. They are essentially cut off from larger society and deprived of natural social needs. Moreover, all aspects of life are conducted in a single location, and all of the inmates' physiological, safety, esteem, and self-actualization needs are under bureaucratic control (Gillespie, 2003). Inmates are stripped of personal possessions, denied privacy, subject to indignities, and exposed to a highly regimented existence.

Lawbreakers, especially violent offenders, deserve punishment. Nevertheless, the conditions within corrections can embitter prisoners and, in some cases, may be counterproductive to rehabilitation (Gillespie, 2003; Miller, 1978; Roberts, 1974). It seems reasonable to believe that we should heed Miller's (1978) advice: *"an individual is in prison as punishment, not for punishment"* (p. 4).

According to Carlson et al. (1999), the correctional system has endeavored to improve prison living conditions since the first generation of penitentiaries. The original architecture included cellblocks designed to confine individual inmates. Cells and corridors were constructed to forestall communication among occupants. Dwellings had few windows, and any available windows were gated and louvered to preclude inmates from looking out onto the street. Facilities were poorly ventilated, dim, unkempt, and filthy. First generation prisons were built and structured to minimize contact between jailers and jailees. Prison guards believed their safety depended on keeping a physical barrier between them and inmates (Carlson et al., 1999).

Overcrowding and the psychological trauma of solitary confinement eventually necessitated desegregation of inmates (Carlson et al., 1999; Peak, 2004). Subsequently, physical and sexual abuse among inmates became a regular occurrence. Second generation penitentiary architecture merely improved remote surveillance of inmates. Living conditions were barely improved, and prisoners and their keepers remained separated (Carlson et al., 1999; Peak, 2004).

Third generation architecture entailed major improvements in interior and living conditions. The plan required better sanitation, illumination, and ventilation; regular maintenance; large common areas; fixed, ungated windows in every prisoner's room; colorfully painted walls; and moveable furniture (Peak, 2004). During the third generation, there was also a change in inmate supervision protocol. Physical barriers between guards and inmates were removed (Carlson et al., 1999; Peak, 2004). In short order, officers went from monitoring to managing prisoners. Correctional staff were expected to maintain custody and control, help inmates cope with incarceration, assist them with institutional problems, and serve as role models for prisoners. These expectations came with minimal training.

The first penitentiary designed according to the new architectural and management standards opened in Contra Costa County, California in the 1970s (Carlson et al., 1999; Peak, 2004). It was anticipated that the new program would reduce the trauma of incarceration; however, the plan did not have the desired effect. Destruction and violence among inmates continued to be prevalent in the prison environment (Carlson et al., 1999; Peak, 2004). Two main explanations have been given for this phenomenon. Both regard subcultures, and both are related to the total institution effect.

The first interpretation comes from the importation model. The main premise of this model is that inmate behavior is formed from what offenders bring into prison (Cullen et al., 1989; Farkas, 1999; Gillespie, 2003; Lambert et al., 2007; Paterline & Petersen, 1999). Simply stated, inmates' norms are an extension of the criminal subculture. When inadequately socialized individuals with similar adjustment issues interact, incivility and mayhem are likely to ensue (Carlson et al., 1999; DiIulio, 1987; Gillespie, 2003). The second explanation is "prisonization," a term coined by Donald Clemmer (1940, 1950). "Prisonization" is based on the theory that conditions within the prison engender a process of socialization that draws inmates away from the values and norms of the institution. In any event, inmates who lack self-responsibility, are in constant fear for their life, and are denied dignity and worth will probably be unable to derive benefit from prison education. In fact, many may forgo the opportunity entirely.

Correctional Officers' Attitudes Toward Inmates and Rehabilitation

Inmate rehabilitation is determined by the administrative machinery of incarceration, the physical plant, and inmate subculture (Clemmer, 1940, 1950; Flynn, 1974; Gillespie, 2003; Roberts, 1974). Efforts are likely influenced by correctional officers as well. There is an abundance of empirical and theoretical information regarding correctional officers' attitudes toward prisoners and rehabilitative ideals (Antonio & Young, 2011; Antonio, Young, & Winegeard, 2009a, 2009b; Bazemore & Dicker, 1994; Crewe et al., 2008; Crouch & Alpert, 1982; Cullen et al., 1989; Hemmens & Stohr, 2000; Jackson & Ammens, 1996; Jurik, 1985; Jurik & Halemba, 1984; Klofas, 1986; Lambert et al., 2009; Lambert & Paoline, 2008; Lambert, Paoline, Hogan, & Baker, 2007; Maahs & Pratt, 2001; Paterline & Petersen, 1999; Paboojian & Teske, 1997; Van Voorhis, Cullen et al., 1989; Warr, 2008; Whitehead, Lindquist, & Klofas, 1987; Young & Antonio, 2009). This knowledge spans over 70 years. Since correctional officers have been characterized as the "other prisoners" (Carlson et al., 1999; Muraskin, 2005; Peak, 2004) it is apropos that importation and prisonization models have also been used to explain this phenomenon.

Much attention has been given to correctional officers because they are the largest group of prison workers (Bureau of Labor Statistics, 2011). Furthermore, their contact with inmates is direct and prolonged. To the extent that this is true, genuine implementation of rehabilitation programming can not be achieved without the acquiescence and participation of correctional officers. The literature emphasizes three sets of factors that effect treatment orientation among these workers: personal characteristics, career variables, and institutional attributes.

Personal Characteristics

Historically, the position of correctional officer was occupied by White males from rural areas and small towns. Commonly, these officials had limited education and lacked significant employment opportunities. For these reasons, their interest in corrections was motivated by job security (Carlson et al., 1999; Farkas, 1999; Josi & Sechrest, 1999; Lambert et al., 2007; Paboojian & Teske, 1997; Peak, 2004). Since the 1980s, the penal system has made earnest attempts to diversify the workforce. It was hoped that these concerted efforts would reduce officer-to-inmate brutality, increase overall skill in managing prisoner behavior, and result in improved relations between jailers and jailees. These notions were governed by importation-differential experience theory (Van Voorhis et al., 1991). This model argues that an array of cultural (i.e., personal and career) characteristics influence officers' attitudes and behaviors toward prisoners. The most frequently investigated demographic variables are sex, race, educational attainment, and age. Scientific investigations of these factors have largely drawn mixed conclusions.

Sex

Prior to the 1970s, there were no women correctional officers in male penitentiaries. Although they could serve as officers in female and juvenile institutions, they were restricted from official duty in male facilities. The argument was that women were incapable of managing male prisoners. In addition, their presence was regarded as both enticing to male inmates and a violation of their privacy. Ultimately, women were recruited and employed in male prisons because it was assumed that this would lead to improvements in direct inmate supervisions. Men and women are socialized differently, and this results in different attitudes, perceptions, and behaviors. (Lambert et al., 2007). More specifically, women are socialized to be caregivers. Therefore, they are more likely than males to choose a career in corrections because they want to rehabilitate inmates. Furthermore, they are more likely than their male counterparts to exercise effective interpersonal skills and acute sensitivity in their interaction with inmates (Farkas, 1999; Lambert et al., 2007; Paboojian & Teske, 1997).

While some investigations have found no significant relationship between officers' sex and attitudes toward inmates (Jurik, 1985; Jurik & Halema, 1984; Kjelsber, Skoglund, & Rustad, 2007; Paboojian & Teske, 1997; Paterline & Petersen, 1999; Whitehead, Lindquist, & Klofas, 1987), there is some evidence to the contrary. Jurik (1983) found that among officers in her study, females were significantly more likely than males to have taken a job in corrections because they wanted to help inmates. The study also concluded that female correctional officers reported more positive attitudes toward prisoners. However, this finding should be taken with caution since female officers were more likely to have: (1) come to corrections for intrinsic reasons, (2) more education, and (3) fewer contact hours with inmates as compared to their male counterparts. In another investigation that included a survey of security staff at five correctional facilities and one training academy in a rural mountain state, Kifer and her colleagues (2003) found that female officers were more likely than male officers to favor rehabilitation as a goal of corrections.

Overall, the empirical literature has determined that male and female correctional officers generally differ in their treatment orientation toward inmates; however, as one study revealed, attitudes toward rehabilitation and readiness to inflict punishment on prisoners are not mutually exclusive events. With respect to this matter, Farkas (1999) found that female officers were more supportive of rehabilitation programs in the prison setting than male correctional officers; nevertheless, her study indicated that female officers held more punitive attitudes toward inmates than their male counterparts. A specific explanation for this finding is that, to be successful, female correctional officers overcompensate and comport to stereotyped norms (Farkas, 1999). In another way, this evidence can be interpreted by the effect of prisonization on any correctional officer.

Race

Racial turmoil between security staff and inmates within men's correctional facilities, in particular, has been an empirical rule (Carlson et al., 1999; Paboojian & Teske, 1997; Peak, 2004). Although, jailers and jailees typically came from the same socioeconomic background, they traditionally differed disproportionately with respect to race. Prison officers were almost exclusively White, and inmates were, and still are, disproportionately Black and Latino (Farkas, 1999; Josi & Sechrest, 1998; Paboojian & Teske, 1997; Peak, 2004). At least up until the time of the Attica State Prison revolt, correctional facilities were racially hostile environments.

Since the 1980s, there have been major initiatives to recruit and hire African American and Latino correctional staff (Paboojian & Teske, 1997). It was presumed that this strategy would minimize racial conflict between inmates and their keepers (Paboojian & Teske, 1997; Peak, 2004). It stands to reason that: (1) ethnic minority prisoners will feel more comfortable with similarly situated staff, and (2) Black and Latino officers will be more identified with and hold more positive attitudes toward inmates.

Like sex, findings regarding the relationship between race and attitude are rather inconclusive. Some investigations into the association between officers' race and attitude found no statistically significant relationship between these variables (Bazemore & Dicer, 1994; Crouch & Alpert, 1982; Klofas, 1986). Many studies, however, have shown that race explained varying orientations among correctional officers. Specifically, the empirical rule is that ethnic minority officers are more supportive of treatment programs (Cullen et al., 1989; Jackson & Ammen, 1996; Jurik, 1985; Maahs & Prat, 2001; Paboojian & Teske, 1997; Van Voorhis et al., 1991; Whitehead & Lindquist, 1989). These findings must be viewed with caution for at least two reasons. First, most studies that have examined race as an explanation for correctional officers' attitudes neglected to statistically control for variations within and between race groups due to other potentially confounding variables (i.e., other personal characteristics, career variables, and institutional attributes). Second, just as Farkas (1999) discovered in regards to sex, an analysis of race and attitude by Cullen and colleagues (1989) established that support for rehabilitation and punitive attitudes toward inmates were not mutually exclusive.

Education

Before the third period of prison management, contact between correctional officers and prisoners was limited and brief. Custodial staff were posted in control rooms and behind barriers where they kept watch over jailees. The new generation of administration was characterized by prolonged, direct contact and management of prisoners (Carlson et al., 1999; Lariviere & Robinson, 1996; Muraskin, 2005; Peak, 2004) . Unfortunately, passage from a "hands off" philosophy to direct supervision included minimal in-service training. Moreover, although the educational standard has increased with the professionalization of the field, it is barely adequate for the essential duties required for the job (Carlson et al., 1999; DiIulio, 1987; Josi & Sechrest, 1998; Miller, 1978). It is assumed that correctional officers with postsecondary educational credentials will be more enlightened about human behavior and the social environment and, thereby, more favorable toward rehabilitative ideals. In addition, it is supposed that they will be better able to control inmate activity by use of liberal tactics (Carlson et al., 1999; Peak, 2004).

To date, research has been unable to link educational level with officers' attitudes toward treatment. There is evidence suggesting that education explains orientation toward restoration (Jurik, 1985; Kifer et al., 2003; Paboojain & Teske, 1997; Stohr, Hemmens, Kifer, & Schoeler, 2000); yet, other investigations found no relationship between education and support for inmate rehabilitation (Hemmens & Stohr, 2000; Maahs & Pratt, 2001). The relationship between educational attainment and punitiveness becomes even more complex when considering job satisfaction and organizational commitment to custody and control. Research done in Canada (Lariviere & Robinson, 1996) as well as the United States (Kifer et al., 2003; Lambert & Paoline, 2008) indicates that there is a complex association between institutional commitment to custody and control, punitiveness, support for rehabilitation, and job satisfaction among correctional officers. The precise nature and importance of this relationship has yet to be settled.

Age

Since 1980's *Ruiz v. Estelle* (Crouch, 1985; Justice, 1990), the federal mandate to increase the number and diversity of frontline security staff, there has been major change in the sociodemographic characteristics of correctional personnel (Paboojian & Teske, 1997). One of the changes has been the shift in entry age. Younger officers have been routinely recruited and hired as custodial staff. Studies, for example, have failed to uncover a priori link between chronological age and treatment orientation; yet, it is the only personal characteristic that has consistently been associated with attitudes toward working with prisoners. Apart from Crouch and Alpert (1982) and Kjelsberg et al. (2007), age is evidently positively correlated with attitudes toward inmate rehabilitation (Cullen et al., 1989; Farkas, 1999; Jurik, 1985; Kifer et al., 2003; Lariviere & Robinson, 1996; Paboojian & Teske, 1997; Ward & Kupchik, 2010). Perchance, older (veteran and rookie) officers have less apathy toward treatment programming in the prison setting because they are less likely to associate competence as a security officer with culturally dominant notions of masculinity (Lambert et al., 2007).

Career Variables

Career variables, such as position, prior military background, and years of experience in corrections have also been used to study importation-differential experience theory and treatment orientation among prison workers.

Position

There are a variety of jobs in the penal system. The Federal Bureau of Prisons lists in excess of 40 job titles on their website (www.bop.gov/jobs/index.jsp) . The warden oversees operation of the entire institution. He or she sets policy and procedure for the facility. However, the warden does not run the jail alone. A superintendent's orders are implemented by an array of personnel (Cullen et al., 1993; Federal Bureau of Prisons, 2011).

The nature of employment in a correctional facility range from mainte-nance to food service, business to health care, legal to clerical, and teach-ing to security. Because custodial staff are frontline workers in prison, and they comprise the majority of correctional personnel, a lot of research attention has been given to them. Owing to the history and nature of pris-oner supervision, inmate-keeper relations, and extrinsic job motivation among security officers, it is granted that they generally have less positive attitudes toward inmates and are less supportive of human service work in the prison setting than other correctional personnel (DiIulio, 1987; Lam-bert et al., 2009; Lariviere & Robinson, 1996; Peak, 2004).

Studies indicate clearly that correctional officers are less empathic toward offenders (Kjelsberg, 2007; Kifer et al., 2003), have more punitive dispositions toward inmates (Lariviere & Robinson, 1996), and are more apathetic toward rehabilitation ideals (Antonio & Young, 2011) than other correctional personnel. However, these postures may be influenced, as well as confounded, by role stress and role ambiguity. Evidence suggests that correctional officers are generally perplexed and distressed by their dual mission of punishment and rehabilitation (Ward & Kupchick, 2010; Antonio & Young, 2011; Farkas, 1999). Many custodial workers support treatment for inmates before reentry into society; nevertheless, they do not favor rehabilitation as a role in their interaction with prisoners. This may explain why security staff members are generally more dissatisfied with their work than other personnel (Kifer et al., 2003; Lariviere & Rob-inson, 1996).

Military Background

Law enforcement, including corrections, is organized along semimili-tary lines (DiIulio, 1987; Peak, 2004). Traditional and contemporary inmate supervision have usually been approached in military fashion. In a correctional environment characterized by a paramilitary approach, abso-lute deference and obedience are expected from prison inmates. Under the new administration of supervision and management, however, officers are required to balance strict enforcement of rules, flexibility in decision making, and tact in their interactions with jailees. Correctional officers are not allowed to physically or verbally abuse inmates; nevertheless, some officers are overly authoritative and punitive (DiIulio, 1987; Peak, 2004; Roberts, 1974). It is expected that officers with a background in the military are not only more likely to be regimented and inflexible in their interactions with inmates but are also likely to hold less positive attitudes toward prisoners and rehabilitation (Paboojian & Teske, 1997).

There is a dearth of empirical knowledge concerning prior military service and perceptions of inmate rehabilitation among correctional offi-cers. One documented investigation was found. In 1997, Paboojian and

Raymond published an article in the *Journal of Criminal Justice*. Their study examined attitudes regarding various inmate treatment programs among 319 preservice officers in Texas. Among other things, the research revealed that military experience was not significantly related to attitude toward programming.

Years of Experience

Prison jobs are highly stressful and dangerous—especially for security staff (Carson et al., 1999; DiIulio, 1987; Farkas, 1999; Josi & Sechrest, 1998; Lambert et al., 2007; Muraski, 2005; Peak, 2004). By its nature, the work is unpleasant and trying. Correctional officers work closely with criminals and degenerates. They bare witness to utterly reprehensible behavior on a regular basis. They are exposed to the monotony of numbering, counting, checking, and locking. Moreover, custodial workers contend with divergent and conflicting tasks and goals. After everything else has been considered, they put their own welfare in jeopardy to maintain safety and security for inmates, staff, and visitors. It stands to reason that length of employment would be associated with attitudes toward inmate rehabilitation. More specially, it is logical to expect that officers with the most tenure would be more jaded and, therefore, less supportive of the treatment orientation.

The weight of the evidence shows that the amount of tenure that a correctional officer has determines his/her treatment orientation. However, years of experience is negatively associated with attitudes toward human services in the prison environment (Antonio & Young, 2011; Farkas, 1999; Jurik, 1985; Kifer et al., 2003; Ward & Kupchik, 2010). On account of the potentially high degree of correlation between age and years of experience, it is not possible to decipher whether these two factors have independent effects on correctional officers' attitudes toward inmates and/or restorative incarceration. Whatever the case may be, the association between tenure and attitudes have been explained by the maturation process. It is presumed that with time and experience, older and more experienced officers have a better understanding of their dual role as custodian and human service provider and are more confident in their ability to negotiate both roles than younger and newer employees (Antonio & Young, 2011; Kifer et al., 2003).

Institutional Attributes

If attitudes toward rehabilitative ideals are determined by personal characteristics and/or career variables, than human service work and support for educational programming among correctional officers could be influenced by the recruitment and hiring processes. The preponderance of the scientific literature, however, suggests that this may not be the case. In general, research shows that the treatment orientation of correctional officers is effected by institutional attributes (Carlson et al., 1999; Cullen et al., 1993; Farkas, 1999; Kifer et al., 2003; Lambert et al., 2007, 2009; Paterline & Petersen, 1999). Even if, to some degree, support for treatment is predicted by race, sex, educational attainment, and/or pre-service training, longitudinal evaluations of staff attitudes and support for inmate human service programming show that interest in restoration significantly decrease within the first year of employment (Antonio & Young, 2011; Antonio et al., 2009a, 2009b; Young & Antonio, 2009). This occurrence has been explained by the deprivation thesis, which posits that the type of institution in which one works affects outlook on inmate rehabilitation. The ideology of prisonization among correctional officers has been subsumed under this model. Irrespective of one's personal treatment orientation, the rehabilitative mission of corrections management is mainly compromised by frustration and deprivation in the work environment. Variables such as type of detention facility (Kiefer, 2003), sex of inmates (Antonio & Young, 2011; Kjelsberg et al., 2007), size of institution (Lariviere & Robinson, 1996), and security classification (Antonio & Young, 2011; Jurik, 1985; Lariviere & Robinson, 1996) beget sufficient conditions for the emergence of a counterculture among security staff.

With respect to type of detention facility, for instance, Kifer and her partners (2003) discovered that staff working in jail settings were less likely than staff employed in prisons to favor rehabilitation. A reasonable assumption for this occurrence is the difference between jails and prisons in regards to sentencing and inmate turnover, as well as how that affects the perceived dangerousness of corrections work. Perceived dangerousness and the seemingly incompatible nature of security and rehabilitation has also been used to explain why security staff working in male only prisons (Kjelsberg et al., 2007), large institutions (Lariviere & Robinson, 1996), and maximum-security facilities (Lariviere & Robinson, 1996; Jurik, 1985) have more punitive attitudes toward inmates and are less supportive of prison rehabilitation than their counterparts.

Given current prison conditions, particularly crowding and violence, it is unreasonable to expect correctional officers to take on the role of human service provider. Safety concerns for self and others create tension between officers' treatment orientation and inmate management techniques (Farkas, 1999). One adapts to the dangerousness of the job. In a treacherous prison environment, officers may develop a common commitment to custody and control by any means necessary.

THE HUMAN SERVICE CORRECTIONAL OFFICER

Although there have been many changes in both the philosophy and purpose of incarceration, the fact remains that the primary objective for correctional officers has always been to maintain safety and discipline within the prison environment – not to reform individuals or to prepare them to be better performing citizens upon discharge (Carlson et al., 1999; Miller, 1978; Muraskin, 2005; Peak, 2004). Nevertheless, security and treatment are not inevitably incompatible goals. In fact, a successful educational program is not possible without instituting methods and procedures to maintain safety and order within the prison environment (DiIulio, 1987; Gillespie, 2003; Miller, 1978; Roberts, 1974). Individuals who are unsettled by the constant presence or imminence of danger are not likely to benefit from educational programming. This issue can be addressed by segregating inmate-students from the general population (Gillespie, 2003). Besides, to a more immediate extent, security and control are expedient for protecting inmate-students and teaching staff from potential aggressive horseplay, taunts, and threats in the classroom setting (DiIulio, 1987). Notwithstanding the preceding considerations, effective security and control does not have to be driven by paramilitary approaches. In reality, repressive tactics are counterproductive to self-improvement (DiIulio, 1987; Gillespie, 2003; Peak, 2004).

In consideration of the compatible nature of security and treatment, an unfortunate feature of all education-based incarceration initiatives has been the total compartmentalization of roles among correctional officers and teachers. It is seemingly feasible, as well as advantageous, for custodial and human services personnel to *work together* to provide an atmosphere that is conducive to the rehabilitation of offenders. It is a matter of course, however, for correctional officers to primarily function as watchmen. In addition, individuals generally come to the field with that professional orientation in mind (Carlson et al., 1999; Josi & Sechrest, 1998; Kiefer et al., 2003; Miller, 1978; Peak, 2004). By the latter fact itself, a two track career model – that is a course laid out for correctional security officer and another for correctional human service officer —is indicated for a harmonious work relationship between custodial and teaching staff and, thereby, successful implementation of educational programming in the prison environment (Farkas, 1999).

CONCLUSIONS AND IMPLICATIONS

The social and economic costs of recidivism are excessive. Relapses into criminal behavior violate human security. Furthermore, rearrest, reconviction, and reincarceration of offenders oppose the greater economic good of society on account of public expenditures for law enforcement, legal defense, and imprisonment (or alternatives to incarceration). Of course, there is also the larger cost to society in terms of productivity losses for victims and institutionalized offenders.

In general, there is good evidence of a causal link between education and criminal behavior (Lochner & Moretti, 2004). More specifically, the empirical literature indicates that prison education programs have promise and possibility as a crime prevention measure (Lawrence, 1974; Lochner & Moretti, 2004; Vacca, 2004; O'Neil, MacKenzie, & Bierie, 2007; Zgoba et al., 2008; Siegel et al., 2003). Although prison superintendents and jailers are generally supportive of reformative educational strategies (BJS, 2008; Cullen et al., 1993), many, if not most, offenders reenter society from prison unskilled, undereducated, and likely to recidivate (NIJ, 2011). This is particularly true for violent offenders (Lochner & Moretti, 2002).

To that extent, the merit of prison-based education is called into question. A review of the current state of knowledge regarding this matter reveals that factors within the prison environment influence the effectiveness of incarceration-based educational programming. Absolutely, inmate rehabilitation efforts are affected by the inmate subculture as well as the administrative and authoritarian machinery of incarceration (Gillespie, 2003). In the prison milieu, inmates customarily consider deputies as the foremost authorities of the institution. By that fact, correctional officers' attitudes toward inmates and tuition behind bars is likely to impact treatment outcomes (Antonio & Young, 2011; Crewe et al., 2008; Kiefer, 2003; Paboojian & Teske, 1997; Warr, 2008).

Since inmate rehabilitation efforts are largely influenced by security staff, the type of officer one desires in a prison education program is determined by what one expects to achieve with and for the incarcerated individual. The kind of persons needed to provide the type of intervention program that will bring about life-changing behavior are, in some ways, very complex individuals. Empirical evidence counters intuition regarding the influence of sociodemographic variables on expressed attitudes toward inmates and educational ideals among correctional officers. For the most part, characteristics such as race, sex, educational attainment, and military experience do not significantly predict officers' attitudes toward prisoners or their support for corrections-based education.

The preponderance of information derived from scientific observation suggest that perceptions and behaviors of security staff and, thereby, the restorative educational mission of corrections management, is mainly compromised by deprivation in the work environment. There are many obstacles that complicate and impede the educational process in a correctional facility. Most of all are the methods and procedures that are used to maintain order and safety (DiIulio, 1987; Miller, 1978; Muraskin, 2005).

There is "nothing wrong with putting safety first" (Miller, 1978, p. 33); the question is: Are security and treatment necessarily incompatible goals? No, especially if one considers that a successful prison education program is contingent on procedures that insure order and safety in the classroom setting as well as the general environment (DiIlio, 1987; Muraskin, 2005).

Perhaps the fundamental issue is contamination. That is, exposing inmate-students and deputies that might be disposed to favor education behind bars to the pressures and problems caused by the general experience of residing and working in a prison environment. If this is the case, administrative restructuring may be the solution. Procuring a separate facility from general population that serves as an educational building and living quarters for inmate-students would probably be beneficial. Moreover, developing a two tract career system for deputies (Antonio & Young, 2011; Kiefer et al. 2003)—that is security versus human services corrections officers—might be sufficiently valuable. Staff on the latter track could be involved in implementing and supporting educational plans for offenders.

Deviant individuals need educational programming that not only focuses on academic, vocational, and social skills training. Transformational behavior change requires a positive environment that facilitates the process of rehabilitation. Although teaching staff is charged with delivering educational instructions to inmates, custodial staff have the power of affecting the practical impact and outcome of that tutelage. Antonio and Young (2011) explained it well; they postulated that corrections officers "have the best opportunity to reinforce lessons learned; provide opportunities for inmates to apply and practice skills; and give inmates opportunities to observe staff modeling ideal reactions to real-life situations" (p. 2).

Deputies who do not agree with rehabilitative initiatives in the prison setting can thwart the effectiveness of the educational process (Kifer et al., 2003). Educational programs may be most effective when each and every staff member involved believes that the inmate can change. Accordingly, they should believe that the inmate is worthy of change, can make a good person and citizen, and is worth one's investment of time. The philosophy of expectation and change is the glue that holds the whole project together and drives the program in all its phases—staffing, student assessment, delivery of services, and rewards for achievement. Corrections officers are indispensible members of the team; there should also be sincere and total commitment on the part of deputies toward the project and its success.

The correctional system has failed to reduce recidivism rates in any significant way inasmuch as prison education has not been given an adequate chance to succeed (Miller, 1978; Peak, 2004). The cycle of crime has implications for personal development to the extent that reoffending and serial incarceration affects the social functioning of individuals, as well as their capacity to self-actualize and perform a positive function in society. Moreover, this phenomenon has repercussions for public safety and public economics. Therefore, it is worthwhile to increase the efficacy of tuition behind bars.

REFERENCES

Adams, K., Flanagan, T., Marquart, J., Cuvelier, S., Fritsch, E., Gerber, J., ... Burton, V. (1994). A large-scale multidimensional test of the effect of prison education programs on offenders' behavior. *Prison Journal, 74* (4), 433-449.

Antonio, M. & Young, J. (2011). The effects of tenure on staff apathy and treatment orientation: A comparison of respondent characteristics and environmental factors. *American Journal of Criminal Justice, 35,* 1-16

Antonio, M., Young, J., & Wingeard, M. (2009a). Reinforcing positive behavior in a prison: Whose responsibility is it? *Journal of Offender Rehabilitation, 48,* 53-66.

Antonio, M., Young, J., & Wingeard, M. (2009b). When actions and attitude count most: Assessing perceived level of responsibility and support for inmate treatment and rehabilitation programs among correctional employee. *Prison Journal, 89,* 363-382.

Bazemore, G., & Dicker, T. (1994). Explaining detention worker orientation: Individual characteristics, occupational conditions, and organization environment. *Journal of Criminal Justice, 22,* 297-312.

Bureau of Justice Statistics. (2010). *Prisoners in 2009.* (NCJ Publication No. 231675). Washington, DC: U.S. Department of Justice.

Bureau of Justice Statistics. (2008). *National prisoner statistics program: Census of state and federal correctional facilities, 2005.* (NCJ Publication No. 222182). Washington, DC: U.S. Department of Justice.

Bureau of Justice Statistics. (2004). *State prison expenditures, 2001.* (NCJ Publication No. 202949). Washington, DC: U.S. Department of Justice.

Bureau of Labor Statistics. (2011). *Occupational outlook handbook, 2010-2011 edition: Correctional officers.* Retrieved from http://www.bls.gov/oco/ocos156.htm

Carlson, N., Hess, K., & Orthmann, C. (1999). *Corrections in the 21st century: A practical approach.* Belmont, CA: Wadsworth.

Clemmer, D. (1940). *The prison community.* New York, NY: Holt, Rinehart, & Winston.

Clemmer, D. (1950). Observation on imprisonment as a source of criminality. *Journal of Criminal Law & Criminology, 41,* 311-319.

Crewe, B., Bennette, J., & Wahidin, A. (2008). Introduction. In J. Bennett, B. Crewe, & A. Wahidin (Eds.), *Understanding the prison staff* (pp. 1-13). Portland, OR: Willan.

Crouch, B., & Alpert (1982). Sex and occupational socialization among prison guards: A longitudinal study. *Criminal Justice and Behavior, 9*, 159-176.

Cullen, F., Lutze, F., Link, B., & Wolfe, N. (1989). The correctional orientation of prison guards: Do officers support rehabilitation? *Federal Probation, 53*, 33-42.

DiIulio, J. (1987). *Governing prisons.* New York, NY: The Free Press.

Farkas, M. (1999). Correctional officers' attitudes towards inmates and working with inmates in a "get tough" era. *Journal of Criminal Justice, 27*(6), 495-506.

Federal Bureau of Prisons. (2011). Careers with the Bureau of Prisons. Retrieved from http://www.bop.gov/jobs/index.jsp

Flynn, E.E. (1974). Environmental variables: Their impact on the correctional process. In A. Roberts (Ed.), *Correctional treatment of the offender* (pp. 45-71). Springfield, IL: Charles C. Thomas.

Gillespie, N. (2003). *Prisonization: Individual and institutional factors affecting inmate conduct.* New York, NY: LFB Scholarly.

Hemmens, C., & Stohr, M. (2000). The two faces of the correctional role: An exploration of the value of the correctional role instrument. *International Journal of Offender Therapy & Comparative Criminology, 44*, 326-346.

Jackson, J., & Ammen, S. (1996). Race and correctional officers' punitive attitudes toward treatment programs for inmates. *Journal of Criminal Justice, 24*, 153-166.

Josi, D., & Sechrest, D. (1998). *The changing career of the correctional officer: Policy implications for the 21st century.* Woburn, MA: Butterworth-Heinemann.

Jurik, N. (1985). Individual and organizational determinants of correctional officer attitudes towards inmates. *Criminology, 23* (3), 523-539.

Jurik, N., & Halemba, G. (1984). Gender, working conditions and the job satisfaction of women in a non-traditional occupation: Female correctional officers in men's prisons. *Sociological Quarterly, 25*, 551-566.

Justice, W. W. (1990). The origins of *Ruiz v. Estelle. Stanford Law Review, 43*(1), 1-12.

Kifer, M., Hemmens, C., & Stohr, M. (2003). The goals of corrections: Perspectives from the line. *Criminal Justice Review, 28*(47), 47-6.

Kjelsberg, E., Skoglund, T., & Rustad, A (2007). Attitudes towards prisoners, as reported by prison inmates, prison employees, and college students. *BMC Public Health, 7*(71), 1-9.

Klofas, J. (1986). Discretion among correctional officers: The influence of urbanization, age, and race. *International Journal of Offender Therapy and Comparative Criminology, 30*, 111-121.

Lambert, E., Hogan, N., Moore, B., Tucker, K., Jenkins, M., Stevenson, M., & Jiang, S. (2009). The impact of the work environment on prison staff: The issue of consideration, structure, job variety, and training. *American Journal of Criminal Justice, 34*, 166-180.

Lambert, E. & Paoline, E. (2008). The influence of individual, job, and organizational characteristics on correctional staff job stress, job satisfaction, and organizational commitment. *Criminal Justice Review, 33*, 541-564.

Lambert, E., Paoline, E., Hogan, N., & Baker, D. (2007). Gender similarities and differences in correctional staff work attitudes and perceptions of the work environment. Western *Criminology Review, 8*(1), 16-31.

Lariviere, M., & Robinson, D. (1996). *Attitudes of CSC correctional officers towards offenders* (CSW Research Report No. R-44). Ottawa, Ontario, Canada: Correctional Service of Canada.

Lawrence, R. E. (1974). Vocational rehabilitation of the offender. In A. Roberts (Ed.), *Correctional treatment of the offender* (pp. 45-71). Springfield, IL: Charles C. Thomas.

Lochner, L., & Moretti, E. (2004). The effects of education on crime: Evidence from prison inmates, arrests, & self-reports. *American Economic Review, 94*(1), 155-189.

Maahs, J., & Pratt, T. (2001). Uncovering the predictors of correctional officers' attitudes and behaviors: A meta-analysis. *Corrections Management Quarterly, 5*, 13-19.

Marquart, J. W., & Crouch, B. M. (1985). Judicial reform & prisoner control: The impact of *Ruiz v. Estelle* on a Texas penitentiary. *Law & Society, 19*(4), 557-558.

Miller, E. (1978). *Jail management*. Lexington, MA: Lexington Books.

Muraskin, R. (2005). *Key correctional issues*. Upper Saddle River, NJ: Pearson-Prentice Hall.

National Institute of Justice. (2010). *Reentry: Research findings*. Retrieved from http://www.ojp.usdoj.gov/nij/topics/corrections/reentry/research-findings.htm

O'Neill, L., MacKenzie, D. L., & Bierie, D. M. (2007). Educational opportunities within correctional institutions: Does facility type matter? *The Prison Journal, 87*(3), 311-327.

Paterline, B., & Petersen, D. (1999). Structural and social psychological determinants of prisonization. *Journal of Criminal Justice, 27*(5), 427-441.

Paboojian, A., & Teske, R. (1997). Pre-service correctional officers: What do they think about treatment? *Journal of Criminal Justice, 25*(5), 425-433.

Peak, K. (2004). *Justice administration: Police, courts, & corrections management* (4th ed.). Upper Saddle River, NJ: Pearson-Prentice Hall.

Roberts, A. R. (1974). Alternative strategies to offender rehabilitation: A prison option system. In A. Roberts (Ed.), *Correctional treatment of the offender* (pp. 5-44). Springfield, IL: Charles C. Thomas.

Siegel, L. J. (2007). *Criminology: Theories, patterns, & typologies* (9th ed.). Belmont, CA: Thomson Wadsworth.

Siegel, L. J., Welsh, B. C., & Senna, J. J. (2003). *Juvenile delinquency: Theory, practice, & law* (8th ed.). Belmont, CA: Thomson Wadsworth.

Sourcebook of Criminal Justice Statistics Online. (2009a). *Adults on probation, in jail or prison, & on parole: United States, 1980-2009*. Retrieved from http://www.albany.edu/sourcebook/pdf/t612009.pdf

Sourcebook of Criminal Justice Statistics Online. (2009b). *Rate of sentenced prisoners under jurisdiction of state & federal corrections authorities: By region & jurisdiction, 1980, 1984-2009*. Retrieved from http://www.albany.edu/sourcebook/pdf/t6292009.pdf

Stohr, M., Hemmens, C., Kifer, M., & Schoeler, M. (2000). We know it, we just have to do it: Perceptions of ethical work in prisons and jails. *Prison Journal, 80*, 126-150.

Vacca, J. (2004). Educated prisoners are less likely to return to prison. *Journal of Correctional Education, 55*(4), 297-305.

Van Voorhis, P., Cullen, F., Link, B., & Wolfe, N. (1991). The impact of race & gender on correctional officers' orientation to the integrated environment. *Journal of Research in Crime & Delinquency, 28*, 472-500.

Ward, G., & Kupchik, A. (2010). What drives juvenile probation officers? Relating organizational contexts, status characteristics, and personal convictions to treatment and punishment orientations. *Crime & Delinquency, 56*, 35-69.

Warr, J. (2008). Personal reflections on prison staff. In J. Bennett, B. Crewe, & A. Wahidin (Eds.), *Understanding the prison staff* (pp. 17-29). Portland, OR: Willan.

Whitehead, J., & Lindquist, C. (1989). Determinants of correctional officers' professional orientation. *Justice Quarterly, 6*, 69-87.

Whitehead, J., Lindquist, C., & Klofas, J. (1987). Correctional officer professional orientation: A replication of Klofas/Toch measure. *Criminal Justice & Behavior, 14*, 468-486.

Wilson, D., Gallagher, C., & MacKenzie, D. (2000). A meta-analysis of corrections-based education, vocation, and work programs for adult offenders. *Journal of Research in Crime & Delinquency, 37*(4), 247-368.

Young, J., & Antonio, M. (2009). Correctional staff attitudes after one year of employment: Perceptions of leniency and support for inmate rehabilitation. *Corrections Compendium, 34*, 9-17.

Zgoba, K., Haugebrook, S., & Jenkins, K. (2008). The influence of GED obtainment on inmate release outcome. *Criminal Justice & Behavior, 35*, 375-387.

CHAPTER 6

DISRUPTIVE INNOVATION

The Role of Technology
in Advancing Educational Achievement
Among Inmate Populations

Brian D. Fitch, Brian Mattson, and Jeff Mullhausen

The chapter explores the technologies currently being used to deliver educational programming in correctional settings. This includes an overview of the benefits derived from the proper application of educational technology and, more specifically, a review of data on computer-aided instruction (CAI). The chapter considers the challenges facing modern correctional institutions, as well as the ways technology has been used to overcome such obstacles. The discussion concludes with a model for evaluating the effectiveness of educational technologies in correctional environments based on the components common to most instructional system design (ISD) models.

Advances in technology have revolutionized the ways we interact, work, and entertain (Noeth & Volkov, 2004). Technology offers promising answers to a host of important educational issues as well, including innovate ways of reaching isolated and remote populations, addressing different learning styles, and assessing important learning outcomes (Borden & Richardson, 2008; Schacter, 1999). Consequently, there has been consid-

Education-Based Incarceration and Recidivism:
The Ultimate Social Justice Crime-Fighting Tool, pp. 103–117
Copyright © 2012 by Information Age Publishing
All rights of reproduction in any form reserved.

erable discussion among educators and scholars about how these innovations can best be used to enhance the learning experiences of disenfranchised and underserved populations—especially incarcerated students.

The United States has long been criticized for its high crime rate, especially violent crime. Critics have recently turned their attention to the nation's weak and, in some instances, deteriorating status as an educated society. Thus, it has been argued that the United States is both a highly criminal and undereducated society (Tewksbury & Vito, 1994). And while the correlation between education and crime has prompted considerable debate regarding data quality and research methods (Cho & Tyler, 2008), the educational needs of many underserved populations, including the more than 2.4 million inmates housed in federal, state, and local jails, continue to go unmet. Data suggest that approximately 59% of federal inmates, 75% of state prison inmates, and 69% of county jail inmates failed to complete high school. In fact, 35% of the current jail population reports dropping out of high school because of academic or behavioral problems—or because they generally lost interest (Harlow, 2003).

It has been suggested that criminality serves as a substitute for a legitimate career, with established links between underemployment, criminal lifestyle, and low basic educational achievement (Blumstein, Cohen, Roth, & Visher, 1986; Thornberry & Christenson, 1984). In 1982 the annual cost of operating the U.S. criminal justice system was estimated to be about $36 billion dollars. By 2003 the annual expenditures for similar services increased to more than $185 billion (Hughes, 2006). To make matters worse, current economic conditions in the United States are forcing many local jails and state prisons to curtail a variety of services, including, in many cases, vital areas of correctional education.

While the consequence of these choices are difficult to predict, high levels of recidivism—in some cases, as much as 70% (Langan & Levin, 2002)—require new and innovative ways of educating incarcerated individuals, assessing critical skills, and connecting former inmates with meaningful employment. Studies have consistently linked correctional education with higher levels of postrelease employment and lower levels of recidivism (Aos, Miller, & Drake, 2006), suggesting that the amount of time an inmate spends in school can significant reduce the probability of criminal activity (Lochner, 2003).

Clearly, the primary function of corrections is to help inmates become better citizens, not just better inmates (Brockway, 1912/1966). Current advances in technology offer a variety of tools capable of transforming the ways we develop, deliver, and assess education—especially correctional education. CAI and other forms of technology have the ability to individuate the educational process to accommodate the learning style and interests of each student. However, to be effective, technology must be deliberately identified and purposely integrated with particular focus on computer literacy, technological access, and teacher pedagogical beliefs (Borden & Richardson, 2008).

This chapter examines how technology can best be used to provide educational opportunities in correctional settings, including county jails. We explore how technology is being used currently to enhance correctional education. This includes an overview of research on performance and educational outcomes, as well as a review of the opportunities and challenges presented in correctional settings. We conclude with a model for evaluating the effectiveness of educational technology, while considering methodological approaches that can be used to facilitate a more robust understanding of the ways planning and program design can improve educational outcomes.

DEFINING TECHNOLOGY IN CORRECTIONAL EDUCATION

Despite limited research on technology within correctional education, a substantial body of data exists on student achievement within general education, including both K-12 and higher education (Baker, Gearhart, & Herman, 1994; Kulik, 1994; Sivin-Kachala, 1998). These findings provide a framework for implementing technology to improve correctional education outcomes, as well as targeting the underlying reasons for the high dropout rate of inmates from primary education. Technology further offers methods of educational delivery and assessment that differ from the primary education system, where many inmates' educational challenges first emerged (Winters, 2000).

Educational Technology Defined

Technology is generally defined as the tools, techniques, and systems used to solve problems or attain specific goals (Baker, 2000). These procedures can be used to enhance the reliability of existing functions or services, or be developed to serve new goals. Educational technology represents a method of delivering information and instruction with specific possibilities and limitations (Glennan & Melmed, 1996; Jones & Paolucci, 1999). As an innovative tool, technology is implemented along a continuum, from minor modifications of familiar designs to the development of radical new systems. It is important to note, however that all technology achieves its goals at the expense of some other outcomes (Baker, 2000).

Computer-aided instruction (CAI) has emerged as a popular and rapidly growing area of educational technology (Noeth & Volkov, 2004). There are currently four primary models for computer use in the classroom. The first model, the one-computer classroom, offers two principle approaches to integration: teacher use and student use (Dockterman, 1998). The teacher may use the computer as a workstation or to deliver content to the larger class, or allow the students to use the computer as a single learning station. The second model, the multicomputer classroom, rotates students along a group of computer stations throughout the course of the school day (Gwaltney, 2003). This type of schedule allows each student access to a computer several times a week or, in some cases, even daily. The third model, the computer lab, provides one computer per student—with computers typically fixed in rows, an arrangement that can make it difficult for the teacher to monitor student work (Lim, Pek, & Chai, 2005).

The fourth and final model, the one-to-one classrooms, provides laptop computers for every student (Goodwin, 2011). Students use their laptops to complete in-class assignments and, in some cases, are encouraged to take their laptops home—thus allowing learners to take a more active role in their own learning. Data from one-to-one laptop programs has yielded positive results on both student learning and curriculum development (Rockman et al., 1997, 1998, 2000)—with the most significant outcomes associated with math, science, and language arts (Bebell & Kay, 2010; Holcomb, 2009; Sivin-Kachala, 1998).

Unlike computer delivery systems, digital assessment is a way of evaluating a student's educational needs, as well as measuring progress. Digital assessments can assist with identifying student weaknesses, addressing different earning styles, providing immediate feedback, and evaluating achievement (Borden & Richardson, 2008; Fletcher-Flinn & Gravatt, 1995; Squires & McDougall, 1994). The information provided by these assessments allows teachers to focus instruction on areas of common weakness in the classroom, while providing students with valuable feedback and interventions targeted at specific areas of weakness.

Elman (2004) anticipated a time when assessments would be embedded within the learning context, effectively serving as seamless, integrated partners in the learning process. Embedded assessments are capable of providing formative and diagnostic information that can be used to provide feedback, reinforce learning, and assess areas in need of further attention. Teachers can use this type of platform to provide individualized assessment, curriculum development, and performance tracking.

One valuable tool that has emerged to help teachers and administrators better manage the education process is the learning management system, a software application that automates the administration, tracking, and reporting of student grades, projects, and assignments (Ellis, 2009). Learning management systems can assist teachers with centralizing, personalizing, and delivering educational content—enabling educators to better measure the impact, effectiveness, and cost of educational technology over extended periods of time. By linking technology with specific outcomes, educators can select the tools best suited to address specific student needs, thereby reducing costs while increasing the overall effectiveness of educational programming.

Technology and Student Outcomes

A variety of meta-analytic studies have validated the efficacy of technology in all major subject areas, from preschool to higher education, as well as special needs children (Kulik, 1994; Sivin-Kachala, 1998). Technological interventions have been linked with improved test scores, reduced dropout rates, and fewer discipline problems (Greaves, Hayes, Wilson, Gielniak, & Peterson, 2010a); improved attitudes toward learning (Sivin-Kachala, 1998); reductions in the time necessary to learn new materials (Kulik, 1994); and positive gains on constructed, standardized, and national tests (Schacter, 1999). Additionally, technology has also been found to increase teacher enthusiasm about instruction (Mann, Shakeshaft, Becker, & Kottkamp, 1999).

Schools that have implemented a one-to-one ratio of computers to students have experienced improvements in other key areas as well. For example, Project Red (Greaves, Hayes, Wilson, Gielniak, & Peterson, 2010b) studied the effects of technology on five key learning outcomes at 997 U.S. schools. Data from the study suggest that schools with one computing device per student performed significantly better than schools with higher ratios, such as three students per computer. More specifically, schools with a properly implemented one-to-one ratio demonstrated a 62% increase in high-stakes test scores, a 48% reduction in disciplinary problems, a 41% decrease in drop-out rates, and a 39% increase in college enrollment (Greaves et al., 2010a).

Yet, while technology offers the ability to improve the quality of learning and teaching in a variety of educational settings, including corrections, merely purchasing the latest technological innovations is not enough. Data indicate that the success of computers and other educational technologies is affected by a host of factors, such as student characteristics (Cuban, 2003; Tyack & Cuban, 1995), professional development (Greaves et al., 2010a), software design (Sivin-Kachala, 1998), institutional culture (Ertmer, 1999), teacher attitudes (Ertmer, 2005; Hermans,

Tondeur, Valcke, & van Braak, 2006), and student access to technology (Bauer & Kenton, 2005; Hew & Bush, 2007).

Despite these limitations, a number of technologies have demonstrated the ability to evaluate students' cognitive capabilities at higher levels of functioning (Wall, 2004; Winters, Mathew, Booker, & Fleeger, 1993). This is attributed, at least in part, to recent advances in technology that offer a variety of measures capable of moving beyond simple multiple-choice and free text options to include running simulations, encouraging collaborative learning, and allowing access to resources formerly reserved for scholars, historians, and scientists (Kerrey & Isakson, 2000). The difficulty, however, resides in isolating any single component to determine its effectiveness. Indeed, depending on how technology is designed and delivered, the components to be assessed can vary dramatically.

Technological Tools and Correctional Education

Technology—and, more specifically, personal computers—offer a number of advantages not found with more traditional forms of educational instruction (Gannon & Lapham, 2010; Winters, 2000; Winters et al., 1993):

1. Computers are nonjudgmental.
2. Computers have limitless patience.
3. Computers give students continuous feedback and reinforcement.
4. Computers allow students to work at their own pace by removing many of the typical time constraints.
5. Computer software can effectively diagnose each student's weakness.
6. Computer software can deliver customized lessons to address deficiencies.
7. Computers provide students with regular drill and practice of academic skills.

Borden and Richardson (2008) identify several correctional institutions employing a mix of synchronous and asynchronous technology to deliver learning and distance learning. Synchronous tools permit real-time communication between students, effectively allowing learners at different physical locations to connect at a single point in time (Jones & Paolucci, 1999). The two principal methods of synchronous communication are Videoconferencing and web-based delivery. While synchronous communication allows people to connect in real time, by definition, it requires all participants to be at the same point in time, a limitation which can, in some instances, make it difficult to employ.

In contrast, asynchronous technology does not require the sender and receiver to be concurrently engaged in communication (Anderson, 2009). This form of communication is well suited for correctional education because it allows for instruction over a period of time with the teacher and students occupying different locations and time zones. Web-based asynchronous communication offers a variety of delivery methods, such as web pages, interactive tutorials, quizzes, Blackboard discussions, and noncommercial Moodle systems that make learning available to students anytime of the day or night (Pullen & Snow, 2007).

The Internet has become increasingly popular as an educational tool because of its ability to provide students with instant access to resources and information (Anderson, 2009). Indeed, asynchronous education via the Internet is found in growing numbers of colleges and universities. Increasing numbers of institutions offer not only courses, but entire programs of study online, with current statistics suggesting that over 50% of larger institutions (those with over 7,500 students) offer at least one entire degree program online (Allen & Seaman, 2006).

The growing popularity of distributed education has the potential of reaching large numbers of disenfranchised or disadvantaged populations, including large number of formerly incarcerated individuals (Batchelder & Rachal, 2000; Borden & Richardson, 2008). Students trained in these modalities are better able to navigate the digital world that now dominates business and vocational opportunities. Thus, it stands to reason that any legitimate effort to educate inmate populations should provide greater access to these opportunities if students are to stand any chance of success.

The Challenge of Implementing Technology in Correctional Education

While the use of educational technology has the potential to improve instruction and learning, there are several challenges facing correctional institutions that include geographic location, learning style, security, and criminal subgroups (Borden & Richardson, 2008). Studies suggest that the successful use of technology requires administrators and educators to identify the appropriate curricula and technologies (Earle, 2002), increase teacher knowledge and technological skills (Hew & Bush, 2007), develop meaningful ways of blending curriculum with technology to stimulate higher-order thinking (Moursund, 2002), and develop a culture that promotes the use of technology and other innovative teaching strategies (Ertmer, 2005).

Unfortunately, many of today's correctional institutions were built during the early to mid-twentieth century. Design requirements and housing considerations have evolved significantly over the course of time. Administrators interested in implementing educational programs can find themselves hamstrung by limited space and resources. With the number of inmates growing substantially over the past few decades (Minton, 2010; West, 2010), many institutions simply lack the necessary classroom space, leaving the educational needs of inmates unmet.

In addition to limited space and resources, a recent study by Batchelder and Rachal (2000) identified at least five unique challenges of CAI in incarcerated settings:

- *Inmate attitude toward evaluation.* Not all inmates in the study shared the same level of enthusiasm as the researchers regarding the use of computers in prison classrooms. In many cases, prisoners were reluctant to participate or take long tests, frequently refusing to participate. This was evidenced by several declines in achievement between pre- and posttest measures.

- *Inmate motivation.* Researchers questioned whether inmates participated in the study because they were eager to learn or simply because they wanted a chance to be removed from their cellblock. Age was another factor worth noting, as younger inmates earned higher achievement scores than older inmates. The researchers surmised that younger inmates might be expected to take their education more seriously if they believed opportunities to advance their employment were still attainable.

- *Teacher support.* To isolate the unique effects of computer-aided instruction on achievement, no teachers were allowed in the classroom. Several of the participants expressed concern at the lack of teacher support. Many stated that they would have felt less intimidated by the instruction if teachers had been included to help them learn to use unfamiliar technological tools.

- *The dynamics of inmate interaction and prison society.* Inmates are particularly sensitive to their privacy. Therefore, it is especially important to offer inmates direct instruction in ways that prevent embarrassment. Gang affiliation and membership can also prevent participation as members may see participation "as cooperating with the system" or "selling out" (p. 331).

- *Quality of software.* Simply put, all software is not created equal. All software has limitation, and different types of software yield different results. The researchers concluded that CAI software used with adults, particularly with inmates, should be geared with a mature theme.

EVALUATING TECHNOLOGY EDUCATION

While it is reasonable to believe that technology will ultimately improve teaching and learning, current evidence regarding the effectiveness of technology and achievement outcomes is mixed (Cuban, 2003). Technology does not operate in a vacuum. Rather, it functions in the context of other interdependent variables that influence teaching and learning (Sivin-Kachala, 1998), including student access to technology, teacher preparation and experience, student background, curriculum content, and instructional methods (Noeth & Volkov, 2004). Thus, the results and conclusions of any technological assessment must be considered in light of the larger systems in which the technology is employed.

There is currently a scarcity of practical guidance about how to best evaluate web-based learning environments (Sheard & Markham, 2005). While research methods for these forms of testing are not new, there has been considerable debate regarding the merits and methods used to evaluate educational technology and, thus, limitations on understanding how effective these technologies are in achieving their intended purposes (Oliver, 2000).

Jones and Paolucci (1999) suggest an approach to evaluating educational technology embedded in the variables common to many pedagogical models. More specifically, they propose a framework based on current ISD practices as the best model for assessing the appropriate application and assessment of technology to various learning domains and teaching requirements. While the specific focus of ISD models can vary, most instructional systems consist of three major components: performance objectives (input), delivery system (process), and learning outcomes (output) (Rothwell & Kazanas, 1998).

The purpose of ISD is to facilitate student learning by establishing and meeting a set of performance objectives (Glatthorn, Bragaw, Dawkins, & Parker, 1998). Performance objectives represent specific, measurable outcomes describing what a student should know, do, or feel at the end of a planned instructional activity. They describe the intended result of instruction rather than the actual mechanics of instruction itself. As such, performance objectives focus on learning outcomes—desired effects on the learner—rather than on the delivery processes instructors should use (Rothwell & Kazanas, 1998).

Properly written and executed performance objectives should consider the following criterion:

- *Learner characteristics*: Performance objectives should be tailored to the learner's needs and abilities (Rothwell & Kazanas, 1998). In some cases, learners may require prerequisite skills or knowledge before they can successfully demonstrate competency. The minimum requirements for a student profile typically include information regarding cognitive style, aptitude and ability, relevant experience, level of education, motivation, attitude, age, and gender (Sells & Glasgow, 1998).
- *Learning domain*: Performance objectives should correspond to one or more learning domain (Jones & Paolucci, 1999). The three learning domains most commonly used in educational assessment are cognitive, affective, and psychomotor. While there are a number of suitable categorizations, Bloom's (1956) taxonomy of learning objectives remains one of the most widely used groupings in education.
- *Performance*: The performance component details what a student should be able to demonstrate at the end of a planned educational activity (Rothwell & Kazanas, 1998). It represents the activity, knowledge, or attitude to be learned during instruction and demonstrated afterward. Absent a measurable change in learning, there is no way for educators to assess any learning that may, or may not, have occurred.
- *Criterion*: This element describes how well a student must perform a particular activity to be considered competent (Mager, 1975). For example, the level of accuracy, percentage score, or maximum number of errors allowed to pass an assessment.
- *Condition*: The condition criteria describes the important conditions (if any) under which the performance will occur (Mager, 1975). This usually refers to some condition where the learner is provided with equipment, resources, or information with which to function—that is, computer or other instructional technology.

The delivery system represents the method (process) used by the instructional system to transfer information and knowledge from the teacher (human or machine) to the student and vice versa (Jones & Paolucci, 1999). The type of delivery system—traditional classroom instruction, self-directed study, or technology—should be made only after the instructional objectives have been clearly identified and specified.

Technology is not a "magic bullet," nor is it necessarily the best delivery system for certain student populations or learning objectives.

The development, delivery, and assessment of proper learning objectives do not happen by accident. By embedding the evaluation of technology in an ISD model, educators can compare the *intended* results of an educational activity with *actual* student scores on specific performance objectives (Rothwell & Kazanas, 1998). In this way, the assessment of performance objectives becomes the major source of feedback on the effectiveness of technology in meeting educational objectives. This information can then be used to evaluate the effectiveness of the ISD, including the incorporation of technology.

CONCLUSIONS AND IMPLICATIONS

Martin, Mattson, & Lynn (2005) assert that the fundamental purpose of technology is to help agencies provide better public service, and should be driven by agency goals and system strategic direction. Thus, the proper use of educational technology requires more than simply knowing how to use the tools, it requires the deliberate identification and purposeful integration of technology into a larger organizational vision. It mandates that teachers and administrators knowingly identify the curricula best suited for educational technology, as well as the tools most appropriate to deliver educational content (Moursund, 2002). Moreover, it requires that teachers receive the necessary training (Greaves et al., 2010a), students secure the needed access to technology (Hew & Bush, 2007), and administrators promote the appropriate use of technology and innovative thinking (Ertmer, 2005).

Advances in technology have the potential of delivering education and assessment that differ from the primary scholastic system, where the learning challenges faced by many students first emerged—a finding that is especially significant with the nation's growing inmate population (Winters, 2000). The proper development and implementation of educational technologies has the potential to educate large numbers of disenfranchised and underserved populations, providing previously unheard of opportunities for academic success and career advancement (Borden & Richardson, 2008). Indeed, the opportunities offered by recent advances in educational technology offer educators, politicians, and corrections officials a unique set of leadership opportunities for social justice.

Unlike many previous occurrences, educational technology has the potential for improving a number of important inmate outcomes, including improved test scores (Greaves et al., 2010a), increased postrelease employment (Blumstein et al., 1986; Thornberry Christenson, 1984), and decreased levels of criminal behavior (Lochner, 2003). Therefore, leaders interested in evidence-based practice and social justice would be well served to focus their efforts on the proper development, implementation, and assessment of educational technology. And, while technology has revolutionized many important areas of our lives, its ability to create a more egalitarian and socially just society remains largely untapped.

REFERENCES

Allen, I. E., & Seaman, J. (2006). *Making the grade: Online education in the United States, 2006*. Needham, MA: The Sloan Consortium.

Anderson, T. (Ed.). (2009). Toward a theory of online learning. In *Theory and practice of online learning* (2nd ed., pp. 33-60). Athabasca, Alberta, Canada: Au Press.

Aos, S., Miller, M., & Drake, E. (2006). *Evidence-based public policy options to reduce future prison construction, criminal justice costs, and crime rates*. Olympia, WA: Washington Institute for Public Policy.

Baker, E. L. (2000). *Understanding educational quality: Where validity meets technology*. Princeton, NJ: Educational Testing Service.

Baker, E. L., Gearhart, M., & Herman, J. L. (1994). Evaluating the apple classroom of tomorrow. In E. L. Baker and H. F. O'Neil, Jr. (Eds.), *Technology assessment in education and training* (pp. 173-197). Hillsdale, NJ: Erlbaum.

Batchelder, J. S., & Rachal, J. R. (2000). Effects of a computer-assisted-instruction program in a prison setting: an experimental study. *Journal of Correctional Education, 51*(4), 324-332.

Bauer, J., & Kenton, J. (2005). Toward technology integration in the schools: Why it isn't happening. *Journal of Technology and Teacher Education, 13*(4), 519-546.

Bebell, D., & Kay, R. (2010). One to one computing: A summary of quantitative results from the berkshire wireless learning initiative. *The Journal of Technology, Learning, and Assessment, 9*(2), 7-59.

Bloom, B. S. (Ed.). (1956). *Taxonomy of educational objectives: The classification of educational goals, Handbook I: Cognitive domain*. White Plains, NY: Longmans

Blumstein, A., Cohen, J., Roth, J., & Visher, C. (eds.) (1986). *Criminal careers and career criminals* (Vol. 1, pp. 1-11). Washington, D.C: National Academy Press.

Borden, C., & Richardson, P. (2008). *The effective use of technology in correctional education*. Proceedings of the John Jay College of Criminal Justice Reentry Roundtable on Education (pp. 1-13). New York, NY: Northstar Correctional Education Services.

Brockway, Z. R. (1966). *Fifty years of prison service: An autobiography*. Montclair, NJ: Patterson Smith. (Original work published 1912)

Cho, R., & Tyler, J. H. (2008, April) *Prison-based adult basic education (ABE) and postrelease labor market outcomes*. Paper presented at the Reentry Roundtable Meeting, John Jay College, New York.

Cuban, L. (2003). *Oversold and underused: Computers in the classroom*. Cambridge, MA: Harvard University Press.

Dockterman, D. (1998). *Great teaching in the one-computer classroom*. Watertown, MA: Tom Snyder Productions.

Earle, R. S. (2002). The integration of instructional technology into public education: Promises and challenges. *Educational Technology, 42*(1), 5-13.

Ellis, R. K. (2009). *A field guide to learning management systems*. Alexandria, VA: American Society of Training and Development.

Elman, L. (2004) The future of school testing: A school district perspective. In J. Wall & G. Walz (Eds.) *Measuring up: Assessment issues for teachers, counselors and administrators* (pp. 657-664). Greensboro, NC: ERIC Counseling and Student Services Clearinghouse.

Ertmer, P. A. (2005). Teacher pedagogical beliefs: The final frontier in our quest for technology integration. *Education Technology Research and Development, 53*(4), 41-56.

Ertmer, P. A. (1999). Addressing first- and second-order barriers to change: Strategies for technology integration. *Educational Technology Research and Development, 47*(4), 47-61.

Fletcher-Flinn, C. M., & Gravatt, B. (1995). The efficacy of computer-assisted instruction (CAI): A meta-analysis. *Journal of Educational Computing Research 12*(3), 219-233.

Gannon, M., & Lapham, M. (2010, December). Computer-assisted literacy education serves as intervention for incarcerated women. *Corrections Today, 72*(6), 50-53.

Glatthorn, A. A., Bragaw, D., Dawkins, K., & Parker, J. (1998). *Performance assessment and standards-based curricula: The achievement cycle*. Larchmont, NY: Eye on Education.

Glennan, T. K., & Melmed, A. (1996). *Fostering the use of educational technology: Elements of a national strategy*. Santa Monica, CA: RAND.

Goodwin, B. (2011). Teaching screenagers: One-to-one laptop programs are no silver bullet. *Educational Leadership, 69*(5), 78-79.

Greaves, T., Hayes, J., Wilson, L., Gielniak, M., & Peterson, R. (2010a). *Project red key findings*. Shelton, CT: MDR.

Greaves, T., Hayes, J., Wilson, L., Gielniak, M., & Peterson, R. (2010b). *The technology factor: Nine keys to student achievement and cost-effectiveness*. Shelton, CT: MDR.

Gwaltney, T. L. (2003). *Year three final report of the Project M (Preparing Tomorrows Teachers to use Technology Grant)*. Wichita, KS: Wichita State University.

Harlow, C. W. (2003). *Education and correctional populations*. Washington, DC: U.S. Department of Justice, Bureau of Justice Statistics.

Hermans, R., Tondeur, J., Valcke, M., & van Braak, J. (2006, April). *The impact of primary school teachers' educational beliefs on class use of computers*. Paper presented at the AERA conference, San Francisco, CA.

Hew, K. F., & Brush, T. (2007). Integrating technology into K-12 teaching and learning: Current knowledge gaps and recommendations for future research. *Education Tech Research, 55*(3), 223-252.

Holcomb, L. B. (2009). Results and lessons learned from 1:1 laptop initiative: A collective review. *Tech Trends: Linking Research and Practice to Improve Learning, 53*(6), 49-55.

Hughes, K. A. (2006). *Justice expenditures and employment in the United States, 2003.* Washington, DC: U.S. Department of Justice.

Jones, T. H., & Paolucci, R. (1999). Evaluating the effectiveness of education technology on learning outcomes: A research framework. *Journal of Research and Computing in Education, 32*(1), 17-28.

Kerrey, B., & Isakson, J. (2000). *The power of the Internet for learning: Moving from promise to practice.* Washington, DC: Web-based Education Commission.

Kulik, J. A. (1994). Meta-analytic studies of findings on computer-based instruction. In E. L. Baker & H. F. O'Neil, Jr. (Eds.), *Technology assessment in education and training* (pp. 3-93). Hillsdale, NJ: Erlbaum.

Langan, P. A., & Levin, D. J. (2002). *Recidivism of prisoners released in 1994.* Washington, DC: U.S. Department of Justice.

Lim, C., Pek, M., & Chai, C. (2005). Classroom management issues in ICT-mediated learning environments: Back to the basics. *Journal of Educational Multimedia and Hypermedia, 14*(4), 391-414.

Lochner, L. (2003). Education, work, and crime: A human capital approach. *International Economic Review, 45*(3), 811-843.

Mager, R. (1975). *Preparing instructional objectives* (2nd ed.). Belmont, CA: Fearon-Pitman.

Mann, D., Shakeshaft, C., Becker, J., & Kottkamp, R. (1999). *West Virginia's basic skills/computer education program: An analysis of student achievement.* Santa Monica, CA: Milken Family Foundation.

Martin, J., Mattson, B. & Lynn, J. (2005). *A guidebook to system innovation: Lessons and tools from the youth service improvement initiative.* Washington, DC: U.S. Department of Justice.

Minton, T. D. (2010). *Jail inmates at midyear, 2009.* Washington, DC: U.S. Department of Justice, Bureau of Justice Statistics.

Moursund, D. G. (2002). Getting to the second order: Moving beyond amplification uses of information and communications technology in education. *Learning and Leading with Technology, 30*(1), 7-9, 48-49.

Noeth, R. J., & Volkov, B. B. (2004). *Evaluating the effectiveness of technology in our schools: ACT Policy Report.* Iowa City, IA: ACT.

Oliver, M. (2000). Evaluating online teaching and learning. *Information Services & Use, 20*(2-3), 83-94.

Pullen, J. M. & Snow, C. (2007). Integrating synchronous and asynchronous internet distributed education for maximum effectiveness. *Education and Information Technologies, 12*(3), 137-148.

Rockman et al. (2000). *A more complex picture: Laptop use and impact in the context of changing home and school access—The third in a series of research studies on Microsoft's anytime anywhere learning program.* San Francisco, CA: Author.

Rockman et al. (1998). *Powerful tools for schooling: Second-year study of the laptop program—A project for anytime anywhere learning by Microsoft corporation notebooks for schools by Toshiba American information systems.* San Francisco, CA: Author.

Rockman et al. (1997). *Report of a laptop program pilot: A project for anytime anywhere learning by Microsoft corporation notebooks for schools by Toshiba America information system.* San Francisco, CA: Author.

Rothwell, W. J., & Kazanas, H. C. (1998). *Mastering the instructional design process: A systematic approach* (2nd ed.). San Francisco, CA: Jossey-Bass.

Schacter, J. (1999). *The impact of educational technology on student achievement: What the most current research has to say.* Santa Monica, CA: Milken Exchange on Educational Technology.

Sells, B., & Glasgow, Z. (1998). *Making instructional design decisions.* Englewood Cliffs, NJ: Educational Technology Publications.

Sheard, J., & Markham, S. (2005). Web-based learning environments: Developing a framework for evaluation. *Assessment & Evaluation in Higher Education, 30*(4), 353-368.

Sivin-Kachala, J. (1998). *Report on the effectiveness of technology in schools, 1990-1997.* Washington, DC: Software Publisher's Association.

Squires, D., & McDougall, A. (1994). *Choosing and using educational software: A teacher's guide.* London, England: Falmer.

Tewksbury, R. A., & Vito, G. F. (1994). Improving the educational skills of jail inmates preliminary program findings. *Federal Probation, 58*(2), 55-59.

Tyack, D., & Cuban, L. (1995). *Tinkering toward utopia.* Cambridge, MA: Harvard University Press.

Thornberry, T. P., & Christenson, R. L. (1984). Unemployment and criminal involvement: An investigation of reciprocal causal structures. *American Sociological Review, 49*(3), 398-411.

Wall, J. E. (2004). Assessment and technology—Allies in educational reform: An overview of issues for counselors and educators. *Measurement and Evaluation in Counseling and Development, 37*(2), 112-127.

West, H. C. (2010). *Prison inmates at midyear, 2009.* Washington, DC: U.S. Department of Justice, Bureau of Justice Statistics.

Winters, C. A. (2000). Promising practices in adult correctional education. *Journal of Correctional Education, 51*(4), 312-314.

Winters, C. A., Mathew, M., Booker, F., & Fleeger, F. (1993). The role of a computer-managed instructional system's prescriptive curriculum in the basic skill areas of math and reading scores for correctional pre-trial detainees (inmates). *Journal of Correctional Education, 44*(1), 10-17.

CHAPTER 7

THE REENTRY PROCESS— LINKING INMATES TO COMMUNITY SERVICES

Parallels to the Transition of Youth With Disabilities to a Quality Adult Life

Jessica Nolan Daugherty, Laura S. Abrams, and Gary Greene

Connecting parolees and probationers with community-based services and resources upon their release from incarceration may be correlated with improved transition outcomes. This chapter reviews research on the transition of incarcerated persons from prisons and jails to the community and provides recommendations for improving the educational outcomes and quality of life of ex-offenders through policies and practices related to transition and aftercare services. Relating reentry to the experience of transitioning youth with disabilities, the authors emphasize the importance of interagency collaboration, wrap-around services, and connection to community-based organizations. The chapter also highlights model transition programs that utilize many of these practices.

In 2011, a record number of people will reenter California communities from state prisons and county jails. A case is currently awaiting a decision in the Supreme Court to honor the previously mandated release of 40,000

Education-Based Incarceration and Recidivism:
The Ultimate Social Justice Crime-Fighting Tool, pp. 119–137
Copyright © 2012 by Information Age Publishing
All rights of reproduction in any form reserved.

prisoners from state adult facilities due to substandard health and safety conditions. According to the *New York Times*, "the ruling is the largest state prison reduction ever imposed by a Federal court over the objection of state officials" (Moore, 2009). This mandated release, in addition to the more than 200,000 inmates that leave California county jails annually and the usual release of approximately 130,000 adult men and women from state prisons, would amount to approximately 370,000 people returning to California communities from adult correctional facilities when the decision passes (Chapman, Grealish, Grassel, Viscuso, & Lam, 2010; Petersilia, 2011). The increasing volume of returnees in the coming years is forcing law enforcement officials and politicians to rethink reentry policies and practices—and more specifically, how reentry can and should be accomplished (Reentry and Recidivism Reduction Workgroup, 2011).

The average probationer or parolee returns to the community following incarceration with little, if any, of the resources necessary to rebuild their lives. Most of these individuals return to their former community or neighborhood with few pro-social supports, persistently high crime rates, limited employment opportunities, substandard housing, and the same often criminally involved peer groups whom the ex-offender spent time with prior to incarceration (Committee on Community Supervision and Desistance from Crime, 2007; Good & Sherrid, 2005). Further, probation or parole systems rarely provide returnees with the comprehensive educational or vocational skills that are needed to advance in the labor market. Thus, existing probation and parole systems typically lose the opportunity to send returnees along a more pro-social or productive pathway (Holl & Kolovich, 2007).

Standard probation or parole services have not comprehensively addressed offenders' reentry needs, yet there are a number of promising transition and reentry programs that provide models for consideration. These programs address the basic needs of returnees and often provide them with vocational skills and opportunities that may help them to become more productive members of society. Further, these programs recognize that the chances for successful reentry are enhanced through an array of vital wrap-around services (i.e., coordinated services tailored to the risks, needs, and strengths of the individual such as drug treatment programs, vocational training, case management, and housing) (Holl & Kolovich, 2007). A more complete discussion and examples of model transition programs are presented later in this chapter.

OVERVIEW OF CHAPTER

This chapter is organized as follows. First, we present an overview of typical reentry systems in California. This is followed by a presentation of the various reentry needs of probationers and parolees. Next, we discuss what is entailed in reentry planning and transition planning. Subsequently, we relate this discussion of needs and services to policies concerning the transition of youth with disabilities from school to quality adult life. Here we focus on principles that are used with the youth with disabilities population that can be applied to the reentry of prisoners and ex-offenders. We conclude the chapter by offering conclusions and implications for reentry services.

Existing Reentry Systems

Although returnees share some overarching requirements for successful reentry, the needs of returnees vary widely across individuals. As such, one key to successful reentry is to provide each individual with comprehensive, individualized reentry planning that begins during incarceration (Holl & Kolovich, 2007). Unfortunately, many California Counties do not apply these practices, and recidivism rates for adults paroled from state prison average 67% (Chapman et al., 2010). Using Los Angeles County as a case example, the authors describe a typical reentry process. This information is derived from interviews with key informants, including jail personnel, ex-offenders, and other community and government stakeholders interviewed for the Los Angeles County Reentry Blueprint (Abrams, Daughtery, & Freisthler, 2011).

In Los Angeles County jails, most transition or reentry planning and programming occurs in the final days or weeks before release. In some cases, a reentry plan is not established until the individual is already released and returned to the community. This uneven format fails to provide a fluid transition from incarceration back to the community, most notably because it does not provide enough time for service providers to collaborate, for the returnee to understand their reentry plan, or for the basic needs of the returnee to be addressed (Abrams et al., 2011). Additionally, the current system does not consistently assist returnees or their families with assistance in navigating the "system," or with links to prosocial resources, which may also inhibit their chances of success (Abrams et al., 2011).

The account of "Steve's" (a pseudonym) experiences with reentry from both state prisons and county jails can be considered typical for many offenders. Steve is a member of a reentry organization that offers at 2-year residential self-help program. According to Steve, during their time at this organization, residents receive a General Equivalency Diploma and are trained in marketable skills such as construction, landscaping, and clerical work. Beyond academic and vocational training, residents learn social and interpersonal skills that allow them to live successfully in mainstream society. Steve had been in and out of state and county facilities for years before finding a way out. He was a user of methamphetamine and committed many crimes related to the attainment of the drug. His experience provides valuable insights into the existing reentry system and the needs of returnees.

According to the key stakeholders interviewed in Los Angeles County, the current reentry process varies for individuals released from county and state prison facilities in California. Due to extreme overcrowding in recent years, adults who are housed in Los Angeles County Jails are released based on jail capacity. Few reentry services are available in Los Angeles County Jails. According to jail staff, an individual usually "wakes up and is told they are being transferred to the Inmate Reception Center for release (Community Transition Unit, Los Angeles County Sheriff's Department, Personal Interview. February 15). This decision is based on the need to control overcrowding and as such overshadows the need for more thoughtful postrelease planning (Abrams et al., 2011).

> Having been released from either county jails or state prisons more times than I can recount, I can't say with any conviction that I've ever been offered any help upon release. While incarcerated (in prison) I often heard from other inmates that help was available, however, nobody ever seemed to have any concrete evidence or facts that would substantiate their claims … merely rumor. Prison is like that. Although I've always wanted help, I never knew where to find it or whom to ask. In retrospect, I've come to realize that it did exist, it simply wasn't made readily available at the times when I was being released. It seems like it is not any more available now, but strides are being made.
>
> As far back as I can recall, I've never had a case manager or known that one existed. Maybe they were reserved for the more "special cases"; those not deemed a danger to society. I don't know. Furthermore, I've never been assigned to a Parole Officer who offered any assistance, unless it was pertaining to my being reincarcerated. In many instances, my parole officer in juxtaposition with his team, would show up at my place of residence at odd hours of the night and morning to perform a "routine search." Never once did the same cadre of officers show up at any time of the day to offer any help, job training, educational opportunities, or anything remotely resembling the aforementioned … never. It quickly occurred to me that my Parole Officer's primary function was to re-arrest me, to get me off the street and back in prison. I can only presume that it was easier to have me in prison than to monitor me from the streets.
>
> Never once was I offered a resource list, nor was housing made available to me. Consequently, I was instructed to return back to the county of my commitment, which often placed me right back in harms way—same neighborhood, same people, same results. As for drug treatment, nothing of the sort was ever offered or discussed. In my experience, rehabilitation and/or drug treatment have never been an integral part of the release process by

either state or county (and I was an individual that could have benefited greatly from such services).

Having paroled from prison on four separate occasions, the process has remained consistent; "Here's $200, good bye." I have never met with a case-worker, pre or post parole, nor has my counselor (CCII), prior to release, ever offered any assistance or postrelease alternatives. Consequently, I always felt as though my days were numbered, whether I adhered to my parole stipulations or not. So, going on the run and absconding always seemed like a better alternative than laying in wait for the inevitable.

I can only imagine how different my life might have been had any real help been afforded to me at any point in my four separate terms in and out of prison and the countless times in and out of county jail. All I know is that when I finally was offered help via this organization, that is, a chance at meaningful, deliberate assistance at changing the way I lived, the very way I thought about myself and my choices, and the consequences of those choices, I did change. I changed so much, in fact, that I have dedicated the last 5 years and at least the next 3, and possibly many more years, at this organization to helping others just like me to get that same help. It has liter-ally saved my life and the same opportunity could change many other lives that are mired in the system the same way that I was. Ironically, as a direct result of my decision to come to this program, it costs the taxpayers abso-lutely nothing because the program is self-supporting through our busi-nesses. I think that's a change we can all live with. (Steve)

The investigation of the reentry systems and strategies in Los Angeles County found additional variations and systemic problems with uniform implementation of reentry protocols:

At Twin Towers Correctional Facility, the release process "begins at 12:01 A.M. While individuals are sitting and waiting to be released, the Commu-nity Transition Unit counselors ask them about their housing, transporta-tion, and rehabilitation plans. Probation does not necessarily set these adults up with follow-up services in the community. Adults who are released from county jail have 24 hours to report to their probation officer, however, many are now being released without any probation, due to the implemen-tation of nonrevocable parole. (Abrams et al., 2011, p. 41)

Following release, field-based probation officers are probationers' pri-mary access to critical reentry services such as housing, employment, edu-cation, and income support. Unfortunately, knowledge of these reentry services varies widely across individual probation officers who are often challenged by large caseloads and lack of training in supportive reentry services (Abrams et al., 2011).

It is noteworthy that Los Angeles County Sheriff Lee Baca recently authorized the creation of an on-site resource center at the Los Angeles County Twin Towers Correctional Facility. This program will provide basic support in the form of identification, transportation, and temporary lodging for current inmates, as well as people outside of custody. Additionally, the drop-in resource center aspires to add a federally funded health care center in the coming years

The system is slightly different in California state facilities. The Los Angeles County Young Offender Reentry Blueprint reports,

> Approximately 210 days prior to release, a correctional counselor reviews an inmate's paperwork and determines a residence plan, employment plan, and reviews the caseworker evaluation. The assigned parole officer then reviews the packet, develops conditions of parole, creates a treatment plan, and determines if the inmate will be released "fully funded" (with $200) or "half funded" (with $100). Once released, the returnee must report to the designated parole officer at a designated address in their neighborhood within 24 hours (Abrams et al., 2011, pp. 41-42).

Similar to probationers from the county system, the main connection that parolees have to reentry services is a parole officer, who may offer inconsistent or scant attention to reentry services or planning. It is noteworthy that parole reentry services may improve in the near future due to pending policy changes. Soon, all field parole officers will be trained to administer the COMPAS assessment—a computer-based risk and needs assessment showing all available services, while providing a breakdown of the client's specific criminogenic needs. Through a more comprehensive understanding of individual needs, officers are better positioned to recommend effective services. Additionally, plans are in place to reduce state parole officers' caseloads from 70 to 48 parolees (California Department of Corrections and Rehabilitation, 2010).

Reentry Needs of Probationers and Parolees

Many people think of incarceration as the punishment for a particular crime or set of crimes, and that after the time is served, the sentenced individual has a clean slate and a reasonable chance for succeeding in life postincarceration. Unfortunately, for most returnees, the biggest challenges and barriers to their success exist outside prison and jail walls (i.e., in their own communities) (Good & Sherrid, 2005). Many formerly incarcerated individuals return to their communities lacking the most basic needs such as housing, healthcare, employment, and a valid form of identification. They are often unsure of where they will sleep, how they will make money to purchase food and other essential provisions, and fear neighborhood violence and gangs (Good & Sherrid, 2005). Additionally, a significant number of ex-offenders face mental illness, health problems and drug addition, yet are released with no treatment plan and no healthcare (Davies et al., 2009). Without addressing these basic needs, many released adults return to similar patterns of criminal behavior and incarceration. In the state of California, the total 3-year recidivism rate for all adult felons released during fiscal year 2005-2006 was 67.5% (Chapman et al., 2010).

Returnees also face many obstacles in obtaining legal employment. Formerly incarcerated adults typically have limited vocational skills and often lack the basic skills needed to attain and maintain employment, such as how to participate in a job interview or create a resume (Good & Sherrid, 2005). An added challenge is that numerous state licensing requirements and federal and state laws bar employment in some positions or force applicants to indicate their record on employment applications (Davies & Tanner, 2003; Uggen, Manza, & Behrens, 2004). Additionally, many formerly incarcerated individuals return to communities with limited employment options and high rates of unemployment (Kubrin & Stewart, 2005). Challenges related to attaining employment often lead to criminal activity and conversely, scholars have linked employment to reductions in recidivism (Holl & Kolovich, 2007).

In addition to the aforementioned reentry barriers, returnees face challenges related to educational attainment. First, many returnees are far from attaining a high school diploma or General Equivalency Diploma. According to the U.S. Department of Justice (2003), "an estimated 40% of state prison inmates, 27% of federal inmates, 47% of inmates in local jails and 31% of those serving probation sentences have not completed high school or its equivalent, compared to about 18% of the general population (correctional education). Those who recognize the benefit of continuing their education and skills may not have the time to put into classes because they have to find employment to raise money to provide for their family's basic needs. According to stakeholders in Los Angeles, other young adult returnees lack knowledge about their educational options or do not understand how to navigate the system to enroll in lower-cost courses or courses that will lead to a degree that will help them to succeed in the marketplace (Abrams et al., 2011).

Due to the varied and often extensive postincarceration needs of inmates, each returnee may benefit from a more individualized reentry plan. Such a plan supports them in the reentry process and if implemented and followed, can help to prevent recidivism.

Transition of Youth With Disabilities From School to Quality Adult Life: What can be Learned and Applied to Prisoners and Ex-Offenders?

Youth with disabilities in the United States do not fare well in a number of important adult life transition outcomes compared to the nondisabled population (Blackorby, & Wagner, 1996, 2005). The challenges faced by youth with disabilities are remarkably similar to incarcerated individuals. However, compared to ex-offenders, the transition problems of youth with disabilities can more aptly be described as "entry" versus "reentry" difficulties. A concerted federal effort in the past 15 years has sought to improve the transition from school to adult life for youth with disabilities in the United States (Individuals With Disabilities Education Act, 1997). Much can be learned from this initiative that can be applied to reentry issues. This comparison is meant to serve as a model of what federal legislation and careful policy consideration can accomplish in offender reentry.

Individuals with disabilities in the United States have historically inferior postschool adult life outcomes compared to nondisabled individuals. Similar to incarcerated populations, individuals with disabilities often face employment discrimination. Findings from the National Longitudinal Transition Studies substantiate this claim (Blackorby & Wagner, 1996, 2005). Youth with disabilities also have significantly lower high school graduation rates, employment, hourly wage, participation and completion of postsecondary education, independent living, and overall satisfaction with adult life compared to their nondisabled peers. Many adults with disabilities live at or below poverty levels and are dependent on government support for their basic needs.

Like ex-offenders, youth with disabilities in transition are optimally served by wrap-around services. Research evidence on best practices in transition for this population has consistently cited that coordinated services tailored to the risks, needs, and strengths of individuals has a significant effect on improving the adult outcomes of transition-aged youth with disabilities (Kochhar-Bryant & Greene, 2009). Examples of beneficial wrap-around services for youth with disabilities include employment development, supported employment, supported living, community mobility training, independent living and daily living skills, and social and interpersonal skills development (Kochhar-Bryant & Greene, 2009). A comprehensive review of the components involved in the transition of youth with disabilities from school to adult life follows.

Legal Requirements for Transition of Youth With Disabilities

The 2004 Individuals with Disabilities Education Act (IDEA) and its predecessors mandated that transition services language be included in the Individualized Education Plan (IEP) for all youth with disabilities beginning at age 16. The transition services portion of the IEP is often referred to as the Individualized Transition Plan (ITP). Goals in the ITP must address instruction, employment and other postsecondary education and training, as well as community adjustment, independent living, daily living skills, and provide a valid vocational evaluation. Specific links with outside adult transition support agencies are also required in the ITP (Kochhar-Bryant & Greene, 2009).

Transition Assessment for Youth With Disabilities in High School

The federal IDEA act requires transition assessment to determine the interests, preferences, and needs in all transition services language requirements of a youth with a disability (see previous section). This assessment data is subsequently supposed to be used to develop transition goals in the ITP.

Communication and Linkages With Postsecondary Transition Services Agencies

As previously discussed, the 2004 IDEA act requires that ITPs include specific links to adult transition service agencies capable of providing support to youths with disabilities after graduating or completing high school. Examples of such programs and agencies include: vocational rehabilitation, regional centers that provide ongoing services, disabled student services programs at colleges and universities, the Department of Mental Health (DMH), and independent and supported employment services and programs. IDEA also mandates that a Functional Summary of Performance (SOP) document be prepared for a youth with a disability prior to exiting high school containing important information that can be used by postschool support agencies to determine eligibility for needed transition services.

Transition-Based Educational Programming and Basic Needs for Youth With Disabilities

IDEA mandates that high schools provide transition-aged youth with disabilities educational experiences that prepare them for adult life (Kochhar-Bryant & Greene, 2009). Examples include instruction leading to entrance into college or university, career and vocational training to prepare them for competitive employment, community experiences (e.g., transportation, community awareness, mobility training), independent living, recreation and leisure skills, and daily living skills.

Family Involvement for Youth With Disabilities

IDEA mandates the involvement of families in the transition assessment process, drafting, and monitoring of transition goals in the ITP of youth with disabilities. Scholars and policy makers cite this element of family inclusion as a best practice in transition (Greene, 2009). IDEA requires that special education personnel communicate with families on a quarterly basis regarding the progress made by a youth with a disability toward meeting their annual IEP and ITP goals. This communication must include discussion of whether these goals have been met, are to be continued, or revised. IDEA also states that if the school or other transition service agency does not provide the previously decided upon services designated in an ITP, parents have the right to reconvene the IEP team to address the originally stated ITP goals.

What can be Learned and Applied to Prisoners and Ex-Offenders?

There are a number of parallels between youth with disabilities and ex-offenders. Both populations face monumental challenges in transitioning to society, as demonstrated by data documenting their poor transition outcomes after completing school or exiting prison (Blackorby, & Wagner, 1996, 2005). Likewise, both populations need similar assessment, planning, educational programming, connection with support agencies and services, and continuing assistance after entering or reentering society.

There is, however, one striking difference between the two populations: transition services and supports in school and beyond are required by federal law for youth with disabilities while they are not mandated for people reentering the community from incarceration (IDEA, 2004). This policy has resulted in improved transition programming and supports for youth with disabilities in public schools in the United States in the past 15 years (Kocchar-Bryant & Greene, 2009). Unfortunately, similar legislation mandating transition programs and supports during incarceration and postincarceration for prisoners and ex-offenders does not exist. The authors have offered this comparison to youth with disabilities as a possible blueprint for changes in federal and state legislation and policy for prison populations. Along these lines, the next section proposes the components of a potentially ideal reentry system.

The Ideal Reentry System

This section describes a model reentry system that begins during incarceration and follows the individual through probation or parole until thorough community reintegration is accomplished. These recommendations emerged from the process of researching and writing the County of Los Angeles Young Offender Reentry Blueprint and through an extensive literature review (Abrams et al., 2011). As explained earlier, the construction of the blueprint entailed interviews with ninety key stakeholders including reentry service providers, jail personnel, ex-offenders, and government stakeholders concerning the best solutions for existing barriers to reentry.

To date, there have been few evaluations of adult wrap-around services. This is somewhat due to the recent discovery of the wrap-around approach, which Wilson explains may be due to the fact that "this approach has only recently (within the last 2-3 years) been imported into the field of corrections. Therefore, insufficient time has passed for abundant literature to accumulate" (Wilson, 2008). Despite the existence of direct evaluations, existing literature supports the potential for wrap-around services to benefit adult parolees. For example, Taxman (2004) stated the claim for wrap-around services while listing critical evidence-based principles for reentry practices, by explaining, "Comprehensive, integrated, and flexible services are critical to address the myriad needs and risk factors that affect long-term success. Offenders typically present diverse deficits and strengths, and programs are effective when they can meet the multiple needs of individuals" (Taxman, 1998). Wilson further supports the case for wrap-around service delivery:

> In addition, research on the elements of effective programming with adult offenders also supports the use of integrated rather than isolated service delivery. These facts, combined with the success of wraparound services with juveniles, lend both theoretical and nascent empirical support for the introduction of wraparound services for adult offender populations. (Wilson, 2008)

Based on the promise of this model for juvenile offenders and other high risk populations, many of the recommendations that follow are based on both suggestions from the community in Los Angeles with the backdrop of a wrap-around case management model.

Steps Recommended During Intake of Inmates

Assessment: At the time of arrest or booking, an individual should be assessed thoroughly with regard to their needs and strengths using a validated assessment tool. Caseworkers should utilize this assessment to develop an individualized case plan for each individual. This assessment case plan should also follow the individual into the reentry period.

Education-Based Incarceration: Each case plan should include opportunities for educational, vocational, and personal advancement in which the individual may choose to participate in academic and/or life skills programs. Educational opportunities could include General Equivalency Diploma and literacy courses as well as opportunities for higher learning based on interests. Vocational courses should teach relevant employable skills that provide opportunities for upward career mobility, as well as basic skills such as interviewing tactics and resume writing. Finally, life skills classes and workshops should be provided that teach anger management, financial literacy, and systems navigation to name a few.

Family Involvement: One of the challenges for returning ex-offenders is that during their period of incarceration, they lose touch with their families and support networks (Holl & Kolovich, 2007). As such, family involvement is a critical part of service planning and reentry programming during incarceration. By keeping families involved, the offender stays connected with loved ones and may maintain critical family support necessary to avoid recidivism upon release.

The California-based Incarcerated Youth Offenders Program (IYO Program) provides a look into an existing California program that incorporates many of the proposed elements of an ideal reentry system. This program provides wrap-around services to youth offenders in correctional facilities and upon release. It is important to note that the IYO Program is currently available to serve youth and there are many differences in the needs of returning youth and adults (Nellis, Hooks Wayman, & Schirmer, 2009).

PROMISING PROGRAM—The California-Based IYO Program

Funded by a federal grant from the U.S. Department of Correctional Education, the IYO program has offered the following wrap around services for nonviolent California youth offenders age 18-25 with a high school diploma or General Equivalency Diploma and less than 5 years to serve until parole: Career assessment and guidance counseling during incarceration; Basic life skills, vocational certification coursework, and college coursework while incarcerated; Prerelease planning and guidance; Linkage with a postincarceration support agency for assistance with housing, employment, and continuing education; and Follow-up monitoring of IYO participant status in the areas of employment, continuing education, and violation for the following intervals after release from prison: 30, 60, 90, 180, 270 days and at 12 months.

Ten-year results of the IYO program have been remarkable with respect to crime recidivism. The average crime recidivism rate for the general parole population in California is roughly 50%, whereas the crime recidivism rate for IYO program participants over 10 years has been roughly 18%. These statistics demonstrate the positive effects of providing individuals with wrap around support services during and after incarceration and linkages to postrelease community support agencies. It is important to note that the IYO program is only offered to those who are considered "model citizens" compared to the general population, which could account for the low recidivism rate. However, the low recidivism rate for the IYO population should still be considered a huge success.

Steps Recommended During Prerelease Reentry Planning/Transition Planning

Follow up on Assessment: The intake assessment should be reviewed and updated as necessary to ensure the individual's needs have remained consistent or to document major changes. Specifically, the reentry plan should address individual's basic needs (i.e., housing, income, documentation), potential risks of the release environment, and educational and vocational skills and plans.

Communicate with Field-Based Parole/Probation Officer: Prior to release, the individual's facility-based case manager should communicate with the designated field-based probation or parole officer in order to discuss the client's needs and case plan. The discussion should solidify the plan to ensure that each client is given a case manager and continuous individualized assessment to track their needs and connect them to resources in or near their local communities.

Connect to Community-Based Providers: There are a number of existing community-based and faith-based service providers outside of jails and prisons that can help support reentry in positive ways beyond the supervision requirements of traditional probation and parole offices. Facility-based case managers should connect individuals with local community based organizations that best address the returnee's continuing needs that such as, for example, substance abuse programs, mental health services, vocational training, and housing assistance. These connections should be communicated to the field-based probation or parole officer as part of the reentry plan. This collaboration with outside service providers has the potential to take some of the strain off of probation and parole officers and provide them with more time to see to the latest needs of clients rather than the basic needs that could and should be taken care of prior to release.

Basic Needs Addressed: As mentioned earlier in this chapter, many adults reenter the community without a valid form of identification, money, or basic provisions. At minimum, the facility should provide all individuals with the basic documentation needed to attain employment and housing. This includes a current state identification card, birth certificate, and Social Security card, if applicable. Transportation is another difficult expense for many returnees, making it difficult to attend meetings with probation or parolee officer, or to participate in job interviews. Therefore, returnees should be provided with a means of transportation for six months post release, such as a subsidized 6-month bus pass or prepaid public transportation tokens.

PROMISING PROGRAM—Homeboy Industries

Homeboy Industries assists at-risk and formerly gang-involved youth and young adults to become positive, contributing members of society through job placement, training, and education. Founded by Father Greg Boyle, the nonprofit organization works to place clients in jobs because, "Nothing stops a bullet faster than a job." To assist in job placement, Homeboy acquires its own enterprises to serve as training and employment options for the most difficult-to-place individuals. Homeboy's businesses include the Homeboy Bakery, Homeboy Silkscreen, Homeboy Maintenance, Homeboy Merchandise, Homegirl Café, and Homeboy Catering. In the course of a year, Homeboy will employ 150-200 in the businesses and other job training positions.

Every employee and client who participates in job-readiness training also receives wrap-around services that may include case management, education, job training, employment counseling, legal services, mental health counseling, 12-step meetings, tattoo removal, parenting classes, and domestic violence intervention. Each job trainee works with a Homeboy case manager to design short- and long-term individual service plans that ensure that they receive appropriate services, meet their parole or probation requirements, and address any additional needs or concerns.

To monitor client progress, Homeboy Industries developed the "Secure Base"—a team headed by a client's case manager that includes a mental health counselor, job supervisor, peer navigator, and job developer. Each team has a caseload of 10-20 clients, whom they meet with individually every month. This approach presents a full picture of the challenges facing each client and allows problems to be identified before they intensify. Additionally, the incorporation of a job developer encourages and reinforces forward momentum for clients, setting the tone from the beginning that they will move on to outside employment.

Homeboy currently serves approximately 12,000 clients annually. In 2009, about 8,000 former members from over 800 gangs (of the 1,100 gangs in Los Angeles County) sought specific services from the organization. An additional 4,000 gang-affiliated family and community members have also sought help from the organization. Homeboy has received national and international acclaim as a leading gang intervention model. A

5-year evaluation conducted by UCLA researchers is currently in progress. (Homeboy Industries, n.d.)

There are a number of additional basic needs that must be addressed to reform the current system. However, many of these may be infeasible for state and local governments given current financial limitations (Reentry and Recidivism Reduction Workgroup, 2011). Some of the include: the need to increase the number of viable transition housing for ex-offenders, provide free legal assistance to all returnees, and increase available drug treatment programs.

Employment Plans: Valid employment is essential to successful reentry and desistance from crime (Good & Sherrid, 2005; Holzer, Raphael, & Stoll, 2003). As such, returnees should be connected with local job placement, apprenticeship, training, or educational programs prior to release. Additionally, model programs should be extended and made more sustainable by solidifying their funding. In the future, funding should be included in state and country reentry plans for employment training and placement. Much of this can be accomplished with minimal financial outlays by partnering with government and community-based organizations that provide reentry services and job training/placement. These organizations can provide reentry services within prison and jails, which will then be continued in the community. In addition to employment and vocational support, partnered services might include education, mental health, housing, drug treatment, and additional therapeutic services. Two organizations that provide all of these elements are the nonprofit organization Homeboy Industries and the government funded Los Angeles County Probation Department's Day Reporting Center.

Steps Recommended During Period on Probation and Parole

The parole or probation officer should connect returnees to needed services in the community, such as substance abuse treatment, counseling, employment, and housing based on individual assessments. Currently, a parole or probation officer's responsibilities and considerable caseload make it difficult, if not impossible, to provide the time and attention necessary to adequately address these needs. Nonetheless, these services may be critical to helping ex-offenders rebuild and reestablish their lives. Some of this can be accomplished by using a place-based resource directory, listing all available and relevant reentry services by geographic area, as well as collaborating closely with other community based service providers.

PROMISING PROGRAM—The LA County Probation Department's Day Reporting Center

The Day Reporting Center (DRC) was created in 2007 to serve returning young adult males in the Florence-Firestone area, ages 18-24, who are gang involved and at high risk of recidivism. The DRC provides a host of services in one location necessary to transition these young male adults away from crime and gang activity to more stable mainstream lives and employment.

The DRC recognizes that their clients need job training before they enter the workforce, but that they also need an income for survival. Therefore, the DRC pays clients, through the Department of Public Social Services' (DPSS) General Relief program, to attend life skills, education, and vocational classes and then connects them to further education or employment after they complete the program. The program consists of three phases designed to address the issues mentioned above. In Phase One, clients receive a thorough risk and needs assessment and motivational counseling. Phase Two provides cognitive behavioral treatment, life skills classes, and case management. In Phase Three, clients receive vocational and education training, on the job training, and continued case management. All of the classes are taught by a trained probation officer in a small group, are participatory in style, and are based around relevant topics the clients can relate to. Some of the classes include, anger management, GED attainment, "how to deal with baby mama drama", Internet skills, and getting motivated to change.

The DRC has been very successful at attaining on the job training contracts with various employers. The DRC model pays a percentage or all of the employee's wages to the employee while they are being trained for up to three months. This is different than the government funded Workforce Investment Act (WIA) programs because the WIA programs reimburse employers at the end of the program rather than at the front end as the DRC does. In addition, funding for WIA programs is subject to a federal audit, which often deters small businesses from hiring ex-offenders.

To date, 185 clients have enrolled in the program and 100 clients have graduated at a cost of $9000.00 per probationer. Upon graduation, all clients have been placed in a job or educational program. Currently, 69 clients remain in the program. (Los Angeles County Department of Probation, n.d.)

Probation/Parole Officer Communicates with Designated CBOs: Field-based parole or probation officers must communicate with community-based service providers to stay informed of any major developments or changes in service. Such collaboration helps to prevent and reduce duplication of effort. Meanwhile the collaboration alleviates some of the probation or parole officers' responsibilities as the CBO can help to connect the client to other needed services such as public benefits and childcare.

Connect Returnee to Employment and Education: The parole or probation officer and community based service provider should assess the created employment plan and follow-up with designated service providers. In the case that the returnee has not contacted the designated service providers, the parole or probation officer and CBO should work together to connect returnees to necessary services such as employment, training, or apprenticeship programs.

Steps Recommended During Return to the Community

Prior to terminating any case, the parole or probation officer should ensure that clients have a community-based case manager who will provide ongoing mentoring, assistance, and connections to services. This case manager will provide a place for returnees to come for assistance if they need something once their period on probation/parole is completed.

CONCLUSIONS AND IMPLICATIONS

In conclusion, a comprehensive reentry strategy for adults must assess and identify the individual needs of returnees and follow through on an individual release plan (Abrams et al., 2011). Some ex-offenders will need vocational training, whereas others will require specialized services such as anger management courses or domestic violence counseling. Others may still require substance abuse treatment or mental health medication and housing, so reentry planning must be able to address a variety of individual needs.

Reentry planning and implementation should continue as the individual transitions from incarceration to the community. Incarceration in no way models the day-to-day life of average people and many returnees quickly fall back to their old ways upon their release. For example, a returnee may be drug free, willing to work, hopeful, and eager to reunite with their families, yet may crumble under the daily pressures of drugs, unemployment, hopelessness, and the stigma and alienation they may experience upon release. To date, there is a true lack of federal policies or mandates around reentry from incarceration. We must recognize that some offenders may not be ready to shut the "revolving door." However, a consistent and sound reentry system ought to be in place for those who are willing to take it—be ready to move forward with their lives in a positive direction. It seems fitting to conclude the chapter with the words of Steve, a former offender who stated:

I can only imagine how different my life might have been had any real help been afforded to me at any point in my four separate terms in and out of prison and the countless times in and out of County jail. All I know is that when I finally was offered help via this organization, that is, a chance at meaningful, deliberate assistance at changing the way I lived, the very way I thought about myself and my choices, and the consequences of those choices, I did change. (Steve)

REFERENCES

Abrams, L. S., Daugherty, J., & Freisthler, B. (2011). *County of Los Angeles Young Offender Reentry Blueprint*. Los Angeles, CA: UCLA School of Public Affairs, Department of Social Welfare.

Blackorby, J., & Wagner, M. (1996). National longitudinal transition studies-1, Longitudinal post school outcomes of youth with disabilities: Findings from the National Longitudinal Transition study. *Exceptional Children, 62*(5), 399-413.

Blackorby, J., & Wagner, M. (2005). *National longitudinal transition studies-2*. Retrieved from http://nlts2.org/pdfs/str6_completereport.pdf

California Department of Corrections and Rehabilitation. (2010). CDCR releases online community resource directory of local services for parolees. Retrieved from http://cdcrtoday.blogspot.com/2010/11/cdcr-releases-online-community-resource.html

Chapman, S., Grealish, B., Grassel, K., Viscuso, B., & Lam, L. (2010). *Adult institutions outcome evaluation report*. Retrieved from: http://www.cdcr.ca.gov/Adult_Research_Branch/Research_Documents/ARB_FY0506_Outcome_Evaluation_Report.pdf

Committee on Community Supervision and Desistance from Crime. (2007). *Parole, desistance from crime, and community integration*. Washington, DC: The National Academies Press.

Davis, L., Nicosia, N., Overton, A., Miyashiro, L., Derose, K. P., Fain, T., … Williams, E. (2009). *Understanding the public health implications of prisoner reentry in California, Phase I report*. Santa Monica, CA: Rand Corporation.

Davies, S., & Tanner, J. (2003). The long arm of the law: Effects of labeling on employment. *The Sociological Quarterly 44, 3,* 385-404.

Good, J., & Sherrid, P. (2005, October). *When the gates open: Ready4Work, A national response to the prisoner reentry crisis*. Philadelphia, PA: Public/Private Ventures.

Holl, D., & Kolovich, L. (2007, September). *Evaluation of the prisoner reentry initiative interim report*. Washington, DC: U.S. Department of Labor.

Holzer, H. J., Raphael, S., & Stoll, M. A. (2003). *Employment barriers facing ex-offenders*. New York, NY: New York University Law School.

Homeboy Industries. (n.d.). About us: Homeboy history. Retrieved from http://www.homeboy-industries.org/about.php

Individuals With Disabilities Education Act Amendments of 1997, Pub. L. No. 105-17, 20 U.S.C. Sec. 1400 *et seq.* (1997).

Individuals With Disabilities Education Act of 2004, Pub. L. No. 108-446, 20 U.S.C. Sec. 1400 *et sec.* (2004).

Kochhar-Bryant, C. A., & Greene, G. (2009). *Pathways to successful transition for youth with disabilities: A developmental process* (2nd ed.). Upper Saddle River, NJ: Pearson Education/Merill.

Kubrin, C. E., & Stewart, E. (2006). Predicting who reoffends: The neglected role of neighborhood context in recidivism studies. *Criminology, 44*(2), 165-197.

Los Angeles County Probation Department. (2010) "Adult Day Reporting Center Fact Sheet. Los Angeles, CA: Author.

Moore, S. (2009, August 4). California prisons must cut inmate population. *The New York Times.* Retrieved from http://www.nytimes.com/2009/08/05/us/05calif.html

Nellis, A., Hooks Wayman, R., & Schirmer, S. (2009). *Back on track: Supporting youth reentry from out-of-home placement to the community.* Retrieved from http://www.sentencingproject.org/doc/publications/CC_youthreentryfall09report.pdf

Petersilia, J. (2011). *Challenges of prisoner reentry and parole in California* (California Policy Research Center, Brief Series). Retrieved from http://www.rbtaylor.net/50_read_paroleincalif.html

Reentry and Recidivism Reduction Workgroup. (2011). *Smart on crime: Reentry and recidivism reduction workgroup briefing.* Retrieved from http://smartoncrimepolicy.org/reentryandrecidivismreduction.html

Taxman, F. S. (1998). *Reducing recidivism through a seamless system of care: Components of effective treatment, supervision, and transition services in the community.* Washington, DC: Office of National Drug Control Policy, Treatment and Criminal Justice System Conference. (NCJRS 171836).

Uggen, C., Manza, J., & Behrens, A. (2004). Less than the average citizen: Stigma, role transition, and the civic reintegration of convicted felons. In S. Maruna & R. Immarigeon (Eds.), *After crime and punishment: Pathways to offender reintegration* (pp. 258-290). Devon, England: Willan.

U.S. Department of Justice. (2003). *Education and correctional populations.* Washington, DC: Author.

Wilson, K. J. (2008). *Literature review: Wraparound services for juvenile and adult offender populations.* Davis, CA: Center for Public Policy Research, University of California, Davis.

PART III

PROMISING AND PROVEN "BEST PRACTICES": GLOBAL PERSPECTIVES

CHAPTER 8

MAXIMIZING BENEFITS OF CORRECTIONAL EDUCATIONAL PROGRAMS

Best Practices

M. C. Esposito, Anthony H. Normore, and Arthur A. Jones

The positive outcomes associated with providing educational programs to inmates include reduced recidivism rates, increased employment opportunities, and greater adjustment to society upon reentry are well documented within the extant literature. Although widely implemented within the state and federal correctional settings, educational programs vary greatly both in scope and fidelity of implementation. Central to implementing strong educational programs is a clear understanding of the factors which increase their effectiveness. As such, this chapter synthesizes the types of educational programs currently implemented within the correctional setting (e.g., basic skills, vocational, and postsecondary), reviews the effectiveness of such programs, identifies key factors increasing the likelihood such programs are effective, and summarizes best practices specific to educational-based incarceration. These authors hold that the identification of best practices will enable correctional facilities across the nation to implement more effective correctional educational programs, thus maximizing the benefits associated with such programs.

Education-Based Incarceration and Recidivism:
The Ultimate Social Justice Crime-Fighting Tool, pp. 141–160
Copyright © 2012 by Information Age Publishing
All rights of reproduction in any form reserved.

So it seems that at the heart of both a good approach to adult education and good penal policy is recognition of people's full humanity, their individuality, autonomy and potential, and acceptance of them as full members of the larger society. (Warner, 2007, p. 181).

National figures indicate that more than one in every 100 adults is currently incarcerated (Pew Center on States, 2008). In fact the "United States incarcerates more individuals than any country in the word" (Pew Center on States, p. 5). The most recent statistics available indicate that the United States has an imprisonment rate of 738 per 100,000 of the general population (Walmsley, 2007). By contrast, at the international level the rates for France are 85 per 100,000, those for Germany are 95 per 100,000, and the median rates for Western and Southern Europe are 90 per 100,000 (Walmsley, 2007). All the foregoing apply to penal institutions generally, and include jail inmates or pretrial detainees. These staggering figures are frequently attributed to high rates of recidivism—with recent estimates suggesting that more than half of the individuals released from prison will be reincarcerated within 3 years of their release date (Lattimore & Visher, 2009).

Given that nearly 700,000 inmates are released from prison each year (Harlow, 2003), and more than 11 million people are estimated to pass through U.S. jails (Freudenberg, 2007), efforts aimed at reducing recidivism are of national significance.

The growing body of literature specific to reduced recidivism rates indicates a clear agreement that pivotal to reducing recidivism is the implementation of effective correctional educational programs. Generally speaking, the preponderance of evidence suggests that individuals who participate in educational and vocational programs are less likely to recidivate (Jensen & Reed, 2006; Przybylski, 2008). As such, this chapter will provide a brief overview of the positive postrelease outcomes associated with effective correctional education programs, followed by an overview of the types of educational programs offered within the prison and jail systems. Further, we include literature that focuses on program effectiveness with regard to reducing recidivism rates, and conclude with recommendations regarding the best practices for correctional educational programs.

POSITIVE OUTCOMES ASSOCIATED WITH IMPLEMENTATION OF EDUCATIONAL PROGRAMS

The majority of correctional facilities offer education programs (MacKenzie, 2008). Over 60% of U.S. jails have some form of educational program (Freudenberg, 2007). The primary impetus for correctional education is reduced recidivism. The extant literature examining recidivism and participation in prison education programs evinces considerable agreement that participation in such programs has a significant impact on reducing reincarceration rates. However, as MacKenzie (2008) notes, absent from the literature is a theoretical framework explaining the connection between education and postrelease outcomes. The relationship between participation in educational programs and reduced recidivism rates has been attributed to wide rage of variables from increased problem solving skills (Correctional Association of New York [CANY], 2009), greater employment opportunities (Gaes, 2008), increased self-esteem (Contardo & Erisman, 2005), manageable prison environment (CANY, 2009), and increased cognitive skills (MacKenzie, 2008). Although there is much support for any of the above mentioned outcomes, this chapter will review research specific to employment opportunities, increased cognitive skills, and self-esteem. These authors hold that these three variables are most relevant to best practices related to education-based incarceration (EBI).

Employment

According to Meyer, Fredericks, Borden, and Richardson (2010), "The relationship between educational progress and a range of economic and noneconomic outcomes for individuals and for society is well documented" (p. 149). In general, convicted offenders when compared to the general population have lower education attainment and fewer job skills (Harlow, 2003). Dramatically reduced recidivism rates are empirically evident for those inmates employed after release (Winterfield, Coggeshall, Burke-Sorer, Correa, & Tidd, 2009). The ability to find and maintain employment is critical to successful reintegration in to society (Solomon, Osborne, LoBuglio, Mellow, & Mukmal, 2008). Intuitively it reasons that education is closely related to ones ability to secure employment. The questions within an educational context then becomes, what factors specific to education are related to employment, and what is the exact nature of the relationship? Gaes (2008) suggests that obtaining a certificate such as a high school diploma or General Education Diploma (GED) while incarcerated sends positive signals to potential employers about the offenders work habits and ability to complete tasks. Gaes further suggests that the relationship between EBI programs and employment for minority individuals results in an increase in wages of 10 to 15%. This is important because 50% of inmates have minor children at the time of their incarceration (Contardo & Erisman, 2005). It stands to reason then, that increased wage earning potential benefits not only former inmates but also their families.

Increased Cognitive Skills

The relationship between educational program and reduced recidivism rates results from inmate's increased cognitive skills. MacKenzie (2008) demonstrates that these programs are associated not only with increases in social cognition, but in executive functioning thus diminishing behaviors associated with criminal activity. The literature examining the relationship between correctional education programs and increased cognitive skills has focused primarily on the completion of postsecondary education programs. A recent report by the CANY (2009) reviews this relationship, stating enhanced problem-solving skills is among the "principal benefits" (p. ii) of college programs within correctional settings. Although a paucity of literature exists which delineates explicitly this important relationship, the authors of this chapter contend there is sufficient evidence to support increased cognitive skills as a positive outcome associated with educational programs.

Increased Self-esteem

One of the most promising outcomes related to correctional-based education is the increase in positive self-esteem (Aspinwall & Taylor, 1992). Increased self-esteem is frequently cited as an outcome of educational programs particularly in the literature specific to postsecondary educational programs (CANY, 2009; Contardo, & Erisman, 2005). Similar to findings in the study conducted by Winterfield et al. (2009), students in Tweksbury and Stengel's (2006) cited esteem as the primary reason for participation in educational programs. Winterfield and colleagues (2009) likewise concluded that participating in postsecondary education (PSE) programs increased inmates' feelings of self-esteem. An increase in one's self-esteem may also serve as a buffer when encountering difficulties within and outside of prison environments (Tewksbury& Stengel, 2006). As Meyer and colleagues (2010) note, self-esteem is a proximal benefit of participating in educational programs which may lessen the harmful impacts of incarceration.

DESCRIPTION OF EDUCATIONAL PROGRAMS

Important to the study of correctional education is an assessment of the various educational programs implemented within the prison and jail setting (Tewksburry & Stengel, 2006). However, as Foley and Gao (2004) note, while researchers support the implementation of educational programs, few data are available describing the educational practices available to incarcerated adults. Most programs that fall under the rubric of education vary. The most widely implemented programs fall under five broad categories: (1) adult basic education; (2) GED/high school diploma; (3) special education programs; (4) vocational education; and (5) postsecondary/college (Foley & Gao, 2004; MacKenzie, 2008). In efforts to add to the literature specific to correctional education, the subsequent sections will describe the above programs in depth, review evidence specific to outcomes associated with each program and conclude with recommendations for implementation.

Adult Basic Educational Skills

Vocational education programs are widely implemented across the United States (Foley & Gao, 2004). Adult basic education programs are designed to improve the literacy skills of individuals who have limited literacy (Przybylski, 2008). Given that the inmate population is significantly less educated and less literate than the general population (Gaes, 2008), the primary focus on these programs is to improve reading, language, and arithmetic skills. These programs are, in essence, designed to provide inmates with a skill set needed to function in a variety of situations (Tercilla & Breazzanio 2010). Basic literacy skills gained through participation in adult basic education programs may magnify the success of other kinds of prison programs offered within correctional facilities, such as secondary or postsecondary academic programs (Gaes, 2008). It should be noted, that English as a second language programs are often included under this type of education. Within this context, English language adult basic education programs are designed to provide English language learners with the skills needed to communicate effectively and more fully integrate into society (Tercilla & Breazzano, 2010)

Secondary Education Programs

According to Foley and Gao (2004), "The attainment of critical educational milestones such as a high school diploma is valuable to both the financial and social-emotional welfare of the individual and society at large" (p. 19). These programs provide instruction focused on secondary curriculum leading to either a high school diploma or a General Education Diploma (GED). Studies investigating the educational attainment of inmates indicate that 60% of inmates do not have a high school diploma or general equivalency diploma (Solomon et al., 2008). Without a high school diploma these inmates are unable to participate in many educational programs both within and outside of the prison system (Hall & Killacky, 2008; Klien & Tolbert, 2007). On a positive note, Meyer and colleagues (2010) found that more than half of the participants in postsecondary education programs received their GED while in prison. This is most promising given that individuals who obtain their GED in prison may continue on to postsecondary educational programs after release.

Special Education Programs

The prison population in general is characterized by having higher rates of specific learning disabilities than the general population (Harlow, Jenkins, & Steurer, 2010). In fact, "rates of learning disability are spectacularly high among prisoners" (Russel & Stewart, 2001, p. 1), with estimates ranging for 30-50% for inmate population compared to 5-15% of the general education population (Tolbert, 2002, as cited in DelliCarpini, 2008). As mandated by federal law (Individuals with Disabilities Education Act [IDEA], 1997; Individuals with Disabilities Education Improvement Act [IDEIA], 2004), individuals identified as having a disability prior to incarceration are entitled to free appropriate education until the age of 21 years old. The mandates stemming from IDEA (1997) and its' subsequent reauthorization in 2004 (amended to IDEIA) guarantee youths with disabilities convicted in adult or juvenile criminal court receive education services until they reach the age of 21, are released from prison, or obtain a high school diploma.

IDEIA limits a student's right to education only when an incarcerated individual/youth poses a proven "bona fide security risk." IDEIA differentiates between jails and prisons stating that a youth convicted as an adult who is incarcerated within a prison is not required to take state wide assessments as mandated by the federal No Child Left Behind Act (Hershberg, Simon, & Lea-Kruger, 2004). This federal legislation requires that schools and districts receiving federal funds, including IDEIA funds, demonstrate adequate yearly progress of students, including those with disabilities, as measured by state wide assessment scores. A review of the literature specific to special education programs suggests that students with disabilities are primarily educated with their nondisabled peers (Foley & Gao, 2004). This placement preference, to educate the majority of students with disabilities "along side" their peers is in accordance with IDEA's (1997) least restrictive environment tenant, which states that students must be educated to the maxim extent possible with their nondisabled peers.

Adults served within the prison system have limited access to special education programs (Wilson, 2004). IDEA specifies educational opportunities be provided to youth. Adults who have disabilities are guaranteed protections under the Americans with Disabilities Act (1990), which prevents discrimination on a "civil rights" basis, guaranteeing access, as opposed to "appropriate education." This is an important consideration because as Wilson notes, this population has been widely ignored and marginalized. Critical to ensuring access to educational programs is the provision of accommodations which would provide access to programs outside the scope of special education for adults who do not qualify for services under IDEA regulations.

Vocational Education

When compared to the general population, convicted offenders have fewer job skills (Harlow, 2003). As such, vocational education programs (VE) are designed to develop occupational awareness and teach skills specific to a singular trade or industry. Because of the extensive need, vocational programs are widely implemented within correctional settings. Finding and maintaining a job is central to successful reintegration in to society (Solomon et al., 2008). As such, VE programs seek to increase job skills and include skills related to applying and securing employment. In reviewing VE programs, Layton-MacKenzie (2008) notes that these programs included classroom based instruction, job training, and apprentice ships. Other VE programs focus on specific or related occupations with some offering external certification (see Tercilla & Breazzano, 2010, for complete review). As described in the subsequent section, postsecondary programs include vocational skills classes but researchers do not categorize VE programs as PSE programs (MacKenzie, 2008). This distinction is currently being addressed in the literature because it has implications for conducting meaningful program evaluation.

Postsecondary Education

PSE programs are those programs which include college level courses and are designed to culminate in a 2- or 4-year degree. Most PSE programs result from partnerships with community and 4-year colleges (Contardo & Erisman, 2005; Przybylski, 2008), with the majority of instruction delivered by community colleges. In their review of delivery models Contardo and Erisman found most instruction use was on site (91%), followed by distance learning via video or satellite (45%) with only very limited numbers of facilities utilizing online learning. The definition of PSE programs has included both academic and vocational education at the post-secondary level (e.g., community college or technical school). Outcomes associated with postsecondary education suggest that the higher the level of education the lower the recidivism rate (Shippen, Crites, Houchins, Ramsey, & Simon, 2005). In short, PSE provide inmates with an opportunity to break the "cycle of inequality and benefit both the formerly incarcerated person and the society in which he or she lives" (Contardo & Erisman, 2005. p. v).

OBSTACLES

The research examining the implementation of EBI programs has identified many barriers, including funding and limited resources (CANY, 2009). The authors of this chapter acknowledge that funding is critical, however we believe it is beyond the scope of this chapter to address adequately these inequities. To this end, the following sections will describe four factors: (1) length of stay, (2) varying educational levels, (3) limited access to technology, and (4) prison climate. Integrated into this section is the examination of student perceptions specific to obstacles. We hold that inmates' perceptions are particularly germane to this discussion because as the recipients of such education, they have firsthand knowledge of the barriers most often preventing them from successfully completing EBI programs.

Educators working in correctional facilities face tremendous difficulties in normalizing the experiences of student-inmates. Lockdowns, transfers between facilities, and restricted movement in facilities limits the time students spend in classrooms which may limit educational experiences (Erisman & Contardo, 2005; Hill, 2008). These authors further acknowledge and support other realities of prisons, corrections, and jail systems where security concerns prohibit use of the Internet by students, thus limiting their ability to access information or use online library resources. According to McKenzie (2008), "Unless education programs are specifically designed to assist in reentry there is little contact between educators within facilities and in the community meaning few offenders receive assistance in continuing their education upon release" (p. 1).

Length of Stay

Inmates incarcerated within the U.S. jail system have lower participation rates in educational programs than inmates in prisons. On average nationally, little more than 14% of jail inmates participate in some form of educational program, most frequently GED or high school programs (Freudenberg, 2007). These lower participation rates are often attributed to shorter lengths of stay. By their very definition, jails are intended to provide short term-custody, with most inmates released within months (Solomon et al., 2008). In Los Angeles County, California, the nation's most populous jail facility, the mean length of stay is approximately 53 days (Mo, 2010). In a jail setting, as opposed to that of a prison, it is essential to concentrate on saturating the educational setting with the best available short-term curriculum. In fact, given those complex restrictions, a number of studies, including meta-analytical surveys (Milkman & Wanberg, 2007) have suggested strongly that, in the phraseology of the Urban Institute and the National Institute of Justice, well-constructed programs of cognitive behavioral studies, if interactive, mentor-based and socially aware, can contribute significantly to recidivism reduction. However, it should again be noted that most jail inmates do not participate in correctional programs.

Comparative and meta-analytic studies suggest that, for short-term and medium-term stay students, the best bet for lasting benefit may be a curriculum that encompasses not only literature-buttressed pedagogy, but also other evidence-based curricula as well. For example, cognitive behavioral treatment (or therapy) can serve as an efficient vehicle for perception-deficit behavioral improvements when applied intensively over relatively short periods of times. A meta-analysis of 69 studies covering both behavioral and cognitive behavioral programs determined that the cognitive behavioral treatment courses are more effective than traditional behavioral counseling, and produce a mean reduction in recidivism of about 30% for treated offenders (Milkman & Wanberg, 2007). Moreover, the specific integrity or quality of a cognitive behavioral treatment program can greatly influence the effect size. Variables include number of sessions, smaller class sizes, the variety of backgrounds of the provider/facilitators, levels of cognitive behavioral treatment training of the provider/facilitators, as well as quality control monitoring (Milkman & Wanberg, 2007 pp. 35-37).

In reviewing the effectiveness of vocational programs, Ward (2009) asserts that length of stay is a critical factor in matching inmates with programs. He suggests a "window of opportunity" exists in which inmates must have sufficient time within a program to achieve the goals of the program. Site coordinator and administrators responses in the Meyer et al. (2010) study support providing sufficient time within programs, with responses calling for "inmates in college programs to avoid institutional transfers while enrolled" (Ward, 2009, p. 172).

Educational Levels

One challenge facing the implementation of educational programs is the varying educational levels of the different inmates (Foley & Gao, 2004). Because so many inmates have had inadequate academic preparation they need remediation prior to participating in educational programs, particularly more advanced PSE programs (Contardo & Erisman, 2005). Meyer and colleagues (2010) found that students enrolled in PSE programs frequently cited inadequate preparation as a challenge to successful participation. Their study further suggests that a lack of college readiness may require a high level of self-discipline to succeed in PSE programs. Students' academic skill levels are also important because enrollment in many PSE programs is contingent upon meeting the college or university admission criteria (CANY, 2009).

Given the varying educational levels, it is critical that programs are matched with the "right" participants, so that individuals are not further marginalized by failure that results from placing them in educational programs which they are ill prepared to meet the demands of. This is especially important for the prison population, because many inmates have experienced years of academic failure prior to entering the correctional setting (Contardo, & Erisman, 2005).

Central to any discussion specific to effective educational programs is the learner. More specifically, what are the unique needs of inmates? Factoring into low levels of academic achievement are individual differences, such as learning style and learning abilities. The literature examining rates of learning disabilities within the inmate population demonstrate that incarcerated youth and adults have significantly higher rates of specific learning disabilities (SLD) than does the general population. Specific learning disability is a general term referring to "a disorder which manifests itself in the imperfect ability to listen, think, speak, read, write, spell or do mathematical calculations" (IDEA, 1997). Greenberg, Dunleavy, and Kutner (2007) estimated that 17% of adult prisoners have been diagnosed with a specific learning disabilities compared to 6% of the population at large. The interest among correctional educators regarding the effective practices specific to adults with specific learning disabilitiess has grown (Taymans & Corley, 2001). The primary impetus for improving correctional educational programs results from the empirical relationship between educational program participation and reduced recidivism rates (Jensen & Reed, 2006; Solomon et al., 2008). Because inmates with disabilities comprise a large percentage of the prison population (Harlow et al., 2010) tailoring programs to meet their unique needs is essential if positive outcomes are to be realized.

Successful programs are those which match individual learning abilities and styles with the correct programs (Jensen & Reed, 2006). The "classrooms" of correctional settings have extremely varied educational levels, educational needs, and experiences (Parkinson & Steurer, 2004). Individualizing instruction to support the various education levels of students is critical. However as DelliCarpini (2008) notes, correctional educators have had limited professional development specific to meeting the unique needs of inmate students.

Technology

In today's high-tech world, it may surprise many to learn that only few correctional facilities use online service delivery models for instructional practices (MacKenzie, 2008). Prisoners are less likely to use computers and have access to computers (Harlow et al., 2010). Given that many universities are going to online instruction limited computer use may prohibit inmates from participating in postsecondary programs. In his review of the literature, Werner (2003) notes that prison systems lag seriously behind the larger society when it comes to technology use. The types of technology used for instructional delivery impact program effectiveness. Given that many inmates, even as they near release, have significantly lower computer literacy than does the general population (Amodeo, Ying, & Kling, 2009) an increased focus on current technology is warranted.

Climate

As Bhatti (2010) so aptly notes in reviewing the literature, "peer pressure can reinforce, challenge or decimate inmates' self-image and future aspirations" (p. 34). Meyer and colleagues (2010) note that encouragement from family and peers is viewed by student prisoners as critical to their success. Although peer support is valuable, many prisoners do not have positive attitudes toward education (Vacca, 2004) and, in turn, discourage others from participating in such programs (Parkinson & Steurer, 2004). Negative attitudes are often the result of years of educational marginalization. Given the high rates of school dropout prior to incarceration many students have not learned the norms required for a setting which fosters learning. In short, the climate or attitude of inmates can either deter or enhance the learning environment. Additional climate issues stem from noise or distractions which make it difficult for inmates to study (Hall & Killacky, 2008). Given that many prisoners have been socially and academically marginalized creating an environment which fosters education is critical to the success of any program.

Another factor to consider with regard to climate is the prison staff. How do staff and officers view education? In discussing institutional culture and attitudes toward correctional education programs, Parkinson and Steuer (2004) note that "correctional officers and other staff view programming as a nuisance or a privilege which inmates are not worthy" (p. 89). Factors such as climate are an important consideration in the learning process, because if we are ever to create environments where students feel safe to transcend identities marred by early school failure (Muth, 2008). Given the central role learning theory plays within any educational setting, the following section will review adult learning theory within the context of a social justice framework.

EDUCATION FOR LIBERATION
AND COMMITMENT TO SOCIAL JUSTICE

As Muth (2008) notes, many U.S. prison classrooms are comprised of top-down models where learners' voices are often silenced. To this end, a learning model that seeks to empower learners thus increases the likelihood correctional educational programs are successful. We highlight emerging themes from the literature that have proven critical in understanding the effectiveness of the teaching, learning, and leadership development process and may be beneficial to those who instruct student-inmates in education based incarceration programs.

From a traditional standpoint researchers have defined the fairly new term "critical pedagogy" as educational theory, teaching, and learning practices that are designed to raise learners' critical consciousness concerning oppressive social conditions (Freire, 1998a, 1998b; Ladson-Billings, 1997; McLaren & Torres, 1999). Freire (1998a, 1998b) argues that critical pedagogy focuses on personal liberatory education through the development of critical consciousness. Serving as a catalyst to the commitment of social justice and to the development of a new social order liberatory education attempts to empower learners to engage in critical dialog that critiques and challenges oppressive social conditions nationally and globally and to envision and work toward a more just society (Shields, 2002). The use of such a dialogical approach in education-based incarceration programs is one strategy that can help educators confront transformative changing social conditions and historical contexts.

We propose that the dialogical approach to learning abandons the lecture format and the "banking approach" to EBI (see Freire, 1998a, p. 58) in favor of dialog and open communication among inmates in an EBI program and instructor where everybody teaches and everybody learns. In preparation for social justice education, critical pedagogy is particularly concerned with: reconfiguring the traditional student/teacher relationship, where the teacher is the active agent, the one who knows—and the students receive, memorize, and repeat information as the passive recipients of the instructor's knowledge. As we move toward a critical pedagogy and a commitment to social justice we envision the classroom as a site where new knowledge, grounded in the experiences of students and teachers alike, is produced through meaningful dialog and experiences (Freire, 1998a, p. 58).

In support of critical pedagogy and a more social constructivist approach to teaching for social justice, important concepts about knowledge and learning emerged from the literature (Gredler & Shields, 2004; Hacking, 1999). Understanding how knowledge is constructed is critical. As Galloway (2007) asserts, knowledge is not something that exists outside of language and the social subjects who use it. In support of earlier research (e.g., Vygotsky, 1978), Galloway suggests that knowledge is a process socially constructed and one that cannot be divorced from learners' social context. Knowledge is constructed by "doing" and from social development experience (Galloway, 2007). Students bring prior knowledge into a learning situation, which in turn forms the basis for their construction of new knowledge (Searle, 1995). In a constructivist framework, learning is not a process of information transmission from instructor to student, but is instead a process that positions students to be involved actively in constructing meaning from multiple stimuli (i.e., real-world examples, problem-solving activities, life skills, and dialogues). This is particularly relevant within the prison context that seeks to reintegrate individuals back into society. If educational programs do not implement real life situations they are likely to fail.

Like many organizations that serve the public good (e.g., institutions of higher education, public schools, etc.) correctional institutions and systems of incarceration are in a position to serve as catalysts of positive adult learning conditions and opportunities that address what it means to make teaching and learning more socially conscious and politically responsive in a time of growing conservatism, racism, and social injustices locally, nationally, and internationally (Decisier, 2006). Positive learning conditions must be in place if adults are expected to adapt to significant changes in practice (Webster-Wright, 2009). As Kegan (2000) suggests, adult learners are:

> not all automatically self-directing merely by virtue of being adults, or even easily trained to become so. [Leaders] seeking self-direction from their adult are not merely asking them to take on new skills, modify their learning

style, or increase their self-confidence. They are asking many of them to change the whole way they understand themselves, their world, and the relationship between the two. They are asking many of them to put at risk the loyalties and devotions that have made up the very foundation of their lives. (p. 67)

It is the educator who has the primary responsibility for creating the learning conditions for the adults in any organization. If he or she is intent on facilitating significant change or transformation within his or her organization, he or she must be knowledgeable about and be able to foster positive learning conditions that will facilitate the learning of adults.

Andragogy: The Art of Teaching Adults

Student-inmates of an EBI program must leave their education programs with andragogical knowledge and skills. In spite of the fact that change, or deep learning, must happen at the level of the individual for the organization to improve, there are no explicit references to andragogy, or the actual teaching of adults within the education literature or within the research on effective education programs (Slayton & Mathis, 2010). In fact, the literature seems to have completely ignored the importance of addressing the essential attributes of productive adult learning. The disconnect between the expectations that educators will build the capacity of education systems , individual classrooms, along with the reality that instructors lack the knowledge and skills to do so must be addressed by education programs. As a result, students will have increased opportunity to improve or transform systems and communities. Thus, we advocate that EBI programs demonstrate a powerful understanding of adult learning and to teach inmates about the specific types of learning that are necessary at the individual level for change to take place.

First, the type of learning required has been broadly described throughout this chapter. According to Slayton and Mathis (2010), all members of the education system or of a specific group must be able to move away from reactive learning, "thinking that is governed by 'downloading' habitual ways of thinking, of continuing to see the world within the familiar categories we're comfortable with" where one is most likely to reinforce preestablished mental models (p. 27). Members of the community must move to deeper levels of learning, creating a deeper awareness of the whole and actions that increasingly serve the whole. This deeper learning cycle aligns with Dewey's stages of observing, discovering, inventing, and producing (Rodgers, 2002, cited in Slayton & Mathis,

2010). It has been described by Schön (1983, cited in Webster-Wright, 2009) as reflection in action and by Cochran-Smith and Lytle (1999) as inquiry as stance.

A central component of this deeper learning process is the use of dialog to transform action. Mezirow (2000) defines dialog as reflective discourse "devoted to searching for a common understanding and assessment of the justification of an interpretation or belief ... a critical assessment of assumptions" and leads "toward a clearer understanding by tapping collective experience to arrive at a tentative best judgment" (p. 10-11). Yet "most adults simply have not developed their capacities for articulating and criticizing the underlying assumptions of their own thinking, nor do they analyze the thinking of others in these ways" (Kegan, 2000, p. 73). In fact, many have never had experiences with the kinds of reflective discourse described above. Based on research conducted by Slayton and Mathis (2010), this interaction is dependent on "members of the community's ability to engage in meaningful participation, be reflective, reason, be open minded and nonjudgmental, ask clarifying questions, promote academic and more complex language, use evidence, build on each other's ideas, develop ideas, evaluate, critique, infer, predict" and "negotiate new individual and collective understanding so that they are able to create meaning, draw conclusions, and create conceptual and procedural understanding" (Slayton & Mathis, 2010, p. 36).

This type of deep learning does not occur without specific forms of support. Andragogy is an integrated framework of adult learning, distinguishable from child learning, that can support and facilitate the type of learning described above (Slayton & Mathis, 2010). Mezirow (1991) defines andragogy as an "organized and sustained effort to assist adults to learn in a way that enhances their ability to function as self-directed learners" (p. 199). Since the initial conceptualization of andragogy, many of the theories of adult learning have become part of what is now considered effective pedagogy for children. Pedagogy is often the language applied to the teaching practices used with both adults and children.

While we relied on theories of adult *and* child learning to develop our definition, we have made a conscious choice to stay with the language of andragogy to keep the focus on the adult learner. Our definition of andragogy draws only on element seven "conducting learning experiences with suitable techniques" from Knowles's (Knowles, Holton, & Swanson, 2005) process model of andragogy. Included in our definition of effective instruction is the instructor's ability to facilitate the adult learner's active construction of meaning and recognize the learner's zone of proximal development (Vygotsky, 1978, cited in John-Steiner & Mahn, 1996) using these different techniques. These techniques include direct and explicit instruction, the modeling (Mezirow, 1991) and the modeling of meta-cognitive strategies (Tharp & Gallimore, 1988), the use of scaffolding techniques (Rogoff, 1990; Stein, Smith, & Silver, 1999; Tharp & Gallimore, 1988), and opportunities for guided and independent practice. Andragogy also includes the identification of learning needs, identification of defined learning objectives, planning the learning program with the learner, and assisting with an evaluation process (Mezirow, 1991).

CONCLUSIONS AND IMPLICATIONS

Unlike many correctional interventions which only reach small inmate populations, instantiations of EBI can impact almost all offenders (Gaes, 2008). This places such programs central to any social justice approach to working with incarcerated individuals. In addressing correctional educational programs we have reviewed extant literature which overwhelming supports the implementation of education programs within correctional facilities. The programs have tremendous benefit to individuals and society. Humanely speaking, "broadening minds through [higher] education is beneficial no matter what the practical outcomes" (CANY, 2009, p. 21). On a more individual level, success in EBI programs maybe the first taste of success individuals may have had within an educational context (Contardo & Erisman, 2005).

We have also highlighted the important role individual differences play in implementing effective EBI programs. These differences include previous levels of education and specific disabilities. Given the important role "teachers" play in the facilitating learning process we propose a framework which departs dramatically from traditional banking system approaches, to ones that foster the active construction of meaning, critical dialog, and understanding of adult learning that challenges oppression. Given that prisons by their nature damage people (Warner, 2007) we must strive to counter the harmful and cyclical effects—education is that tool.

REFERENCES

Americans with Disabilities Act. (1990). Retrieved from http://www.ada.gov/pubs/ada.htm

Amodeo, A., Jin. Y., & Kling, J. (2009). *Preparing for life beyond prison walls: The literacy of incarcerated adults near release*. Retrieved from http://wdr.doleta.gov/research/FullText_Documents/Preparing_for_Life_Beyond_Prison_Walls_The_Literacy_of_Incarcerated_Adults_Near_Release.pdf

Aspinwall, L. & Taylor, S. (1992). Modeling cognitive adaptations: A longitudinal investigation of   the of the impact of individual differences and coping on college adjustment and performance. *Journal of Personality and Social Psychology, 63*(6), 989-1003.

Bhatti, G. (2010). Learning behind bars: education in prisons. *Teaching and Teacher Education, 26,* 31-36.

Cochran-Smith, M., & Lytle, S. L. (1999). Relationships of knowledge and practice: Teacher learning in communities. *Review of Research in Education, 24,* 249-305.

Contardo, J., & Erisman, W. (2005). *Learning to reduce recidivism: A 50-state analysis of postsecondary correctional education policy.* Retrieved from http://www.ihep.org/Publications/publications-detail.cfm?id=47

Correctional Association of New York. (2009). *Education from the inside, out: The Multiple benefits of college programs in college.* Retrieved from http://www.correctionalassociation.org/publications/download/ppp/Higher_Education_Full_Report_2009.pdf

DelliCarpini, M. (2008). Creating communities of professional practice in the correctional education classroom. *The Journal of Correctional Education 59*(3), 219-230.

Erisman, W. & J.B. Contardo (2005). *Learning to reduce recidivism: A 40-state analysis of postsecondary correctional education policy.* Washington, DC: Institute for Higher Education Policy.

Foley, R. M., & Gao, J. (2004). Correctional education: Characteristics of academic programs serving incarcerated adults. *The Journal of Correctional Education 55,* 6-21.

Freire, P. (1998a). *Pedagogy of hope.* New York, NY: Continuum.

Freire, P. (1998b). *Pedagogy of the oppressed* (new revised 20th anniversary ed.). New York, NY: Continuum.

Freudenberg, N. (2007). *Coming home from jail: A review of health and social problems facing US jail populations and of opportunities for reentry interventions.* Paper presented at the Re-Entry Roundtable on Education, Hunter College, City University of New York.

Gaes, G. G. (2008). *The impact of prison education programs on post-release outcomes.* Paper presented at Reentry Roundtable on Education, New York, NY.

Galloway, C. (2007). *Vygotsky's constructivism.* Retrieved from http://projects.coe.uga.edu/epltt/index.php?title=Vygotsky's_constructivism

Gredler, M., & Shields, C. (2004). Does no one read Vygotsky's words? Commentary on Glassman. *Educational Researcher, 33*(2), 22.

Greenberg, E., Dunleavy, E., & Kutner, M. (2007). *Literacy behind bars: Results from the 2003 National Assessment of Adult Literacy Prison Survey.* Retrieved from http://nces.ed.gov/pubs2007/2007473_1.pdf

Hall, R. S., & Killaky, J. (2008). Correctional education from the perspective of the prisoner student. *The Journal of Correctional Education, 59*(4), 68-92.

Hacking, I. (1999). *The social construction of what?* Cambridge, MA: Harvard University Press.

Harlow, C. W. (2003). *Education and correctional populations.* Washington, DC: Bureau of Justice Statistics.

Harlow, C. W., Jenkins, H. D., & Stuerer, S. (2010). GED holders in prison read better than Those in the household population. *The Journal of Correctional Education, 61*, 68-92.

Hershberg, T., Simon, V. A., & Lea-Kruger, B. (2004). The revelations of value-added: An assessment model that measures student growth in ways that NCLB fails to do. *School Administrator, 61*(11), 10-12

Hill, E. G. (2008). *From cellblocks to classrooms: Reforming inmate education to improve public safety.* Retrieved from http://www.lao.ca.gov

Individuals with Disabilities Education Act of 1997, PL.105-17, 20 U.S.C. § 1400 et seq.

Individuals with Disabilities Education Improvement Act of 2004, PL.108-446, 20 U.S.C. § 1400 et seq.

Jensen, E. L., & Reed, G E. (2006). Adult correctional education programs: An update on current status based on research studies. *Journal of Offender Rehabilitation, 44*, 81-98.

John-Steiner, V., & Mahn, H. (1996). Sociocultural approaches to learning and development: A Vygotskian framework. *Educational Psychologist, 31*(3/4), 191-206.

Kegan, R. (2000). What "form" transforms?: A constructive-developmental approach to transformative learning. In J. Mezirow (Ed.), *Learning as formation: Critical perspectives on a theory in progress* (pp. 35-69). San Francisco, CA: Jossey-Bass.

Klein, S., & Tolbert, M. (2007). Correctional education: Getting the data we need. *Journal of Correctional Education, 58*(3), 284-292.

Knowles, M. S., Holton, III., E. F., & Swanson, R. A. (2005). *The adult learner: The definitive classic in adult education and human resource development* (6th ed.). Amsterdam, The Netherlands: Elsevier.

Ladson-Billings, G. (1997). I know why this doesn't feel empowering: A critical race analysis of critical pedagogy. In P. Freire, J. W. Fraser, D. Macedo, T. McKinnon, & W. T. Stokes (Eds.), *Mentoring the mentor: A critical dialogue with Paulo Freire* (pp. 127-141). New York, NY: Peter Lang.

Lattimore, P. K., & Visher, C. A. (2009). The multi-site evaluation of SVORI: Summaryn and synthesis. Retrieved from http://www.svori-evaluation.org /documents/reports/SVORI_Summary_Synthesis_FINAL.pdf

MacKenzie, D. L. (2008). *Structure and components of successful educational programs.* Paper presented at the Reentry Roundtable on Education, New York, NY.

McLaren, P., & Torres, R. (1999). Racism and multicultural education: rethinking "race" and "whiteness" in late capitalism. In S. May (Ed.), *Critical multiculturalism: Rethinking multicultural and antiracist education.* London, England, Falmer Press.

Mezirow, J. (2000). *Learning as transformation: Critical perspectives on a theory in progress.* San Francisco, CA: Jossey-Bass.

Mezirow, J. (1991). *Transformative dimensions of adult learning.* San Francisco, CA: Jossey-Bass.

Meyer, S. J., Fredericks, L., Borden, C. M., & Richardson, P. L. (2010). Implementing postsecondary academic programs in state prisons: Challenges and opportunities. *Journal of Correctional Education, 61*(2), 148-184.

Milkman, H., & Wanberg, K. (2007). *Cognitive-behavioral treatment. A review and discussion for corrections professionals.* Retrieved from www.nicic.org

Muth, B. (2008). Radical conversations: Part one of social constructivist methods in the ABE classroom. *Journal of Correctional Education, 59*(3),261-281.

Parkinson, A. F., & Steurer, S. J. (2004, April). Overcoming the obstacles in effective correctional instruction. *Corrections Today,* 88-90.

Pew Center on the States. (2008). One in 100 behind bars in America 2008. Retrieved from http://www.pewtrusts.org/uploadedFiles/wwwpewtrustsorg/Reports/sentencing_and_corrections/one_in_100.pdf

Przybylski, R. (2008). *Effective recidivism reduction and risk-focused prevention programs: A compendium of evidence-based options for preventing new and persistent criminal behavior.* Denver, CO: Bureau of Justice Assistance through DCJ's Office of Adult and Juvenile Assistance, Bureau of Justice Statistics, the National Institute of Justice, the Office of Juvenile, Justice and Delinquency Prevention, and the Office for Victims of Crime.

Rodgers, C. R. (2002). Seeing student learning: Teacher change and the role of reflection. *Harvard Educational Review, 72*(2), 230-252.

Rogoff, B. (1990). *Apprenticeship in thinking: Cognitive development in social context.* New York, NY: Oxford University Press.

Russell M., & Stewart, J.(2001). Disablement, prison, and historical Segregation. *Monthly Review, 53*(3). Retrieved from http://www.monthlyreview.org/0701russell.htm

Searle, J. (1995). *The construction of social reality.* New York, NY: Free Press.

Shields, C. M. (2002, October). *Towards a dialogic approach to understanding values.* Keynote address presented at the seventh annual conference of Values and Leadership, Toronto, Ontario.

Shippen, M., Crites, S. A., Houchins, D. E., Ramsey, M. L., & Simon, M. (2005). Pre-service teachers' perceptions of including students with disabilities. *Teacher Education and Special Education, 28*(2), 92-99.

Slayton, J., & Mathis, J. (2010). Building the leaders we need: The role of presence, learning conditions, and andragogy in developing leaders who can change the face of public pre-K through 12 education. In A. H. Normore (Ed.), *Global perspectives on educational leadership reform: The development and preparation of leaders of learning and learners of leadership* (pp. 23-45). Bingley, England: Emerald.

Solomon, A. L., Osborne, J. W. L., LoBuglio, S. F., Mellow, J., & Mukamal, D. A. (2008). *Life after lock up: Improving re-entry from jail to community.* Washington, DC: Urban Institute, Justice Policy Center.

Stein, M. K., Smith, M. S., & Silver, E. A. (1999). The development of professional developers: Learning to assist teachers in new settings in new ways. *Harvard Educational Review, 69*(3), 237-269.

Taymans, J. M., & Corley, M. A.(2001). Enhancing services to inmates with learning disabilities: Systemic reform of prison literacy programs. *Journal of Correctional Education, 52*(2), 74-78.

Tercilla, E., & Breazzano, D. (2010, August). Maximizing inmate employment success in the bop. *Corrections Today,* 32-35.

Tharp, R., & Gallimore, R. (1988). *Rousing minds to life: Teaching, learning, and schooling in social context*. New York, NY: Cambridge University Press.

Tewksbury, R., & Stengel, K. M. (2006). Assessing correctional education programs: The students perspective. *Journal of Correctional Education, 57*, 13-21.

Vacca, J. S. (2004). Educated prisoners are less likely to return to prison. *Journal of Correctional Education, 55*(4), 297-305.

Vygotsky, L. S. (1978). *Mind and society: The development of higher mental processes*. Cambridge, MA: Harvard University Press.

Walmsley, R. (2007). *World prison population list* (7th ed.). Retrieved from www.prisonstudies.org

Ward, S. A. (2009). Career and technical education in united states prisons: What have we learned? *The Journal of Correctional Education 60*(3), 191-230.

Warner, K. (2007). Against the narrowing of perspectives: How do we see learning, prisons and prisoners? *The Journal of Correctional Education 58*(2), 170-183.

Webster-Wright, A. (2009). Reframing professional development through understanding authentic professional learning. *Review of Educational Research, 79*(2), 702-739.

Werner, D. (2003). *Correctional education: Theory and practice*. La Verne, CA: Author.

Wilson, D. P. (2004).*The silent victims: Inmates with learning disabilities*. Retrieved from http://www.cjpc.org/wap_silent_victims.htm

Winterfield, L. Coggeshall, M., Burke-Storer, M., Correa, V., & Tidd, S. (2009). *The effects of postsecondary correctional education: Final report*. Washington, DC: The Urban Institute, Justice Policy Center.

CHAPTER 9

INTERNATIONAL AND COMPARATIVE BEST PRACTICE IN EDUCATION-BASED INCARCERATION

Arthur A. Jones, Richard Gordon, and Richard Haesly

This chapter provides a systematic analysis of the most demonstrably successful correctional education programs presently in use in a number of countries worldwide. The discussion encompasses the following: (a) needs assessment instruments and their applications; (b) how governments in other countries adapt their educational offerings to the constrictions inherent in a jail setting, that is, making the most of a short stay; (c) the role of cognitive behavioral therapy (CBT) and related techniques in brief-term applications; and (d) new and innovative educational approaches showing promise. The comparative nature of this international survey reveals a high degree of similarity and a number of common features of successful programs, whether pursued in Canada, Germany, Italy, South Korea, Switzerland, the United Kingdom, or elsewhere. Our investigation of international best practices also highlights the obstacles, and opportunities, that implementing such programs in the American context might face. Finally, the chapter reviews the various methods by which successful outcomes are measured, including recidivism reduction figures and how they are defined; the cost savings of apprehending, prosecuting, and incarcerating offenders when it is shown that certain crimes did not occur due to the intervention of

Education-Based Incarceration and Recidivism:
The Ultimate Social Justice Crime-Fighting Tool, pp. 161–178
Copyright © 2012 by Information Age Publishing
All rights of reproduction in any form reserved.

correctional education; and the measurement of improvements in the quality of life in disparate communities internationally.

"Education is not the filling of a bucket, but the lighting of a flame."
—Heraclitus of Ephesus (535-475 BC)

Any serious treatise on international best practices in the realm of education-based incarceration (EBI) should begin with a statement of recognition: Most present-day obstacles to EBI potential success, whether economic, social, political, or cultural in nature, have long preexisted current efforts at improvement (Decisier, 2006). International best practices must therefore take into account all the specific variables occurring in each country or region under consideration. At the same time, the steady increase in EBI programs that have been implemented in countries around the world (and, as we shall see, the extensive borrowing, with modifications, that occurs across national boundaries) suggest that confident conclusions can be drawn about what works and what does not work in EBI. Equally important, even where overincarceration causes crises in prisons and jails, the reader should not lose sight of the fact that, despite universal challenges and national-level variation, individual improvement must ultimately be the single measurement of educational success.

REVIEW OF LITERATURE

We begin by citing available international statistics of incarceration (Walmsley, 2010). Table 9.1 cites the total incarcerated population in each country, including both convicted prisoners and pretrial (jail) detainees.

These data suggest an important caveat at the outset. The United States, in terms of its incarceration rate per 100,000, is in a different category from other advanced industrial nations. One of the implications of this chapter is, therefore, to encourage U.S. officials to take increased note of the achievements of leading governments internationally in the realm of EBI, its roots, development, and implementation.

The underlying causes for such a high rate of incarceration in the United States are both complex and beyond the scope of our analysis. However, considerable consensus in the scholarly research indicates that one major contributing factor for these record numbers of inmates in the United States, and elsewhere, is the extraordinarily high rate of reconvictions, otherwise termed recidivism (Lambert, 2007). Those recidivism rates vary, in Western and Central Europe, from 70% in the United Kingdom, to 37% in The Netherlands (Lambert, 2007). United States recidi-

Table 9.1.   World Prison Population List

Country	Prison Rate Per 100,000 Population
United States	756
Russia	629
South Africa	335
Latvia	288
Singapore	267
Estonia	259
Lithuania	234
United Kingdom	153
Australia	129
China	119
Canada	116
Netherlands	100
France	96
Belgium	93
Italy	92
Germany	89
Switzerland	76
Sweden	74
Norway	69

Source: Adopted from Walmsley (2010).

vism rates average about 66% nationwide, with the state of California leading at about 70% (Freudenberg, 2006).

Despite this variation, the fact that many inmates find themselves back in jail or prison is one of the primary reasons many jurisdictions have begun focusing on inmate education efforts and postrelease services to reduce these sadly persistent trends (Wilson, Gallagher, & MacKenzie, 2000; Zgoba, Haugebrook, & Jenkins, 2008). However, while much inmate educational efforts and many postrelease services may be driven by the currently high recidivism figures, a large number of nation-states and international organizations have designed and implemented policies that provide education and rehabilitation services to inmates based not only on recidivism reduction precepts, but also on the premise that the vast majority of inmates or convicts suffer from educational and social deficits that cannot be corrected by punishment (Committee of Ministers of the Council of Europe, 2006).

Over the past decade, government and nongovernmental organizations in the United States have engaged in an energetic and highly politicized debate about the costs, effectiveness, and even desirability of rehabilitation as a primary goal of incarceration (see e.g., the extensive virtual library of the Urban Institute at www.urban.org). There are many politicians and even corrections administrators in the United States who find it difficult to justify the expense of EBI programs, despite the benefits that such programs—if carefully designed and implemented—can deliver in terms of lower crime rates, lower recidivism rates, and even economic benefits that far outweigh the costs of designing, implementing, and expanding EBI programs (cf. Batiuk, Lahm, Mckeever, Wilcox, & Wilcox, , 2005). Furthermore, as we review in detail in the next section, many of the multinational (e.g., the European Union) and international organizations (e.g., the United Nations) have suggested that, beyond the cost-benefit calculations of EBI programs, there are also clear and fundamental humanitarian grounds in favor of implementing and expanding educational opportunities for a wide percentage of those who are incarcerated.

We begin our discussion by analyzing the larger humanitarian and human rights issues that the United Nations, the European Union, the Council of Europe, and prominent policy advocate groups worldwide have identified as being central to the need for EBI.

INTERNATIONAL SOURCES OF LAW AND POLICY

As documented in Chapters 2 and 7, EBI programs and policies have generally been driven by a patchwork of state and local legislation; local nonprofits and charitable initiatives; litigation against jail and prison administrations; and state and federal legislation authorizing grants for specific reentry/rehabilitation projects. At the international level, however, the push for more systematic prison and jail education efforts is more directly driven by a shared concern for universal human rights, leading to a relatively more unified policy consensus (Muñoz, 2009).

Various bodies of the United Nations (UN) have been notably active in this area for a number of years. In 1957, the UN Economic and Social Council (ECOSOC) set out the "Standard Minimum Rules for the Treatment of Prisoners," which stresses the need for education and training in correctional settings (Hawley, 2010), followed in 1990 by the adoption by the U.N. General Assembly of the "Basic Principles for the Treatment of Prisoners," which made specific reference to the right of incarcerated persons to take part in "cultural activities and education aimed at the full development of the human personality." Adopted in 1997, Article 7 of the

UN ECOSOC Resolution on International Cooperation for the Improvement of Prison Conditions also refers specifically to access to education and skills training.

Most recently, the Human Rights Council of the UN General Assembly, in 2009, adopted the *Report of the Special Rapporteur on the Right to Education of Prisoners and Detainees*. The Special Rapporteur, Vernor Muñoz, notes that

> Despite variations between penal systems, it is clear that, for all, the provision of education for persons in detention is inherently complex and, where it does take place, it does so in an environment inherently hostile to its liberating potential. (as cited in Muñoz, 2009, p. 5)

Then, addressing the social aspects and impacts of prisoners and detained persons returning to their respective communities, Muñoz (2009, p. 5) argues:

> Although for most of the persons concerned detention will be temporary, it is too frequently forgotten that the consequences of what does or does not happen to those who experience it will also be felt by the community into which the majority of prisoners are released.

As poignantly expressed by one released prisoner: We cannot imprison a person for many years without providing an avenue for change and expect that when he or she returns among us, she or he will have changed. Indeed, change will have occurred but certainly not how it was envisioned. We will have created an envious, frustrated, delusional, pent-up, angry, and dehumanized individual who will certainly seek revenge. (as cited in Muñoz, 2009, p. 5).

According to the UN International Covenant on Civil and Political Rights and the Optional Protocol, Article 6, and reported in the U.N. Special Rapporteur in a review of international law, "All prisoners have the right to take part in cultural activities and education aimed at the full development of the human personality" (Muñoz, 2009, p. 9). To this the author adds, "The right to education is now accepted.... No text allows for forfeiture of this right and, more essentially, forfeiture is not necessitated by the fact of incarceration" (Muñoz, 2009, p. 9). In addition to the foregoing provisions of United Nations resolutions, at pan-European level, the European Convention for the Protection of Human Rights and Fundamental Freedoms, Article 2, states that "No person shall be denied the right to education." Further, in 2006, the Council of Europe, in its role as the publicly constituted European body for human rights, published its revised European Prison Rules which state, in Article 28, that:

- All incarceration institutions shall guarantee all inmates access to educational programs which are comprehensive and meet the individual's needs, while taking into account aspirations of the inmate;
- Inmates with literacy and math deficits, and those who lack basic or vocational education, should be given priority;
- All institutions shall maintain a library with a complete range of both educational and recreational resources; and
- All adult education in institutions shall provide a broad curriculum which ensures a wider scope for critical reflection and personal development, for the cultivation of meaningful and useful knowledge and skills, and that will allow inmates to broaden their perceptions of their role and their future (Committee of Ministers, Council of Europe, 2006) also see Hawley, 2010, p. 6).

SELECTED BEST PRACTICES FROM AROUND THE WORLD

There are myriad EBI programs that have been designed in many different contexts. Historically, international rehabilitation theory and practice have fluctuated radically between the countervailing philosophies of punishment and education (Illescas, Sànchez-Meca, & Genovés, 2001). In the 1980s, research emerged favoring education over the "nothing works" position, which spurred investigation throughout the 1990s (Gendreua & Ross, 1979, 1987; Illescas et al., 2001, p. 47). Based on theoretical and empirical work, two of the most promising areas to emerge have been: (1) programs that draw lessons from CBT and combine those techniques with the development of critical thinking skills; and (2) programs that take lessons from the latest thinking about the strengths and challenges of distance learning. These two areas are not mutually exclusive, and yet they also point to the need to think very carefully about the content of each EBI course and how that content is both derived and delivered.

With deep roots in cognitive behavioral experience, such programs are attentive to the educational challenges that are faced by adult learners, many of whom struggle with cognitive, affective, and behavioral disorders and have often had profoundly negative experiences from early encounters with education. Furthermore, these programs, as they were designed both in the United States and abroad, were created for ethnically diverse inmate populations, which is clearly a necessity for any EBI program in most American jurisdictions.

COGNITIVE BEHAVIORAL THERAPY AND CRITICAL THINKING.

Of the total European incarcerated population of 627,455 in 2009, nearly 150,000 were in pretrial detention (Walmsley, 2010). Pretrial detainees are particularly difficult to provide meaningful education and training opportunities because of the short time frame presented (Hawley, 2010). The problem is pandemic, and presents itself whether the jails and prisons are combined under one roof, such as, Germany, Switzerland, and others (Jehle, 2009), or are separate architectural structures, such as, Italy, the United States, and others (Onnis, 2011).

Cognitive behavioral therapy has its roots in the science of experimental psychology. Beginning in the early 1960s, psychologists, psychiatrists, and other behavioral scientists began multidisciplinary research and sharing to define and interpret cognition, based on empirical results and potentials (Milkman & Wanberg, 2007). Cognitive behavioral therapy is commonly used during the course of treatment to identify and inculcate:

- Peer group contribution in examining experiential bias and helping disconfirm schematic assumptions and distortions;
- Procedures for growing adaptive responses among inmates; and
- Methods, using identity codes, to modify attitudes and assumptions using the subject's own *schemas* (behavioral patterns derived from accumulated experience), and to separate the student's reaction from triggers of previous experiences of cognition and of behavior (Milkman & Wanberg, 2007, p. 59).

A meta-analysis covering 32 CBT programs in five member nations of the European Union found that CBT programs produce, on average, a 12% reduction in recidivism over nontreated inmate groups. The findings also suggested that CBT treatment, if properly applied, was at least 15% more effective than non-CBT programs (Illescas et al., 2001).

Given the broad spectrum of sociopolitical, economic, and historic variables presented by the number of countries under study, one primary benefit of the meta-analytic method is the ability to adduce effective and consistent evidence of best practices worldwide. However, it is important to recognize that "the interrelationship between the variables of the studies may mask the real associations between the effect and each individual moderator variable" (Illescas et al., 2001, p. 58). Several empirical and meta-analytical studies have made a strong case for the particular effectiveness of behavioral and cognitive-behavioral models and therapy (Gendreau & Ross, 1979, 1987). However, Illescas et al. (2001, p. 58) cautions that, "It is essential to bear in mind those aspects of the specific environment that may have an influence on the application of these principles—

in other words, the influence of contextual factors that are difficult to quantify." A useful recommendation of the Illescas et al. (2001, p. 59) meta-analysis provides guidance:

> Those special environmental contingencies are difficult to assess in meta-analytic studies, but they can be appropriately studied through direct primary research, which would undoubtedly help to improve the effectiveness of offender rehabilitation.

The process of adapting existing CBT programs to offset special environmental contingencies has led to a heightened realization in Europe that the sheer heterogeneity of prisoners, jail inmates, and probationers or parolees requires individual educational plans for inmates to address the broad spectrum of environmental contingencies, both within and without, facing correctional facilities. From European-funded conferences, such as Pathways to Inclusion, a consensus has emerged that:

> Offenders need to be supported through an approach which emphasizes *critical literacy* rather than *functional literacy*. While the latter is the ability to read and write, critical literacy on the other hand is a process of transformation through which the learner's cognitive and intellectual development is enhanced and transformed.... [I]t can be a stepping stone to other kinds of education and can have a therapeutic effect. Encouraging the offenders to explore new roles can support them in their effort to rebuild a connection with society. (Hawley, 2010, pp. 10-15)

Of course, functional literacy is only one stone in the mosaic of CBT development. A 2002 "Statement of Findings" (Friendship, Blud, Erikson, & Travers, 2002) measured and evaluated reasoning and rehabilitation enhanced thinking skills, cognitive style, critical reasoning skills, self-control, choices, interpersonal problem-solving skills, and social perspective taking. One of the United Kingdom Home Office's recommendations was to adopt a wider spectrum of offerings geared to address an increasing subset of environmental and/or extraneous variables (Friendship et al., 2002, p.161). More specific environmental influences on programs caused by conditions and/or attitudes of correctional institutions internationally are discussed *infra*.

Next, as to the effectiveness of CBT courses by level of risk, a United Kingdom medium to long-term study of comparative reconviction rates following treatment while incarcerated concluded that in a 2-year, observed series of CBT programs, the recidivism rates for medium-low risk students dropped by 14%. The rates for medium-high risk inmates fell by 11%, controlling for known predictors of reconviction (Friendship et al., 2002).

In Germany, data on recidivism rates has changed relatively little over the past 10-year period. Among adult men and women offenders, only about 33% recidivate within the 4-year period of postrelease tracking and measurement required by law (Jehle, 2009). German formal or traditional classroom education in prison—for example, one lecturer teaching biology to 30 students—has been legally obligatory since 1977 (German Penal Sentencing Act, Articles, 37-52). That same legislation also requires a thorough risk and needs assessment of every inmate upon arrival. A basic curriculum and a reentry plan based on that assessment are obligatory. The curriculum must include three main components: Vocational training, formal (i.e., secondary) education, and "practical life skills, social abilities, and critical thinking." (Penal Sentencing Act, Articles. 37, 38, and 71). The third category of EBI in Germany, of nontraditional "Sozial-training" (CBT), is thus clearly established as a matter of law:

> The instructional programs offered cannot be conceived separately from the other duties incumbent upon correctional authorities: They must be meshed and coordinated with the other treatment, support and therapy measures taken, especially respecting cognitive behavioral therapy and other methods of awakening the inmate's sense of freedom and dignity, together with intensive preparations for release, employment, relief from debt burdens, and housing. (Schwind, Böhm, Jehle, & Laubenthal, 2009, p. 381)

In 2006, a "Federal Reform Bill" was passed by the German Parliament, transferring the authority for prison and jail inmate rehabilitation and education from the federal government to the separate German states. This has led to some variance of policy and practice between and among the German states, although several German Supreme Court decisions had already firmly anchored inmates' educational and welfare rights 33 years earlier (German Supreme Constitutional Court 1973, *in re Art. 2 Sub (1), in Conjunction with Art. 1, German Constitution*). The combined result of the foregoing has been labeled "The right to reintegration." It means that police, detention, or prison authorities have the right to abridge inmates' rights to program participation only on convincing grounds of security. Even here, correctional officers must justify to public supervisory bodies any loss, by any inmate, of personal rights to security and education (Ostendorf, 2010).

The legal theory is that if society cannot help protect those who have no control over their own safety, as jail inmates or prisoners, then it certainly is in no position to guarantee public safety generally. For that reason, and specifically to prevent abuses or neglect on the part of correctional officials, once an inmate has indicated an interest in entering an educational program, that inmate comes under direct protection of the state (Ostendorf, 2010). Police and correctional officers are specifically prohibited from inflicting—by overt act, including negligence, or by expressed attitude—repentance, revenge-based retribution, or denial of educational rights (Ostendorf 2010, citing Art. 2 (2), Federal Reform Act 1973). Such provisions apply expressly when a discernible portion of the inmate's original socialization process (i.e., childhood, primary and secondary education) took place outside the standard social norms and values, which is the case in most economically and resource-challenged ethnic or other minority communities (Föhn, 2010).

In this regard, the German Crime Prevention Council has also issued a position paper setting forth its legal and social advocacy on the topics of short-duration incarceration, and past practices in transition and reentry plans (Klein, 2010). In both instances, the council has conducted studies recommending several urgent improvements. First, special attention must be given to probable short-term inmates, to ensure that their educational and CBT opportunities are not given short shrift; and, second, that sufficient custody escort and/or architectural design be present to ensure that inmates can physically attend the classes for which they have registered or applied (Klein, 2010).

In Italy, responsibility falls upon the individual state (Provinzia) to provide for education and social training of inmates in local jails (Circondariale) (Article 60, Custody Institutions, Federal Law No. 354 of July 26, 1975). Because, as in many other locales, short-term attention to deficits will necessarily take the form of CBT-based participation, regional authorities have cooperatively developed several innovative strategies for the ultimately successful reintegration of former jail inmates:

- Courses of instruction are not only didactic, but also interactive. They should be designed to engage all participants in a unity of purpose as the course progresses;
- Cognitive behavioral improvement is ever-present behind the scenes of the materials presented by the teachers/presenters;
- Respect for alumni of the programs, whether they are still incarcerated or have been released in the meantime, is demonstrated in a pro-active manner by teachers and by correctional officers and staff equally;
- When graduates have demonstrated a capacity for constructive criticism in a manner that can contribute to progress of the group as a whole, they are recruited to serve as mentors; and
- As a group, inmate participants are to be regularly asked to engage in continuing discussions (or debates) about the final goals they

seek in qualifications, skills, ways of thinking, education, and the nature of society in general (Bonomelli, 2009).

A Canadian study reached a set of recommendations similar in many respects to the Italian legislation, including:

- Characteristics of successful correctional education programs include program content that is relevant to the lives of inmate students;
- Students with learning disabilities are easily distracted and do not function well in unstructured group sessions. Group leaders should use a structured format, directive questions, and constant interest monitoring to remain on topic and to engage the offender/students;
- On balance, the learning styles of most offenders require active and participatory methods of participation;
- The application of cognitive skills training is both central and critical to the success of inmate recidivism reduction programs; and
- Motivation and continued attention, when combined, lead to concrete and measurable reductions in recidivism (John Howard Society of Alberta, 2002, p. 5).

Results of this intensified, multidimensional approach to inmates led to a 3-year reduction in recidivism exceeding 30% in at least two student groups: offenders committing mainly sexual and violent offenses, and others who had received continued CBT training in a postrelease, community environment (John Howard Society of Alberta, 2002, p.5).

Remote Education and Information Technology in International EBI

In today's societies, distance learning (remote education) and information technology are assuming an importance and essentiality in EBI. First, digital educational materials and learning networks can be exploited to create new learning opportunities and to implement eLearning in correctional settings. The use of DVD-based materials and closed-circuit television presentations apply new multimedia technologies to improve the quality of correctional learning by facilitating broader access to resources and services, as well as remote exchanges and collaboration among teachers and curriculum developers (Hawley, 2010).

For any eLearning approach, security remains the primary concern for most correctional institutions considering such measures. Most prisons and pretrial detention facilities internationally presently consider it impossible to guarantee the secure use of internet facilities in incarceration. However, there is a growing consensus in some leading countries that breaches in security resulting from Internet access for inmates can be minimized or even eliminated, assuming proper software development and adequate monitoring of use. In a number of facilities internationally, the misuse of electronic learning infrastructure is becoming very rare (Hillmer, 2010).

Distance learning lends itself especially well to "short stay" correctional facilities, wherein large segments of the inmate population are either in pretrial confinement or have been given short sentences. DVD libraries are being used to address the problem of interrupted learning caused by transfers between facilities, lockdowns, or court appearances, as well as release into the community. eLearning libraries also facilitate a much wider and more up to date range of educational subjects and materials than was heretofore possible (Hawley, 2010). Another advantage of distance learning in international correctional settings arises from the important role that immigration plays in educational policy. In Switzerland, non-Swiss born persons make up nearly 29% of the general population, but represent 70% of the prison and jail population (Bundesamt für Statistik, 2009).

In nearly every European country, foreigners are incarcerated in numbers disproportionate to their percentage of the total population (Föhn, 2010). In the European Union as a whole, nationals of a country other than that in which they are residing make up 19.6% of the population, but in many countries represent 40% or more of the prison/ jail population (Council of Europe Penal Statistics, 2010). Many of them, especially those who emigrated from North Africa, the Middle East, and the former USSR, frequently present significant deficits in formal education and local languages (Hostettler, Kirchhofer, Richter, & Young, 2010). Distance learning using DVD-based materials in the inmates' first languages, combined with instruction in the local (national) language or languages, is widely considered to be effective in the following ways:

- Reduction in disturbances such as assaults on staff or other inmates;
- Preparation for reentry into the local community; or
- Preparation for return to the inmate's home country with newly-acquired knowledge, skills and abilities (Hostettler et al., 2010).

A meta-analysis of prison and jail educational programs in five member nations of the European Union (Germany, The Netherlands, Spain, Sweden, and the United Kingdom), Illescas et al., (2001), concluded that general distance learning programs alone, offered to the entire correctional facility populations ("all the subjects") reduced recidivism by 6.8% over a 2-year period. Those programs consisted primarily of educational DVD and television offerings. The effects of distance learning, however, when combined with cognitive behavioral treatment, critical literacy, and remedial courses, both in incarceration and in the community after release, produce significantly better results (Föhn, 2010).

In the United States, the Los Angeles County Sheriff's Department has introduced a "Universal Opportunity" inmate educational program in which eLearning, distance learning, closed-circuit transmission of high-integrity educational programs, self-study workbooks, and other instructional means and methods, will touch every inmate every day of his or her incarceration (www.lasd.org/ebi). Those offerings are accompanied by CBT and by additional, specific interdisciplinary series of courses of interactive instruction. The program is being developed with the active engagement of a newly integrated steering committee, comprising leading academic figures from universities throughout Southern California and elsewhere.

CORRECTIONAL ATTITUDES AND THEIR EFFECTS ON INMATE EDUCATION

First, a note of caution: A thorough assessment of correctional attitudes—whether of individual guards or deputies, or of higher-ranking paramilitary civil servants toward inmate education is demonstrably essential to progress in improving, standardizing, and bringing inmate educational and reentry programs up to date and up to scale. We suggest that the social and political role of correctional authorities, from top to bottom of their respective hierarchies, should be revisited in light of today's societies and of the present state of science.

Second, a note of concern: Just as Canada serves as an example of innovation in the field of inmate education during the past decade, no nation is immune to the vicissitudes of economic and political forces and events. According to figures released by the Correctional Services Canada, 8,775 inmates participated in educational and CBT programs in 2000. By 2009, that number had shrunk to 5,539 (Sapers, 2011). Moreover, those statistics reveal that 40% of inmates who were identified as requiring educational and CBT programs in 2009-2010 did not receive them, as compared to 90% in 2000 who were given access to them (Sapers, 2011).

Despite that setback, Correctional Services Canada launched a new model providing programs to inmates who are new to "the system," thus confirming our observation that the best and most successful programs are those that begin as soon as possible after the inmate's arrival and continue, seamlessly as possible, through postrelease inclusion into community-based CBT, job/activity classes, and drug/alcohol treatment in close interaction with each other.

In the United Kingdom, studies of some 12 or more prisons in England and Wales conducted between 2004 and 2005 found that correctional officers, by their own account, felt confused about their job roles respecting inmate education and rehabilitation (Braggins & Talbot, 2005). In fact, many officers reflected the view that "Until the officers value education for themselves they'll find it difficult to value it for others. Until that's sorted out there won't be any change" (Braggins & Talbot, 2005 , p.53).

Correctional officers in many national jurisdictions feel undertrained, underpaid, undersupported and undervalued in the existing, let alone any increased (EBI) role. This perceived lack of appropriate training and support has led directly to animosity against inmate education (Braggins & Talbot, 2005). Among recommended measures to promote prisoners' learning are:

- Build the common purpose of the entire institution around inmate learning;
- Give all staff the common responsibility to facilitate inmate learning;
- Promotion of inmate education should be made a part of management plans; time budgets; activity options for prisoners;
- Responsibility for inmate education must be made part of initial (e.g., academy) training, professional development and appraisal for custody officers; and
- There should be a formalized range of recognized opportunities for correctional officers, deputies, and custody personnel generally to promote, support, and participate in inmate education, whether as guides, mentors, advisors, support assistants, or skill instructors (Braggins & Talbot, 2005, pp. 8-10).

In a South Korean study, Moon and Maxwell (2004) assessed the attitudes and professional orientations of correctional officers (both prison and jail). As part of the study, they distributed questionnaires to some 350 jail and prison correctional officers, a cohort representing practically the entire employee force in local correctional institutions. Of that total number of study participants, 79% were male and 21% female. Also, 26% worked in jails, the remaining 74% in prisons. They concluded that little concrete effort had been made in South Korea prior to 1998-2000 to develop and implement rehabilitation programs any scale.

One of the objects of the study was to establish the relative individual and organizational variables on officer attitudes (Moon & Maxwell, 2004). One of the conclusions the study reached was that, although in favor of rehabilitation programs, over 60% of the officers surveyed felt that the existing education and rehabilitation offerings were not effective. The authors concluded that the most important influence on an officer's attitude toward rehabilitation were not education or gender, but, rather, the individual's interest in performing a meaningful role in public service, a criteria that predating his or her entry into correctional employment (Moon & Maxwell, 2004).

Conversely, four organizational variables were significantly related to a more punitive orientation: seniority, role problems, job stress, and job satisfaction (Moon & Maxwell, 2004). Surprisingly, employees who have worked longer in correctional institutions were more likely to have a rehabilitative orientation and less likely to have a punitive orientation than their less-tenured cohorts. Just as in the United States, the study found a positive relationship between job satisfaction and a rehabilitative/educational orientation, and a negative relationship between job dissatisfaction and a punitive orientation. Thus, the overall findings of this study should be of interest to administrators developing recruitment strategies (Moon & Maxwell, 2004).

Similar findings were reached by Trinidad and Tobago (King & Bartholomew, 2007) in ascertaining the correctional orientation of the country's correctional officers. Beginning with the results of a prior study commissioned by the Government of Trinidad and Tobago, King and Bartholomew (2007) analyzed local data in light of the relative importance of individual factors as opposed to organizational factors. They conclude that:

These studies have illustrated that officers who experience role conflict at their jobs tend to hold either punitive or custodial orientations. Therefore, the managerial and administrative arms of the prison service need to ensure that their expectations of their officers are clear; as ambiguity in roles seems to be related with the officers adopting either a punitive or custodial orientation (King & Bartholomew, 2007).

A Norwegian study (Kjelsberg, Skoglund, & Rustad, 2007) canvassed 390 jail and prison workers, 59% of whom were correctional officers, the remaining 41% being administrative employees or else teachers, librarians, therapists and psychologists. Perhaps not surprisingly, the study found that prison officers' attitudes toward inmate education were generally negative, whereas employees holding other work positions were significantly more positive (Kjelsberg et al., 2007). The study also concluded that prison officers' attitudes toward inmates are very important: Positive attitudes are critical in facilitating change prior to successful release from incarceration (Kjelsberg et al., 2007). The Kjelsberg study also found that corrections or custody officers may form negative feelings toward inmates from day-to-day contacts involving behavioral issues. Finally, Kjelsberg et al. (2007) found that officers are significantly more positive in those facilities that emphasize inmate education and transformation rather than in facilities that favor mere warehousing.

Thus, ample evidence is available to suggest that the organizational message, coupled with adequate and specific correctional officer training, will continue to be vital in developing effective and successful cultural policies toward inmate learning.

CONCLUSIONS

While education-based incarceration is a relatively recent development in the United States—although, as Chapters 2 and 5 of this book demonstrate, the intellectual and pedagogical roots of such programs stretch back much further—the international developments in this area illustrate that much can be learned by investigating the best practices of EBI programs that have been developed and tested in places as diverse as the United Kingdom, Canada, Germany, Switzerland, Italy, and South Korea. Particularly instructive is that, with the notable exception of the United Kingdom, these countries have federal (or, in the cases of Canada and Switzerland, confederal) political systems, in which significant decision-making power is devolved to subnational territorial units. Thus, these international cases, like the United States, recognize and allow for local variation of general principles when designing public policy solutions to social problems.

In the United States, the fact that most incarceration policies are established at the state, and even local, levels may make the adoption of a nationwide standard challenging in the short or medium term. However, American state and local jurisdictions are increasingly willing to examine the rapidly growing body of empirical evidence that has been collected about the effectiveness of education-based incarceration programs, both at home and abroad. That evidence reveals that, while the task is daunting, societies worldwide are making real gains in terms of lowered recidivism rates, greater respect for the human rights of incarcerated persons, and significant economic benefits resulting from a better-educated and more law-abiding citizenry.

REFERENCES

Batuik, M. E., Lahm, K. F., Mckeever, M., Wilcox, N., & Wilcox, P. (2005). Disentangling the effects of correctional education. Are current policies misguided? An event history analysis. *Criminology and Criminal Justice* 5(1), 55-74.

Bonomelli, R. (2009). *La formazione come strumento di inclusione sociale* [Education as an instrument for social inclusion]. Retrieved from http://www.comunicati-stampa.net/com/cs-76127

Braggins, J., & Talbot, J. (2005). *Wings of learning: the role of the prison officer in supporting prisoner education.* Retrieved from http://www.crimeandjustice.org.uk/opus210/wings-of-learning.pdf

Bundesamt für Statistik. (2009). Retrieved from www.bfs.admin.ch

Committee of Ministers, Council of Europe. (2006). *Recommendations, prisoner education and European prison rules.* Retrieved from https://wcd.coe.int/wcd/ViewDoc.jsp?id=955747

Council of Europe Annual Penal Statistics, Strasbourg, (2010, March). Library No. pc-cp\space\documents\pc-cp, University of Lausanne, Switzerland.

Decisier, M. D. (2006). *Les conditions de la réinsertion socioprofessionelle des détenus en France* [Conditions in social and vocational rehabilitation of inmates in France]. Paris: Conseil Economique et Social.

Föhn, F. (2010). Bildung im strafvollzug Schweiz, Deutschland, Österreich: Ein Vergleich (Unpublished) [Education in incarceration in Switzerland, Germany, and Austria: A comparison]. Wirtschaftsuniversität, Vienna, Austria.

Freudenberg, N. (2006, May). Coming home from jail: A review of health and social problems facing US jail populations and of opportunities for reentry interventions. *Urban Institute Reentry Roundtable, Washington, DC, 2006.* Retrieved from www.urban.org/reentryroundtable/inmate_challenges.pdf

Friendship, C., Blud, L., Erikson, M., & Travers, R., (2002). An evaluation of cognitive behavioral treatment for prisoners, London: UK Home Office.

Gendreau, P., & Ross, R. R. (1979). Effective correctional treatment: Bibliography for cynics. *Crime and Delinquency, 25*(4), 463-489.

Gendreau, P., & Ross, R. R. (1987). Revivication of rehabilitiation: Evidence from the 1980s. *Justice Quarterly, 4*(3), 349-407.

Hawley, J. (2010). *Pathways to inclusion: Strengthening European cooperation in prison education and training.* Brussels, BelguiumEuropean Commission, Directorate General for Education and Culture.

Hillmer, J. (2010). *Rückfallstatistik. Berlin: Bundesministerium der Justiz* [Recidivism data, German Federal Ministry of Justice]. Retrieved from www.bmj.bund.de

Hostettler, U., Kirchhofer, R., Richter, M., & Young, C. (2010, September 30). Bildung im Strafvollzug (Schweiz) Externe Evaluation, Schlussbericht. Retrieved from www.bist.ch

Illescas, S. R., Meca, J. S., & Genovés, V. G. (2001). Treatment of offenders and recidivism: assessment of the effectiveness of programs applied in Europe. *Psychology in Spain, 5*(1), 47-62.

Jehle, J. (2009). *Strafrechtspflege in Deutschland, fakten und zahlen* (5th ed.). Retrieved from http://www.bmj.bund.de

John Howard Society of Alberta. (2002). Inmate education. Retrieved from www.johnhoward.ab.ca

King, K., & Bartholomew, T. (2007, February). *Identifying and predicting the correctional orientation of Trinidad and Tobago's correctional officers: Implications for prison reform.* Paper delivered at the SALISES Conference on Caribbean Development Challenges in the 21st Century, West Indies, St. Augustine.

Kjelsberg, E., Skoglund, T. H., & Rustad, A. B. (2007). Attitudes towards prisoners, as reported by prison inmates, prison employees and college students. *BMC Public Health, 7*(71), doi:10.1186/1471-2458-7-71.

Klein, L. (2010) *Prävention durch haftinterne Bildungsmassnahmen, Hannover: Internetdokumentation des Deutschen Präventionstag* [Crime prevention through educational measures in incarceratio, Hanover, Germany]. Retrieved from www.praeventionstag.de/Dokumention.cms/933

Lambert, K. (2007). *(Ex)-offenders: Effective resettlement or possible re-offending? EQUAL, European Week of Regions and Cities.* Retrieved from http://www.dwp.gov.uk/esf/

Milkman, H., & Wanberg, K. (2007). *Cognitive-behavioral treatment: A review and discussion for corrections professionals.* Retrieved from www.ncjrs.gov/App/Publications/abstract.aspx?ID=240869

Moon, B., & Maxwell, S. R. (2004). Assessing the correctional orientation of corrections officers in South Korea. *International Journal of Offender Therapy and Comparative Criminology, 48*(6), 729-743. doi:10.1177/0306624X04266681.

Muñoz, V. (2009) The right to education of persons in detention. *Promotion and protection of human rights, civil, political, economic, social and cultural rights, including the right to development* (Report of the Special Rapporteur on the right to education, UN Human Rights Council). Retrieved from http://www2.ohchr.org/english/bodies/hrcouncil/docs/11session/A.HRC.11.8_en.pdf

Onnis, M. (ed.). (2011, February 4). La sardegna istituisce il garante dei detenuti [Sardinia implements guarantees for inmates]. *Il Mio Giornale.* Retrieved from http://www.ilmiogiornale.org

Ostendorf, H. (2010). Aufgaben und Ausgestaltung des Strafvollzugs [Objectives and structure of incarceration]. *Informationen zur politischen Bildung Nr. 306/ 2010 (Information for Political Education).* Retrieved from www.bpb.de /publikationen/5U20WD,0,Aufgaben_und_Gestaltung_des Strafvollzugs.html

Sapers, H. (2011). *Fewer inmates taking anti-recidivism treatment programs.* Retrieved from www.daylife.com/topic/Howard_Sapers/conversations

Schwind, H., Böhm, A., Jehle, M., & Laubenthal, K. (2009). Strafvollzugsgesetz: Bund und Länder (5th ed.) [German sentencing laws: Federal and state]. Mönchengladbach, Germany: Forum.

Walmsley, J. (2010). *World prison population list* (8th ed.). London, England: International Center for Prison Studies.

Wilson, D. B., Gallagher, C. A., & MacKenzie, D. L. (2000). A meta-analysis of corrections-based education, vocation, and work programs for adult offenders. *Journal of Research in Crime and Delinquency, 37*(4), 347-368.

Zgoba, K. M., Haugebrook, S., & Jenkins, K. (2008). The influence of GED obtainment on inmate release outcome. *Criminal Justice and Behavior, 35*(3), 375-387.

CHAPTER 10

TEACHING STRATEGIES AND PRACTICES FOR CORRECTIONAL EDUCATION

Sara A. M. Silva, Kimberly B. Hughes, June Kizu, Selene Kurland, and Sylvester "Bud" Pues

The goal of providing educational opportunities for jail inmates is the central focus of this chapter; however, creating appropriate and substantial instructional programming for this population has many inherent problems. The primary obstacle to participation in programs is contingent on length of incarceration that varies greatly from inmate to inmate. Moreover, learning must occur within a stressful environment rife with interruptions due to security issues, court appearances, and medical concerns. The logistical requirements of correctional environment dictate many design dynamics, including method of delivery, materials management, and instructional modalities. As the locus of correctional education shift from academic and vocational instruction to those concentrated on cognitive change and personal growth, innovative curriculum is emerging. This chapter provides an overview of the current tapestry of programs that are endeavoring to modify behavior in order to reduce patterns of repeated incarceration.

The intent of this chapter is to highlight an effective curriculum design that will function within a short-term correctional facility and allow for equal access of all inmates to educational opportunities. According to

Education-Based Incarceration and Recidivism:
The Ultimate Social Justice Crime-Fighting Tool, pp. 179–196
Copyright © 2012 by Information Age Publishing
All rights of reproduction in any form reserved.

Sheriff Leroy Baca of the Los Angeles County Sheriff's Department (LASD), "Education-based incarceration (EBI) is a component of the criminal justice system that is focused on deterring and mitigating crime by investing in its offenders through education and rehabilitation" (LASD EBI, 2010, p.9). This chapter will also provide an overview of existing programs and the required components necessary to achieve a successful EBI Program. Additionally, the need for realigning institutional culture and philosophy with the goals of EBI will be addressed.

As the focus of correctional education shifts from academic and vocational curriculum to one centered on behavioral readjustment, learning objectives must be reevaluated. Programs must be tailored to stressful environments challenged by budgetary constraints, housing limitations, security issues, court appearances, and medical concerns. Adaptations in the design dynamics concerning logistics, method of delivery, materials management, and instructional modalities are essential regardless of specific subject emphasis. All of these factors need to address the special problems inherent in producing educational programs within facilities that house inmates for short periods of time.

INTRODUCTION

Historically, the objective of incarceration was to remove the sinful ways of the accused (Werner, 2003). Offenders were seen as sinners in need of redemption. Prisons were places for punishment; there was no imperative to educate those who were confined within them. This mindset did not change until 1847, when Samuel Gridley Howe posited the idea that prisoners could be changed for the better, in effect reformed, by their incarceration. Howe believed that the "moral sentiments" and "powers of self-government" of prisoners could be readjusted along more acceptable standards (cited in Werner, 2003; McKelvey, 1977, p. 42). This perspective sought new avenues, beyond mere punishment, with which to change prisoners. Correctional personnel focused on the reformation of antisocial behaviors and reeducation of criminal minds in order to achieve real and substantive transformation.

The Education of Adult Prisoners, written by Austin MacCormack (1931), advocated for educational programs within prisons. He believed in the benefits of education during incarceration and argued that gains were possible even when prisoners were confined for short periods. MacCormack suggested that academic education include individualized instruction to accommodate the rapidly changing population and the varying needs of the inmates. His guidelines advocated for educational continuity through links to outside educational centers to enable offenders to continue their education beyond the prison walls. MacCormack's proposed curriculum consisted of vocational training, health education, academic subjects, and literacy and citizenship instruction. While MacCormack saw challenges in implementing educational programs in short-term facilities, he believed that with qualified teachers, well-stocked libraries, adequate classroom space, and a genuine belief in the real possibility of reformation, such educational opportunities would bring forth positive results. Although his methods sometimes proved less than effective, by 1961, MacCormack's correctional education model was ubiquitous throughout the United States (Werner, 2003).

Current views suggest that educational programming must address not only the academic needs of the inmate but also the social, civic, and cognitive issues that contribute to criminogenic behavior and incarceration (MacKenzie, 2008). Rehabilitation in its truest form seeks to invest in the transformation of both the inmate and the institution. To accomplish this, correctional institutions must be guided by the philosophy that inmates can become productive members of society, given sufficient support, guidance, and opportunities for successful educational outcomes (Werner, 2003). When inmates overcome educational limitations, it has a positive influence on their psychological well being (Foley & Gao, 2004) and behavior (Gendron & Cavan, 1990).

Most educational programs within correctional institutions have traditionally consisted of reading, writing, arithmetic, and vocational training (Foley & Gao, 2004). Research has been conducted on the effect of academic programming during incarceration on recidivism, and common trends have emerged (Aos, Miller, & Drake, 2006; Coley & Barton, 2006; MacKenzie, 2008; Phipps, Korinek, Aos, & Lieb, 1999; Przybylski, 2008; Steurer, Smith, & Tracy, 2001; Travis, 2003). There is evidence that the correctional education has a beneficial effect on recidivism (Wilson, Gallager, & MacKenzie, 2000). According to Harer (1995), recidivism rates during a 3-year period following incarceration diminished for those who had spent a minimum of 6 months in a focused program. Forty-six percent of nonparticipants returned to prison, while only 39% of those who participated in these programs met a similar fate (Harer, 1995).

What has been shown is that, for long-term sustainable change to occur, criminal behaviors and associated social and cognitive impairments must be identified and modified. According to Silver (2010), "Whether or not [educating inmates has] anything to do with [why they continue] to come to jail [is unknown], but we are trying to come up with every option we can think of to keep people from repeatedly being put back into the system" (para. 5). The current thought is that if inmates are able to gain skills, which modify their behavior and improve social functioning sufficiently to reduce criminogenic behavior, recidivism may be reduced (MacKenzie, 2008).

Inmate Educational Profile

The California Department of Corrections and Rehabilitation enrolls approximately 54,000 inmates annually in educational programs, roughly 31% of the prison population. Of those who participate, over half are engaged in traditional academic and vocational studies. Most of those engaged in these programs read below ninth grade level (about 63%). Unfortunately, only 7% attend prehigh school level classes and fewer than 4% earn a General Educational Development (GED) test, or vocational certification (Hill, 2008). Approximately 47% of those incarcerated in local jails have not attained a high school diploma or equivalent, as compared with only 18% of the general population (Harlow, 2003). Statistics also show that undereducated individuals are more often sentenced as juveniles.

Institutional Education Profile

In 2003, the Bureau of Justice surveyed adult correctional institutions and determined that education programming was offered in 91% of state prisons and 60% of local jails. These institutions commonly offered adult basic education (literacy), secondary education (GED and high school diploma), college courses, special education, English as a second language, vocational training, and study release programs (Harlow, 2003).

Close examination of these programs yields some interesting conclusions. The data shows that Computer Assisted Instruction, with teacher support, resulted in significant increases in overall achievement. Younger inmates tended to make greater gains than older ones (Smith & Silverman, 1994). Participation in education programs seemed to positively affect the emotional well-being of inmates, with the added benefit of allowing them to act as role models for others. This was demonstrated in the lower instances of infractions against prison rules among those participating in the programs (Harlow, 2003).

A meta-analysis of state correctional institutions revealed that most offered educational programming. Over 60% provided either high school course work or vocational, life, and social skills programs (Kirshstein & Best, 1996 cited in Foley & Gao, 2004). Other studies have shown that although most correctional facilities offer some type of educational programming to their inmates, overall, few jail inmates participate in them—

only 14% as compared to 52% of those incarcerated in state prisons. The numbers of jail inmates taking part in vocational programs was equally diminutive—less than 5% versus almost 33% of those in state prisons (Harlow, 2003).

New Focus of Institutional Education

Over the past 2 decades, correctional education program designers developed a better understanding of the interrelationship of curriculum, instruction, and institutional culture. They began focusing on the link between incarceration, behavior problems, and cognitive issues. Increasingly, programs that target offender behavior pointed to some common attributes of antisocial conduct that can be modified (Andrews & Bosnta, 2003; Gendreau & Andrews, 1990; Gornik, 2002; MacKensie, 2008), including:

- antisocial attitudes, values, and beliefs;
- procriminal association and isolation from prosocial associates;
- antisocial personality patterns (angry, withdrawn, etc.);
- weak problem-solving abilities and social skills;
- problematic home factors (abuse, unstructured or undisciplined environments, criminality or substance abuse in the family);
- low levels of vocational and educational skills; and
- substance abuse.

Many correctional institutions expanded curriculum to include special programs that target social issues (i.e., domestic violence, substance abuse, antisocial behavior, job readiness, cognitive skills development) (Crayton & Neusteter, 2008; MacKenzie, 2008; Steurer et al., 2001). However, it is acknowledged that the successful implementation of these programs is contingent not only on modifying the behavior of the inmates but also the culture of the facilities that house them (Christensen & Clawson, 2006; Gornik, 2002; Mellow, Mukamal, LoBuglio, Solomon, & Osborne, 2008; Solomon, Osborn, LoBuglio, Mellow, & Mukamal, 2008; Travis, 2003).

Correctional Institution Culture

Jails and prisons are components of a larger criminal justice system that includes community police, judges, treatment providers, case managers, counselors, and community resources. "Jail reentry strategies will only work when the culture of the institution supports the end goals and [when] reentry programming, treatment, and operations are thoroughly integrated into everyday activities" (Solomon et al., 2008, p. 40). The National Institute of Corrections defines culture as "the values, assumptions, and beliefs the people in an organization hold, that drive the way they think and behave within [that] organization" (National Institute of Corrections, 2007, p. v). It is important to examine the cultural mindset of correctional officers to evaluate whether they are in alignment with the objectives and delivery of the program (Christensen & Clawson, 2006; Gornik, 2002; Mellow et al., 2008; Solomon et al., 2008; Travis, 2003). "Professionals within criminal justice systems seldom [agree on] correctional strategy and [are often in opposition with] one another in deed as well as perspective" (Christensen & Clawson, 2006, p. 4). The debate often centers on fiscal concerns rather than the benefits to those who are incarcerated. Often community and institutional correctional officers are pitted against one another with regards to punishment versus rehabilitation.

All those in contact with program participants influence the effectiveness of the educational process (Christensen & Clawson, 2006). Success can be achieved only if the culture of correctional institution values reentry services as much as it does the care, custody, and control of inmates. Correctional staff must be embraced by program objectives. This can be difficult if they view rehabilitation duties as additional burdens in an already overloaded work routine (Mellow, 2008).

Since a major part of the implementation of these programs falls on the correctional officers, it is essential to examine and perhaps adjust their beliefs and attitudes (Brazzell, Crayton, Mukamal, Solomon, & Lindahl, 2009). As the objective of incarceration shifts from punishment to rehabilitation, the role of the correctional officer must also reform. They must find a way of reconciling custodial responsibilities (security) with helping inmates to rehabilitate. Staff must adhere to procedures and rules while being interactive and flexible with inmates (Finn, 2000). This complex tapestry of individual priorities and perspectives must align with program objectives.

Program models that are control-oriented hinder rehabilitation and treatment (Craig, 2004). This new multifaceted model is in direct opposition to the historical role of correctional staff. Previously, they were the custodians and controllers of inmates. Correctional personnel manage overcrowded environments that are rife with disruptions (racial and gang violence, substance abuse, mental health problems, sexual deviation, HIV/ AIDS). Long hours (due to understaffing), constant threat of assault, and limited support in emergencies contribute to a stressful professional life

(Brodsky, 1982; Delprino, 2002; Finn, 1998, 2000; Grossi, Keil, & Vito, 1996).

The organizational structure of corrections has traditionally focused on hierarchical control with officers expected to follow orders issued by superiors (Duffee, 1974; Lombardo, 1985). Correctional officers are simultaneously at the bottom of the administrative chain of command, while at the top of the chain that governs the inmates. This can lead to conflicting behaviors and attitudes amongst the officers. Often correctional personnel share negative perceptions of inmates and their capacity to rehabilitate; this can make change difficult, if not impossible (Duffee, 1974; Lombardo, 1985). The California Performance Review found that a code of silence exists in correctional institutions; members are reluctant to report wrongdoing by their peers. This behavior undermines the intent and purpose of correctional institutions and is detrimental to any rehabilitation program (California Performance Review, 2007).

The success of rehabilitative programs is often contingent upon the ability of correctional institutions to change their culture. Organizational values, hiring practices, training, policies, and reward systems need to be evaluated and, in some cases, reconfigured.

ELEMENTS OF EDUCATION-BASED INCARCERATION PROGRAMS

Program Design Challenges: Many challenges exist for those designing EBI programs. Student-inmates may lack educational foundation and requisite skills or be unable to cope with the psychosocial stressors of their environment. Inmates are also vulnerable to peer and staff pressure that may inhibit their ability to attend classes (Mentor, n.d., para. 7). Added to these concerns about student readiness are the obstacles presented by limits on facilities, time, and funding available for educational programs (Brazzell et al., 2009; Coley & Barton, 2006; Hill, 2008; MacKenzie, 2008; Osborne & Solomon, 2006; Solomon et al., 2008).

Design Guidelines: A 2002 Urban Institute report on correctional education concluded that educational and vocational programs work when they address several important factors:

- "[Program design must be] multimodal [and] address multiple needs.… For many individuals, correctional education may need to occur in tandem with substance abuse treatment, cognitive-behavioral therapy, job preparation, and other activities" (Brazzell et al., 2009, p. 20).

- Programs increase postrelease employment and reduce recidivism when they are well designed and effectively implemented (Brazzell et al., 2009, p. 16).
- Designs must promote positive behavior by enhancing cognitive abilities and decision-making skills (cited in Brazzell et al., 2009, p. 17).
- Action must be taken to repair deficits in social cognition (understanding social interactions and the behavior of others), executive cognitive functioning (the ability to plan and implement goal-directed behavior), problem solving abilities, and self-efficacy—all problems associated with criminal and antisocial behavior." (cited in Brazzell et al., 2009, p. 17).
- Employment programs should focus on employable skills, integrated with support programs, and delivered close to the prisoner's release date. Sufficient time is needed for skills and work habits to be internalized. Aftercare services are crucial to support and reinforce newly acquired abilities (Lawrence, Mears, Dubin, & Travis, 2002).

Programming Guideline: Certain preliminary procedural steps are critical to effective program management. Of paramount importance is providing a safe, supportive, and comfortable educational environment. The recruitment of student inmates should include a comprehensive orientation that covers behavioral expectations and realistic outcomes. Finally, a clear assessment of student goals, skill levels, and needs are mandatory to enable the development of individualized learning plans for each student (Brazzell et al., 2009).

Program Implementation: Since the 1980s, correctional education has shifted from a punitive model to a focus on rehabilitation, and now to evidence-based treatments during incarceration. In an effort to reduce recidivism, many jails and prisons offer a wide range of academic classes, vocational programs, social and life skills studies, and substance abuse and mental health counseling (Steurer et al., 2001). Developing a curriculum that is effective despite the short duration of most jail terms—from entry to release into the community or transfer to prison—can be challenging. The critical question arises: Which elements are necessary for positive outcomes, irrespective of length of incarceration? Several meta-analyses of intervention programs have been conducted in an effort to identify what works. Many of these principles have a common set of features (Aos et al., 2006; Brazzell et al., 2009; MacKenzie, 2008; Phipps et al., 1999; Przybylski, 2008).

First, effective programs emphasize individual rehabilitation through skills building, cognitive development, and behavioral change. Achieving cognitive and behavioral change is necessary before other activities can be of value.

Second, the programs must target the multiple needs of the client. Criminogenic behaviors are often related to a network of risk factors, including substance abuse, mental illness, poor education, inadequate social skills, and inappropriate behaviors. Programs need to go beyond the boundaries of the locked facility and continue after the inmate is released from custody.

Third, programs need to be implemented with integrity based on a clear theoretical framework, grounded in research, and delivered by staff in an environment that is aligned with the program. Services should be delivered by qualified, trained staff, who follow standardized protocols. (Brazzell, 2009; MacKenzie, 2008).

Fourth, reliable and appropriate assessment tools should be used to identify needs and appraise risks. The assessments should guide the instructional plan (Aos et al., 2006, Brazzell, 2009; MacKenzie, 2008; Phipps et al., 1999; Przybylski, 2008).

Common Elements: Gehring and Rennie (2008) examined four major schools of thought about correctional education, spanning over 150 years. Their research identified nine important elements. They are:

- *Central to all forms of education is the pedagogy/andragogy continuum:* As the maturity level of both adult and juveniles may not be predicated on their chronological age, a strong knowledge of both pedagogy and andragogy is important. Additionally, a flexibility and willingness to adapt teaching styles to the individual needs of the inmates is required (Genring & Rennie, 2008).

- *Understand that correctional education is more than just vocation education:* While vocational education is essential to developing job-readiness, other components are equally important. To enhance employability, vocational instruction should be delivered in tandem with academic studies (Genring & Rennie, 2008).

- *Social education commonly referred to as life skills, must be a substantial part of any curriculum:* MacCormick's research states that nearly every prisoner needs social education. Social education is the locus around which all other functions of a prison system should function, including facility design and staff/inmate relationships.

- *Correctional education should blend academic and vocational subject matter with curriculum focused on personal development:* Correctional education should include, but not be limited to adult basic, secondary, postsecondary, English as a second language, and vocational education. Prisoners should also be given an opportunity to explore areas of personal enrichment. They would benefit from the availability of art, poetry music, computer applications, and other intellectually stimulating subjects (Genring & Rennie, 2008).

- *Contrary to correctional philosophy, there must be shared responsibility:* Facilities that employed elements of shared responsibility and democratic ideals were successful in the areas of "educational achievement, industrial production, [and a] reduction [in facility violence and drug offenses]. [Also noteworthy were the] improved ... relations between prisons and outside communities" (Gehring & Rennie, 2008, p. 4).

- *Inclusive and multicultural education can expand educational opportunities:* Inmates in need of special and English language education need equal access to educational resources. Multicultural education may facilitate improved relations between prisoners of ethnically diverse backgrounds by promoting tolerance within highly segregated inmate populations.

- *Technology, when properly used, can motivate inmates and provide positive educational opportunities:* In addition to providing marketable job skills, technology provides connectivity beyond the confines of their environment.

- *All inmates must have access to a diverse library:* A well-stocked and accessible library promotes mental development and is the most important feature in any educational program.

- *Correctional educators need access to administrative structure and system configuration:* A collaborative environment should influence all decisions, which are based on relevant research and sound theory.

Current Programs

Foley and Gao's review of 33 experimental and quasi-experimental studies indicated that academically based educational programs were more effective at reducing recidivism than correctional work. The positive affect on the psychological well being of the inmate-students was reflected in a reduction in facility behavioral problems. Common elements included subject matter (adult basic Education, GED, vocational training) and instructional methods (computer-assisted and teacher-directed learning). All programs conducted standardized needs assessments. Special accommodations were made for those with learning disabilities and special education requirements. Instruction was delivered to small groups or via individual instruction. Programs also employed a variety of instructional materials, which addressed the diversity of academic abilities of their students. (Foley & Gao, 2004). The following programs differ in design but share the common intent of reducing recidivism.

Peer-to-Peer Tutorial Program: The Don't Forget Us (DFU) program, administered through the District of Columbia Department of Corrections, is illustrative of the success of peer-to-peer tutoring programs. DFU was designed to enhance academic achievement in Adult Literacy and GED programs participants and is an inmate-driven program based on the "each one, teach one" learning model. The goal of DFU is to provide participants with the skills and knowledge necessary to pass the GED examination. The program segregates participants in two designated housing units within the Central Detention Facility away from the general jail population. Separating participants increases the probability of positive outcomes by limiting exposure to negative and counterproductive pressure. Students work together toward a common goal—usually passage of the GED exam. DFU units follow a strict code of conduct. All students acknowledge full compliance by signing a copy of the rules and regulations. Any infraction results in immediate removal without any option for reentry.

Tutors are carefully selected. They must demonstrate a sincere desire to teach others, exemplary character, and personal academic achievement (GED or higher). A rigorous testing phase confirms their academic abilities and ascertains whether they possess the personality traits required for a leadership role. Tutoring in both English and Spanish is available and tutorial assignments are based on specific GED subject mastery. The Tutor Organization, a self-monitoring component, fosters accountability and guarantees that tutors adhere to program rules and guidelines.

Since its inception in Fall 2007, DFU program participants have maintained a 49% passage rate on the GED exam. Although this figure may seem less than stellar, it is remarkable when one considers the low academic abilities of many incarcerated individuals. Moreover, more than 50% fewer infractions were committed by participants housed in the DFU unit (Correctional Reporter, 2010).

Cognitive behavioral therapy programs: Another approach to correctional education that has demonstrated promise is cognitive behavioral therapy (CBT). CBT seeks to integrate an individual's thought processes with their subsequent behaviors. The premise of CBT is that by enabling someone to envision alternative courses of action, movement toward positive social behavior will occur. A consistent and increasing body of research supports its positive influence on rehabilitation and recidivism rates (Aos et al., 2006; Brazzell et al., 2009, Lipsey & Cullen, 2007; MacKenzie, 2008; Phipps et al., 1999; Przybylski, 2008). CBT incorporates self-concept reformation, anger management, and normalization of family relationships, civic and legal responsibilities, victim awareness, personal health and hygiene issues, and job preparation. CBT uses positive reinforcement, emphasizing self-control and personal responsibility.

CBT programs address criminogenic needs and behaviors. Research shows that CBT increases interest and participation in educational pursuits and substance abuse rehabilitation. (MacKenzie, 2008). In a review of twenty-five CBT programs, the Washington State Institute on Public Policy found that CBT programs decreased recidivism by 8.2%. All CBT programs reviewed were well-defined and provided staff with comprehensive manuals and training regimens. Reasoning and Rehabilitation, Moral Reconation Therapy (MRT), and Thinking for a Change, are three such programs (Phipps et al., 1999).

Reasoning and Rehabilitation teaches social cognitive skills to offenders. The program emphasizes the development of awareness of thought patterns and attitudes. Alternative paths that lead to more positive social behaviors and outcomes are introduced. Over time, offenders' impulsive, reactive thinking patterns are modified and replaced with more thoughtful actions that include acknowledgement of behavioral consequences. Research on the effectiveness of the Reasoning and Rehabilitation program is mixed. An early study using a small sample indicated success with both high- and low-risk offenders. However, follow-up studies have shown no significant effect on participants (Phipps et al., 1999).

MRT is a cognitive-behavioral therapy originally devised for prison-based drug therapy programs. The primary goal of MRT is the moral development of the inmate. MRT is based on the belief that "criminal ... behaviors are defense mechanisms that are a reaction to tension that is a product of conflict between personality and the inner self" (Armstrong, 2003, p. 670). Nine defined stages of moral development are paralleled by nine treatment steps aimed at the participant's evolution to higher levels of moral reasoning. MRT contains both cognitive and behavioral elements. It incorporates evaluations of familial and peer relationships with the development of strategies for responding to life's dilemmas.

Several studies have been conducted on the effectiveness of MRT on reducing recidivism. Study findings reveal a significant reduction on the 5-year rate of incarceration among those participating in this program (37.1% compared to 54.9% of the control group). Questions have been raised about the methodology of these studies, indicating a need for further study before any conclusions about the efficacy of MRT can be definitively drawn (Armstrong, 2003).

Thinking for a Change is an integrated cognitive behavior change program for adult offenders produced by the National Institute of Corrections. It focuses on enhancing the problem solving abilities of participants. A synthesis of cognitive restructuring and cognitive skills interventions provides the means for achieving the desired results. Lesson topics include active listening, finding new thinking, knowing your feelings, understanding and responding to the feelings of others, preparing for stressful conversations, responding to anger, and dealing with accusation (Bush, Glick, & Taymans, 1997).

A study into the effectiveness of the Thinking for Change program indicated a trend toward lower recidivism among program participants. Thirty-three percent fewer subjects who completed the program committed new offenses, compared to those who did not participate. Additionally, technical violations of probation were significantly higher for program dropouts than for completers. Researchers found that those who completed the program had improved problem-solving skills, which may have profoundly influenced their behavioral changes (Golden, Gatchel, & Cahill, 2006).

Anger Management Program: Some programs focus on anger management, which theorizes that violence results from an inability to identify and control disruptive emotions. These programs focus on participants' developing an understanding of how their emotional states, irrational thoughts, reactions to stress, and anger can lead them into violent actions. The goal is for individuals to understand the thoughts and triggers that prompt their aggressive behavior. Participants are given strategies that enable them to reduce stress and mitigate violent thoughts, thereby reducing the probability that they will resort to aggressive behavior. The Cognitive Self-Change program helps offenders recognize their aberrant thoughts and the role they play in antisocial behavior and reasoning. Participants are taught to identify and change the thinking patterns that induce criminogenic behaviors (Phipps et al., 1999).

Multidiscipline Treatment Programs: LASD currently employs several different multidiscipline treatment modules. Among the most successful are the MERIT (Maximizing Education Reaching Individual Transformation) and the SMART (Social Mentoring Academic and Rehabilitative Training) programs.

The goal of the MERIT program is for inmates to develop an understanding of personal commitment, responsibility, and accountability for their life choices. Its curriculum includes: Bridges to Recovery—a two phase domestic violence intervention and recovery program; the Veteran's Program—a two phase individualized program for honorably discharged U.S. military veterans, focused on restoring self-worth, pride and hope; and the Impact program—a therapeutic drug treatment program. Each program is designed to create the cognitive shifts necessary to enable rehabilitation and successful reentry into society (LASD EBI, n.d., pp. 31-32)

The SMART program is a nationally recognized curriculum that addresses those issues that directly effect gay and transgender inmates within the Los Angeles County jail system. Education, health, and life skills components are integrated into a holistic model that is administered by facility staff, volunteers, and community partners. The mutual commitment to the program by both staff and inmates facilitates the rehabilitation process for those involved (LASD EBI, 2010, p. 32-33).

CONCLUSIONS AND IMPLICATIONS

The duration of incarceration in most jail facilities is short. It is estimated that few than 20% of jail inmates stay longer than 1 month (Beck, 2006). Most are charged with misdemeanor crimes. For many offenders, their incarceration also marks the first time that social, health, and public safety risks may be identified and addressed. Regardless of the effectiveness of any correctional programs, prisoners are rarely involved in them very long. For that reason, access to community-based services that mitigate risks and attend to the needs of former offenders are a critical factor in reducing recidivism. Once released, inmates often reenter the same environment that prompted the criminal behavior in the first place. They may also face continuing substance abuse, physical or mental health problems, homelessness, and unemployment issues (James, 2004; Osborne & Solomon, 2006; Solomon et al., 2008).

Although nearly 75% of the inmates in state prisons lack a high school diploma, an unequivocal connection between inadequate education and criminal behavior has yet to be substantiated (Harlow, 2003; MacKenzie, 2008). Even if an immutable connection between academic achievement and eventual incarceration is proven, there are certainly additional factors that cause an individual to peregrinate, often repeatedly, the distance between law-abiding citizen and outlaw. Lack of education does not necessarily predispose someone to a life of crime. Many undereducated people live their lives within the bounds of socially accepted behavioral norms.

The issue of recidivism is complex. No panacea, educational or otherwise, exists will easily resolve it. Until all the root causes of antisocial behavior are discovered, it is doubtful that any educational program will be the sole vehicle to achieving substantive changes in inmate behavior. With that understanding, the ideas presented here may still prove useful as a framework. They are a guide to some of the basic elements necessary to producing correctional programs that offer some benefit to inmates during their brief time in jails.

The odds of inmates committing crimes after release and reentering a correctional facility are better than 50% (Pew Charitable Trusts, 2011). If changes in correctional institutions are not forthcoming, these dire statistics will continue. While anecdotal evidence suggests that some educational programs are proving effective in changing criminal behavior and reducing recidivism, additional research and testing is required. The multiprong strategy that will produce significant, universal, and indelible effects has not been devised.

Absent these postrelease options, it is doubtful that the programs available to prisoners during their incarceration will have any long-term effect on their life choices (Solomon et al., 2008). Reducing recidivism requires more than coursework during jail-time; it necessitates a transformation in a prisoner's postincarceration world. According to the Urban Institute, nearly half of the prisoners surveyed expressed trepidation about returning to their former neighborhoods. Paradoxically, current policy either encourages or mandates that individuals return to their last county of residence (Lawrence et al., 2002). This one action sets the stage for repeated failure. A simple change of postincarceration environment may be an integral part of limiting the cyclical nature of repeated incarceration.

A long-term assessment of the benefits derived from education acquired during incarceration is needed. Tracking former inmates and evaluating these effects may help us garner insight into the relative effectiveness of EBI program components. Such information is vital if we are to construct meaningful programs in the future. Without verifiable data, we resort to speculation and anecdotal observations to design curriculum and programs. Considering the cost of recidivism, in both money and human lives, a more scientifically based foundation must be established for programming decisions.

Whether we approach this problem altruistically or practically, a solution needs to be found. Ultimately, comprehensive programs may be the answer. Our task is to discover the key in each situation within the brief time inmates are available to us. This mission necessitates assessment of individual needs, application of appropriate remediation, reinforcement of remedies beyond prison walls, and transposition of detrimental environmental influences. It is an alchemic undertaking but one necessary for our goal of human transformation.

REFERENCES

Andrews, D. A., & Bonta, J. (2003). *The psychology of criminal conduct.* Cincinnati, OH: Anderson.

Aos, S., Miller, M., & Drake, E. (2006). *Evidence-based adult corrections programs: What works and what does not.* Retrieved from http://www.wsipp.wa.gov/pub

Armstrong, T. A. (2003). The effect of moral reconation therapy on the recidivism of youthful offenders. *Criminal Justice and Behavior, 30*(6), 668-687.

Beck, J. J. (2006). *The importance of successful reentry to jail population growth*. Retrieved from http://www.urban.org/projects/reentry-roundtable/upload/beck

Brazzell, D., Crayton, A., Mukamal, S.A., Solomon, A. L., & Lindahl, N. (2009). *From the classroom to the community: Exploring the role of education during incarceration and reentry*. Washington, DC: Urban Institute Justice Policy Center.

Brodsky, C. M. (1982). Work stress in correctional institutions. *Journal of Prison and Jail Health, 2*(2), 74-102.

Bush, J., Glick, B., & Taymans, J. (1997). *Thinking for a change: Integrated cognitive behavior change program*. Washington, DC: The National Institute of Corrections, U.S. Department of Justice.

California Performance Review. (2007). *Ethics and culture*. Retrieved from http://cpr.ca.gov/Review_Panel/Ethics_and_Culture.html

Christensen, G., & Clawson, E. (2006). *Our system of corrections: Do jails play a role in improving offender outcomes?* Retrieved from http://www.urban.org/reentryroundtable/cji_jails_draft.pdf.

Coley, R. J., & Barton, P. E. (2006). *Locked up and locked out: An educational perspective on the U.S. prison population*. Princeton, NJ: Educational Testing Service.

Correction Reporter. (2010). *DC doc education program*. Retrieved from http://www.correctionsreporter.com/2010/06/05/dc-doc-inmate-education-program/

Craig, S. C. (2004). Rehabilitation versus control: An organizational theory of prison management. *International Journal of Offender Therapy and Comparative Criminology, 53*(3), 348-365.

Crayton, A., & Neusteter, S. R. (2006). *The current state of correctional education*. Retrieved from http://www.urban.org/projects/reentry-roundtable/upload/crayton.pdf

Delprino, R. P. (2002). *Work and family support services for correctional officers and their family members: A national survey* (NCJ Publication number 192292). Washington, DC: National Institute of Justice, U.S. Department of Justice.

Duffee, D. (1974). The correction officer subculture and organizational change. *The Journal of Research in Crime and Delinquency, 11*(2), 155-172.

Finn, P. (1998). Correctional officer stress: A cause for concern and additional help. *Federal Probation, 62* (2). 65-74.

Finn, P. (2000). *Addressing correctional officer stress: Programs and strategies*. Retrieved April 2, 2011 from http://nicic.gov/?q=Finn%2c+P.%2c+(2000)%2c++Addressing+correctional+officer+stress%3a+programs+and+strategies

Foley, R. M., & Gao, J. (2004). Correctional education: Characteristics of academic programs serving incarcerated adults. *The Journal of Correctional Education, 55*(1), 6-21.

Gehring, T., & Rennie, S. (2008). *What works, and why? And what doesn't work, and why? The search for best practices in correctional education*. Retrieved from http://www.csusb.edu/coe/programs/correctional_ed/documents/WhatWorks.short.pdf

Gendreau, P., & Andrews, D. A. (1990). Tertiary prevention: What the meta-analysis of the offender treatment literature tells us about "what works." *Canadian Journal of Criminology, 32*(1). 173-184.

Gendron, D., & Cavan, J. J. (1990). Managing a successful inmate-education program: Why and how? *Community College Review, 18*(1), 31-39.

Golden, L. S., Gatchel, R. J., & Cahill, M. A. (2006). Evaluating the effectiveness of the National Institute of Corrections' "Thinking For A Change" program among probationers. *Journal of Offenders Rehabilitation, 43*(2), 55-73.

Gornik, M. (2002). *Moving from correctional program to correctional strategy: Using proven practices to change criminal behavior.* Retrieved from http://www.unafei .or.jp/referencematerials/135th/135thweb/English_pdf/ V%20Correctional%20Programmes/1%20General%20Effective% 20Correctional%20Interventions/017624.pdf

Grossi, E. L., Keil, T. J., & Vito, G. F. (1996). Surviving the joint: Mitigating factors or correctional officer stress. *Journal of Crime and Justice, 14*(2), 103-120.

Harer, M. D. (1994). *Recidivism among federal prisoners released in 1987.* Retrieved from http://www.bop.gov/news/research_projects/published_reports /recidivism/oreprrecid87.pdf

Harer, M. D. (1995). *Prison education program participation and recidivism: A test of the normalization hypotheses.* Retrieved from http://www.bop.gov/news/research _projects/published_reports/recidivism/orepredprg.pdf

Harlow, C. W. (2003). *Education and correctional populations.* Bureau of Justice Statistics Special Report (NCJ 195670). Washington, DC: U. S. Department of Justice, Bureau of Justice Statistics.

Hill, E. G. (2008). *From cellblocks to classrooms: Reforming inmate education to improve public safety.* Retrieved from http://www.lao.ca.gov/2008/crim/inmate _education/inmate_education_021208.pdf

James, D. J. (2004). *Profile of jail inmates, 2002.* Retrieved from http://www.ojp .usdoj.gov/bjs/pub/pdf/pji02.pdf

Kirshstein, R., & Best, C. (1996). *Survey of state correctional education systems: Analysis of data from 1992 field test.* Washington, DC: Pelavin Research Institute.

Lawrence, S., Mears, D., Dubin, G., & Travis, J. (2002). *The practice and promise of prison programming.* Washington DC: Urban Institute.

Lipsey, M. S., & Cullen, F. T. (2007). The effectiveness of correctional rehabilitation: A review of systematic reviews. *Annual Review of Law and Social Science, 3,* 297-320.

Lombardo, L. X. (1985). Group dynamics and the prison guard subculture: Is the subculture and impediment to helping inmates? *International Journal of Offender Therapy and Comparative Criminology, 29*(1), 79-90.

Los Angeles County Sheriffs Department. (2010). *Education-based incarceration.* Retrieved from http://www.lasdhq.org/releases/1-EBI/E.B.I.pdf

MacCormack, A. H. (1931). Education in the prisons of tomorrow. *The Annals of the American Academy of Political and Social Science—Prisons of Tomorrow, 152*(1), 72-77.

MacKenzie, D. L. (2008, February). *Structure and components of successful educational programs.* Paper presented at the Reentry Roundtable on Education, John Jay College of Criminal Justice, New York.

McKelvey, B. (1977). *American prisons: A history of good intentions.* Montclair, NJ: Patterson Smith.

Mellow, J., Mukamal, D., LoBuglio, S. F., Solomon, A. L., & Osborne, J. (2008). *The jail administrator's toolkit for reentry.* Retrieved from http://www.ojp.usdoj.gov/BJA/pdf/ToolkitForReentry.pdf

Mentor, K. W., & Wilkinson, M. (n.d.). *Literacy in correction.* Retrieved from http://kenmentor.com/papers/literacy.htm

National Institute of Corrections. (2007). *Building culture strategically: A team approach for corrections.* Retrieved from http://ncic.gov/Library/Files/021749.pdf

Osbourne, J., & Solomon, A. L. (2006). *Jail reentry roundtable meeting summary.* Retrieved from http://www.urban.org/uploadedpdf/411368_jrr_meeting_summary.pdf

Pew Charitable Trusts. (2011). *Pew Center on the States, state of recidivism: The revolving door of America's prisons.* Retrieved from http://www.pewcenteronthestates.org/uploadedFiles/Pew_State_of_Recidivism.pdf

Phipps, P., Korinek, K., Aos, S., & Lieb, R. (1999). *Research findings on adult corrections' programs: A review* (Doc. No: 99-01-1203). Olympia, WA: Washington State Institute for Public Policy.

Przybylski, R. (2008). *What works. Effective recidivism reduction and risk-focused prevention programs: A compendium of evidence-based options for preventing new and persistent criminal behavior.* Denver, CO: Bureau of Justice Assistance through DCJ's Office of Adult and Juvenile Assistance, Bureau of Justice Statistics, the National Institute of Justice, the Office of Juvenile, Justice and Delinquency Prevention, and the Office for Victims of Crime.

Silver, R. (2010). *Washington county commissioners approve jail GED training program.* Retrieved from http://www.kjrh.com/dpp/bartlesvillelive/washington-county-commissioners-approve-jail-ged-training-program1302118153717

Smith, L. G., & Silverman, M. (1994). Functional literacy education for jail inmates: An examination of the Hillsborough County jail education program. *Prison Journal, 74* (4), 415-434.

Solomon, A. L., Osborne, J. W. L., LoBuglio, S. F., Mellow, J., & Mukamal, D. A. (2008). *Life after lockup: Improving re-entry from jail to community.* Washington, DC: Urban Institute, Justice Policy Center.

Steurer, S., Smith, L., & Tracy, A. (2001). *Three state recidivism study.* Lanham, MD: Correctional Education Association.

Travis, J. (2003, November). *In thinking about "what works," what works best?* Presented the Margaret Mead Address at the National Conference of the International Community Corrections Association held in Indianapolis, Indiana. Retrieved from http://jpc.urban.org

Werner, D. (2003). *Correctional education: Theory and practice.* LaVerne, CA: The University of LaVerne.

Wilson, D. B., MacKenzie, D. L., & Mitchell, F. G. (2000). A meta-analysis of corrections-based education, vocation, and work program for adult offenders. *Journal of Research in Crime and Delinquency, 37* (4), 347-368.

PART IV

IMPLICATIONS FOR THE FUTURE
OF CORRECTIONAL EDUCATION

CHAPTER 11

SUMMARY, IMPLICATION, AND RECOMMENDATIONS

Anthony H. Normore, Brian D. Fitch, and Sarah Camp

The term *social justice* is an elusive construct, politically loaded, and subject to numerous interpretations (Jean-Marie, Normore, & Brooks, 2009). Its foundation is rooted in theology and social work and it has deep roots in educational disciplines like curriculum and pedagogy (Apple, 1996; Freire, 1998). Social justice has also been studied in law, philosophy, economics, political science, sociology, psychology, anthropology, and public policy (Brooks, 2008). However, it is a relatively new term to fields of educational leadership (Shoho, Merchant, & Lugg, 2005) and correctional education (Camp, 2008; Meloy, 2006). Social justice has become a major concern for educators in many disciplines and is driven by many factors (e.g., cultural transformation and demographic shift of Western society, increased economic gaps of underserved populations, and public accountability pressures and high stakes testing) (Kumashiro, 2004); and rates of recidivism in county jails and prisons (Karpowitz & Kenner, 2004; Lawrence, Mears, Dubin, & Travis, 2002; Wolford, 1989).

In a similar vein, *education-based incarceration* (EBI) and correctional education take a penetrating look at the needs and challenges of society's disenfranchised—the denizens of our streets, the emotionally and physically incarcerated, our children in juvenile hall and in unsettled homes. It is

Education-Based Incarceration and Recidivism:
The Ultimate Social Justice Crime-Fighting Tool, pp. 199–208
Copyright © 2012 by Information Age Publishing
All rights of reproduction in any form reserved.

incumbent to encourage public awareness of the causes that underlie the destructive cycles plaguing these populations, including the abuse and neglect that cycle through generations. When effectively addressed through education the economic burden on society is lightened and an advocacy to increase understanding engenders a humane response. Interestingly enough, when connecting EBI to social justice several issues come to mind. As mentioned earlier, definitions of social justice are based on a variety of factors, like political orientation, religious background, and political and social philosophy (Welsh & Farrington, 2007). If a postmodernist is asked to define this concept, he or she is likely to tell you "it's a fairytale that is not in any way achievable in any form of society." Consequently, a general definition of social justice is hard to arrive at and even harder to implement. In essence, social justice is concerned with equal justice, not just in the courts, but in all aspects of society. Social justice demands that people promote a just society where people have equal rights and opportunities; everyone, from the poorest person on the margins of society to the wealthiest deserves an even playing field.

Camp (2008), in *An Explanatory Mixed Methods Content Analysis of Two State Level Correctional Institutions*, denoted "the emphasis of correctional programming may vary because the ideology of prison leadership did not remain the same throughout time, as well as the purpose of prisons. This may be caused by societal and political shifts of opinions throughout time" (Camp, 2008, pp. 10-11). Furthermore, if it difficult to put social justice into practice, imagine how difficult it is putting into practice relating it to social justice to the criminal justice system because the U.S. citizens are unable to share a common view of their correctional system (Camp, 2008; DiIulio, 1992). Also, she stated the correctional justice system in the United States was described as dysfunctional and its citizens are unsure about its purpose. For instance, the United States wants the correctional system to punish or to desist and seek harm on the guilty; to rehabilitate or to become law-abiding citizens; to deter to discourage future acts of crime; to incapacitate or to prevent others from being victimized; reintegrate, to return to society as productive law abiding citizens (Camp, 2008; DiIulio, 1992). Yet, they desire for the criminal justice system with human treatment and enforcing constitutional rights, as well as implementing with cost containment and without weakening of the federal and local governments (Camp, 2008; DiIulio, 1992).

According to Camp (2008) and others (e.g., Bosworth, 2002), "researchers, policy makers, and educational program administrators in the field of corrections must remember that the purpose of education is rehabilitation intended" (Camp, 2008, p. 50) to enhance public safety and social order (American Correctional Association, 1986; Camp, 2008). Camp further iterated that:

One could surmise that it is necessary that the proper design of prerelease materials be provided to the offenders for the purposes of helping them become law-abiding citizens and preventing them from recidivating (Karpowitz & Kenner, 2004). Prisons then should increase opportunities for offenders to be released as law-abiding citizens. Hence, it would behoove researchers, policy makers, and educational program administrators in the field of corrections to investigate the materials, specifically, the prerelease curricula for adult offenders to see if they provide information that aided offenders in becoming law-abiding citizens. Such research would provide opportunities for correctional facilities to learn how to maximize their correctional training or rehabilitative functions. (Camp, 2008, p. 50)

Los Angeles County: Context of Education-Based Incarceration

For years, inmates have served their sentences in county jails and prisons throughout the nation with little, if any, educational or vocational training to prepare them for successful transitions back into our communities. This practice has resulted in high rates of recidivism among large numbers of previously incarcerated individuals. As Camp (2008) reports:

Over 60% of the offenders represented in the only two major recidivism studies in 1983and 1994 were rearrested within 3 years (Bureau of Justice Statistics, 2002). Data collected for "the 1994 recidivism study estimated that within 3 years, 51.8% of prisoners released during the year returned to prison either because of a new crime for which they received another prison sentence or because of a technical violation of their parole" (Bureau of Justice Statistics, 2002, para. 7). Furthermore, current views of recidivism rates according to Hughes, Beck, and Black (2001) stated that every year approximately 630,000 criminal offenders reenter society. Less than half were noted that they would avoid trouble for up to 3 years upon release from prison. Many of the released offenders were also noted that they would commit such offences that were violent and/or serious offences when under parole supervision (Camp, 2008, p. 1).

Yet, law enforcement agencies throughout the nation continue to do the same thing over and over again while expecting different results. EBI offers a viable alternative, which focuses on providing inmates the skills necessary to live productive, crime-free lives outside of custody (Bosworth, 2002; Camp, 2008).

According to Fitch (2010), Los Angeles County Sheriff, Lee Baca, long ago recognized the inherent problems with "warehousing" inmates then placing them back into the community. "Yet, society continue[s] to lean toward locking up offenders and throwing away the key" (Meloy, 2006) rather than focusing on the rehabilitation of offenders (Camp, 2008, p. 64; Carlson, Hess, & Orthmann, 1999). "Getting tough on crime" increases the hardships of the correctional system that translate to a burden on society pertaining to a wide array of sociological topics (e.g., family, economics, educations, etc.) (Camp, 2008). As a result of Sheriff Baca's vision and leadership, the Los Angeles County Sheriff's Department is a national leader in educational training, currently offering more than 60 educational, vocational, and life-skills courses to the more than 15,000 inmates housed in the department's nine jail facilities—not including religious study, health education, and family outreach programs. While the results of these programs are promising, law enforcement officials may be understandably hesitant to expend the diminishing monies, resources, and personnel necessary to implement educational programming.

Relevance of Education-Based Incarceration

Probably the most common concern voiced by those who oppose EBI is the idea that criminals should be punished for their offenses (Gehring, 2000). This is a legitimate concern—and not to be taken lightly. Criminals, so the argument goes, should be locked up and made to pay for their offenses. What should offenders do who are removed from society and placed in a confined paramilitary environment? More specifically, what is punishment and what is the most productive method of releasing a law-abiding citizen?

There are a many ideologies that date as far back as 1700 BCE that define punishment (Allen & Simonsen, 1998; Camp, 2008). The first known punishment is retribution. Classic retribution is defined as a brutal or violent punishment according to the gravity of the crime, otherwise known as "an eye of an eye, a tooth for a tooth" based on the desire for revenge (Allen & Simonsen, 1998; Camp, 2008; Walker, 1991). Hence, the fear of the severity of the punishment would deter criminals from committing future crimes and others from committing crimes (Camp, 2008). She explained further that retribution was replaced with Europe's 18th century idea of a social contract. The social contract was an agreement between the citizens and the government allowing the government to be the dominant force. During this era, punishment was defined as controlling the operations of the offender via isolations controlling and manipulating the body, mind, and soul to become law-abiding citizens (Camp, 2008; Foucault, 1995). Foucault (1995) hypothesized that" punishment, according to the law, showed that social and political power could transform, suppress, coerce, destroy, and threaten citizens if they deviated from the law or the norm" (cited in Camp, 2008, p. 32). Camp iterated that the deterrence model "evolved from the social contact and emphasized that the punishment should not exceed the crime" (p. 32).

Camp (2008) further elaborated that the social contract was then transformed into rehabilitation. She reported, in the beginning that U.S. history of modern ideologies of punishment, rehabilitation was described as treatment for disorders enlisting psychiatrists and sociologists to fix offenders to be law-abiding citizens. This type of rehabilitation did not last and was replaced with incapacitation or otherwise described as "locking them up and throwing away the key" (p. 37). Camp indicated that "America had reverted back to the classical philosophy of retribution pertaining to determinate or fixed sentences and incapacitation became a part of the current ideology of punishment" (p. 37).

In spite of getting tough on crime or warehousing offenders, correctional facilities are not winning the battle of releasing law-abiding citizens, but instead are "escalat[ing] the challenges of the correctional system (e.g., overcrowding and incarceration costs)" (Camp, 2008, p. 64).

The United States's correctional history it is know for its getting tough on crime attitude implemented with numerous frameworks, treatments, goals and models is not the answer to releasing law-abiding citizens (Camp, 2008). A prime example is the state of California. The Supreme Court ordered the prison population to be reduced (Supreme Court of the United States, 2011). Yet when done, will there not still be a burden of overcrowding on local law enforcement and criminal justice system, not to mention on the local level will there not be less correctional programs? Consequently, "ideologies of punishment shift throughout time according to political, economical, and social reasons, they open the doors to improve correctional education" (Camp, 2008, p. 195) relating to the improved rehabilitation ideology; hence, the EBI program. Improving educational programs for offenders appears to the most productive method of releasing a law-abiding citizen in assisting the decrease of recidivism rate and overcrowding of correctional institutions (Camp, 2008).

Yet, some people still believe that inmates should be "punished" for their crimes by county jails and state prisons focusing their limited resources on punishment and not education by forming chain gangs, providing cold food, and eliminated frills like television believing offenders are less likely to reoffend. While such perspectives maybe understandable, they seldom achieve their intended effect. The goal of education-based incarceration and/or correctional education programs is to reduce recidivism rates and aid offenders in adapting to society and becoming productive citizens (Hendricks, Hendricks, & Kauffman, 2001). According to Mentor and Wilkinson (2006), "research consistently demonstrate[d] that quality education is one of the most effective forms of crime prevention"

(p. 1). Educational skills and knowledge helped to deter people from committing criminal acts. As a result, education programs decreased the likelihood that people would return to crime and prison (Camp, 2008, p. 3).

The Cost of Education-Based Incarceration

Law enforcement agencies throughout the nation are concerned about the best uses of their limited monies, personnel, and resources. In this era of shrinking local economies, state budget deficits, and staffing shortages, where do police agencies obtain the funding to educate inmates? Surprisingly enough, the Los Angeles Sheriff's Department does not rely on monies from the general fund to finance EBI. The department receives approximately $30 million in annual revenue through contracts with vendors responsible for telephone service, vending machines, and inmate commissary. Additionally, the agency receives about $6 million each year in average daily attendance reimbursement from the state of California, as well as about $200,000 per year from its Jail Enterprises unit—which is responsible for commercial printing, signs, and textiles (Fitch, 2010).

While EBI is funded wholly by inmate welfare funds, the real cost saving are found in reducing the number of inmates who return to custody. According to an article entitled "The High Price of Public Safety," which appeared in the *Orange County Register* on December 6, 2009, the annual cost of housing an inmate in the California prison system is $58,356. Thus, every inmate who transitions successfully to civilian life provides taxpayers with significant cost saving. Similarly, for every inmate who reenters the community with the necessary skills to find gainful employment, there is a corresponding decrease in the number of crimes. Less crime, in turn, translates into enhanced feeling of public safety and greater confidence in law enforcement, while strengthening those neighborhoods against poverty, distrust, and gangs.

REFLECTIONS: IMPLICATIONS AND RECOMMENDATIONS

It is now time for correctional agencies, other government agencies, institutions of higher education, teachers in all walks of life, and society, in general, to take a step forward in collaborative efforts to help reduce the overwhelmingly high rates of recidivism and restore law-abiding citizenship for productive lives. As Camp (2008) indicated, "not all offenders may be helped through improved education, but at least it is a positive attempt to improve society" (p. 196). Partnerships among public sector institutions who are seriously engaged in designing effective programs for EBI not only would improve the public safety and social order of individual states, but also the nation as a whole if they "communicate and share prerelease [or correctional programming/EBI] information" (Camp, 2008, p. 196). Camp further iterates, "The more states that are involved, the greater the effect of not only improving the design of prerelease materials and educating offenders, but also the offenders would become more prepared when involved in the reentry programs" (p. 197). Research (e.g., Layton-McKenzie, 2008; Przybylski, 2008) indicates that education programs such as basic education, General Education Diploma, postsecondary and vocational are effective in reducing recidivism and increasing future employment.

In Camp's (2008) study on correction institutions and prerelease handbooks for curriculum design, she recommended that reentry personnel, or in our terms, EBI program personnel "could establish relegations with a local college or university and inquire about researching prerelease handbook curriculum design" (p.197) and that "such a relationship could lead to other research projects, internships, and foster a positive relationship between the correctional system and the educational community" (p. 197). In response to Camp's recommendation, the EBI unit in Los Angeles is currently working with professional educators to evaluate the department's educational and vocational programs, develop a comprehensive profile of the jail population, identify learning needs, investigate best practices, and develop adult-based instructional methods. Currently, educators from California State University, Dominguez Hills; Los Angeles Unified School District; California State University, Los Angeles; and California State University Long Beach—to name a few—have volunteered their time as part of a curriculum development and review committee. Although it is still too early to tell what the results of these efforts will be, the Los Angeles County Sheriff's Department is understandably optimistic about the partnership.

Clearly, EBI is not for everyone. Certain inmates will undoubtedly refuse to participate, while others will be precluded from contributing because of their preference for violence or their history of jail discipline. Yet for those who choose to partake, EBI can be a life-altering experience in support of social justice where education enables "people to become productive members of society, both as citizens sharing in democratic processes and as workers in the economy" (Camp, 2008, p. 197).

When applying the definition of social justice it is important to feel that even when removed from society and placed in a confining paramilitary environment, Camp (2008), stated offenders deserve an opportunity to improve themselves. In this instance, improvement relates to correctional programming in order to become law-abiding citizens. She asserted many correctional educators operate on the belief that behaviors, attitudes, and ideas. Hence, anything from brutal punishment to incapacitation may not help offenders to reach their potential of becoming a law-abiding citizen (Camp, 2008). She denoted that with suitable curricula of correctional programs, correctional programming can help offenders change their behaviors, attitudes and ideas appears to be a better method of improving society as a whole. This is what makes the correctional system or more specifically, correctional education to known as "correctional" (Gehring, 2003) for the employment of correctional education can reform offenders in prison (Camp, 2008).

Camp (2008) further stressed that "in the end, it is a win-win situation for all: offenders, society, correctional institutions, and local graduate colleges and universities that decide to take part in this endeavor" (p. 197). Hopefully, as more agencies adopt the EBI model, providing offenders opportunities to successfully become law-aiding citizens (Camp, 2008), we can finally begin to reduce the devastating effects of recidivism nationwide.

REFERENCES

Allen, H. E., & Simonsen, C. E. (1998). *Corrections in America* (8th ed). Upper Saddle River, NJ: Prentice Hall.

American Correctional Association. (1986). *Public policy for corrections.* College Park, MD: American Correctional Association.

Apple, M. W. (1995). *Education and power.* New York, NY: Routledge.

Bosworth, M. (2002). *The U.S. federal prison system.* Thousand Oaks, CA: Sage.

Brooks, J. S. (2008). Freedom and justice: Conceptual and empirical possibilities for the study and practice of educational leadership. In I. Bogotch, F. Beachum, J. Blount, J. S. Brooks, & F. W. English, *Radicalizing educational leadership: Toward a theory of social justice* (pp. 61-78). Amsterdam, The Netherlands: Sense.

Bureau of Justice Statistics. (2002). *Reentry trends in the U.S.* Retrieved from http://www.ojp.usdoj.gov/bjs/reentry/recidivism.htm

Camp, S. (2008). *An explanatory mixed methods content analysis of two state level correctional institutions' pre-release handbook curriculum designs, looking through the lenses of two philosophical orientations of education.* Saarbruken, Germany: VDM Verlag Dr. Muller.

Carlson, N. A., Hess, K. M., & Orthmann, C. M. H., (1999). *Corrections in the 21st century: A practical approach.* Belmont, CA: Wadsworth.

DiIulio, J. J., Jr. (1992, December). *Rethinking the criminal Justice system: Toward a new paradigm.* Washington, DC: Bureau of Justice Statistics.

Fitch. B. D. (2010). Education-based incarceration: The ultimate crime fighting strategy. *Deputy*

Foucault, M. (1995). *Discipline and punishment: The birth of the prison.* New York, NY: Vintage Books.

Freire, P. (1998). *Pedagogy of hope.* New York, NY: Continuum.

Gehring, T. (2000). Recidivism as a measure of correctional education program success. *Journal of Correctional Education, 51*(2), 197-205.

Gehring, T. (n.d.). *The history of correctional education.* Retrieved from http://www.ceanational.org/aboutce/history.htm

Hendricks, C., Hendricks, J. E., & Kauffman, S. (2001). *Literacy, criminal activity, and recidivism.* Retrieved from http://www.americanreadingforum.org/01_yearbook/html/12_Hendricks.htm

Jean-Marie, G., Normore, A. H., & Brooks, J. (June, 2009). Leadership for social justice: Preparing 21st century school leaders for a new social order. *Journal of Research on Leadership Education, 4(1).* Retrieved from http://www.ucea.org/current-issues/

Joseph, B., & Saavedra, T. (2009, December 6). The high cost of public safety: How the spiraling costs of police and prisons emptied California's pocketbook. *The Orange County Register,* p. News 1.

Karpowitz, D., & Kenner, M. (2004). *Education as crime prevention: The case for reinstating Pell grant eligibility for incarceration.* Annandale-on-Hudson, NY: Bard College.

Kumashiro, K. K. (2004). *Against common sense: teaching and learning toward social justice.* New York, NY: RoutledgeFalmer.

Lawrence, S., Mears, D., Dubin, G., & Travis, J. (2002). *The practice and promise of prison programming.* Washington, DC: The Urban Institute.

Layton-MacKenzie, D. (2008). *Structure and components of successful educational programs* (Unpublished doctoral dissertation). Department of Criminology and Criminal Justice University of Maryland.

Meloy, M. (2006). *Sentencing the guilty.* Retrieved from http://www.ncsall.net/?id=560

Mentor, K., & Wilkinson, M. (2006). *Literacy in corrections.* Retrieved from http://kenmentor.com/papers/literacy.htm

Przybylski, R. (2008). *Effective recidivism reduction and risk-focused prevention programs: A compendium of evidence-based options for preventing new and persistent criminal behavior.* Washington, DC: Bureau of Justice Assistance through DCJ's Office of Adult and Juvenile Assistance, Bureau of Justice Statistics, the National Institute of Justice, the Office of Juvenile, Justice and Delinquency Prevention, and the Office for Victims of Crime.

Shoho, A. R., Merchant, B. M., & Lugg, C. A. (2005). Social justice: Seeking a common language. In F. W. English (Ed.), *The SAGE handbook of educational leadership: Advances in theory, research, and practice* (pp. 47-67). Thousands Oaks, CA: SAGE.

Supreme Court of the United States: Brown, Governor Of California, Et Al. V. Plata Et Al. (2011). Retrieved from www.supremecourt.gov/opinions/10pdf/09-1233.pdf

Walker, N. (1991). *Why punish?: Theories of punishment reassessed.* Oxford, England: Oxford University.

Welsh, B. C., & Farrington, D. E. (2007.). *Preventing crime: What works for children, offenders, victims, and places.* New York, NY: Springer.

Wolford, B. I. (1989). Correctional facilities. In S. B. Merriam & P. M. Cunningham (Eds.), *Handbook of adult and continuing education* (pp. 356-368). San Francisco, CA: Jossey-Bass.

ABOUT THE AUTHORS

Laura S. Abrams is an associate professor and chair of the doctoral program in social welfare at the UCLA School of Public Affairs. Dr. Abrams is the principal investigator of the "Juvenile Justice and Reentry Project" which seeks to identify and implement research-based solutions for pressing policy and practices related to incarcerated youth. Her research has examined the integration and practice of treatment programs in juvenile correctional facilities and the process of identity change for young offenders. She is conducting research aimed at understanding how neighborhood-rooted interventions can improve reentry experiences and outcomes for young people. Dr. Abrams is the author of over 35 peer-reviewed journal articles on at-risk youth. Her first book on the juvenile justice system will be published by Rutgers University Press in 2012.

Leroy D. Baca joined the Los Angeles County Sheriff's Department in 1965 as a deputy sheriff. He was elected as sheriff of Los Angeles County in 1998, and is currently serving his fourth term. The Los Angeles County Sheriff's Department is the largest sheriff's department in the nation, second largest policing agency in the nation, and manages the largest jail system in the country. Sheriff Baca currently commands a staff of more than 18,000 employees, including more than 9,500 sworn members. Sheriff Baca is widely recognized as a national and international expert on a variety of law-enforcement related topics. He is a veteran of the United States Marine Corps and graduate of the University of Southern California, where he earned a doctorate in public administration.

Sarah Camp has worked in the field of corrections since 1995. From 1995 to 1996, she was employed with the South Carolina Department of Corrections as an activities therapist. In 1996, the Federal Bureau of Prisons hired Dr. Camp as a recreation specialist. In 2003, the bureau promoted

209

her as a case manager: first for the Residential Drug Abuse Program and then for the general population. Dr. Camp has earned a masters in criminology and criminal justice and a PhD in educational leadership and policy from Florida State University.

Jessica Nolan Daugherty has worked in various capacities in Los Angeles County to improve the reentry process and decrease crime. Jessica recently finished working on a blueprint for young offender reentry that has the potential to drastically improve how youth and young adults reenter the community post incarceration. As a Dukakis Fellow, she interned in the office of Los Angeles City Councilman Tony Cardenas where she completed an assessment of the City of Los Angeles' ongoing gang prevention and intervention efforts. She began her career as a community organizer and firmly believes that change is only possible with the support and inclusion of the community. She holds a BA from the University of California, Santa Barbara and a master of public policy from the UCLA School of Public Affairs.

Rakel Delevi, PhD, is currently an assistant professor at California State University, Los Angeles in the Department of Child and Family Studies. Some of her teaching interests include intimate relationships, child development, divorce, and family violence. Her main research is on cross-cultural differences in relationships and use of technology in romantic relationships. She is also in private practice as a marriage and family therapist intern and volunteers at the Southern California Counseling Center.

Carolyn Eggleston, PhD, is currently the director of the Center for the Study of Correctional Education at California State University, San Bernardino and a professor of special education. She has spent her career in correctional education and community reentry, as both a practitioner and researcher. She recently opened a program center for returning parolees, which sees 100 clients a day. Dr. Eggleston spent almost 20 years working in corrections as a diagnostician, teacher, school principal, and supervisor. She has written about special needs juveniles and adults, historical issues in corrections, history or the female prisoner, and education and reentry issues for inmates. She serves as the program administrator for the recently opened program center for parolees in San Bernardino CA, a multiservice center for "one-stop" programs for returning California State prisoners.

M. C. Esposito is an associate professor of education at California State University, Dominguez Hills. Dr. Esposito conducts and publishes research in the areas of inclusion, efficacy beliefs, and teacher preparation. Dr. Esposito has conducted workshops in the areas of bullying, inclusion, response to intervention, and complying with special education law. She received her BA and MA from Loyola Marymount University and her PhD from University of Southern California. She holds multiple subject and mild/moderate teaching credentials. She currently serves on the Los Angeles Sheriff's Department Educational Based Incarceration Steering Committee.

Brian D. Fitch, PhD, is a lieutenant and a 29-year veteran of the Los Angeles County Sheriff's Department. He has worked assignments in corrections, field operations, investigations, training, and administration. Dr. Fitch currently oversees the development, implementation, and assessment of the department's education-based incarceration program. Dr. Fitch holds a part-time faculty position in the psychology department at California State University, Long Beach. He is also the recipient of several Los Angeles County Sheriff's Department honors, including an exemplary service award for developing the department's education-based discipline course, a meritorious service award for creating a conflict management course for supervisors, and a leadership award in recognition of developing and facilitating the Deputy Leadership Institute curriculum to more than 500 law enforcement professionals throughout the nation.

Richard Keith Gordon is a professor of education at California State University Dominguez Hills. His research and scholarship is in the areas of urban teacher education, multicultural education, and global minority education. Dr. Gordon currently is responsible for the professional development community seminars held in conjunction with the Urban Teacher Residency Grant. His international experiences include the role of visiting scholar at Tokyo Gakukei University Curriculum Center, delivered the keynote address at the International Conference on Teacher Education in the Philippines, supervisor of over 50 student teachers from the United States and England through the Educators Abroad program. Through the use of interactive technologies he monitored and supervised these students in Japan, South Korea, Peru, Panama, Thailand, and Costa Rica as they embarked on their careers in the grandest of professions. His work with teachers, students, and administrators is invaluable in conceptualizing the breadth and depth of the educative experience around the world.

Gary Greene is a professor of special education at California State University, Long Beach. He has expertise in the area of transition of youth with disabilities, has published two textbooks on this subject, and conducted numerous state and national presentations on this topic. For the past 10 years Dr. Greene has served as the program evaluator of the

Incarcerated Youth Offenders program for the California Department of Corrections and Rehabilitation The focus of the Incarcerated Youth Offenders program is to provide support services to youth offenders while in prison and upon release in order to reduce crime recidivism as they transition back into society.

Richard Haesly is an associate professor of political science at California State University, Long Beach. His research interests include nationalism and national identities, political psychology, and comparative politics research methods. His interest in education-based incarceration began when he had the pleasure of teaching in two correctional facilities in North Carolina through the Department of Continuing Education at the University of North Carolina, Chapel Hill in 1998 and 1999.

Kimberly B. Hughes is the department chair/academic coordinator of adult secondary education. She teaches academics subjects, parent education and GED for Harbor Community Adult School, a division of Los Angeles Unified School District. As a consultant, Ms. Hughes works with nonprofit organizations, universities, and local school districts in the areas of curriculum development and implementation. Prior to becoming an educator, Ms. Hughes served in the private and public sectors as a financial advisor, gerontologist, and librarian. She has presented at conferences locally, nationally, and internationally. Her areas of research include financial gerontology, charter schools best practices, incarceration education, and pregnant and parenting teens educational outcomes.

Arthur Jones, JD, Drjur, is an American and international lawyer with education in the United States (BA, modern European Languages and political science, magna cum laude, Phi Beta Kappa; subsequently, juris doctor); and in Germany (Rotary International Scholar, Germanic history and literature; Fulbright Scholar, postdoctoral studies, international and comparative law). He has over 37 years of professional experience and residence in some 14 European countries. He is widely published internationally in best policing practices, antiterrorism, labor law, and social policy. He is also author of a work of historical fiction, *The Goths: Children of the Storm* (2009). He is engaged in research and development of education-based incarceration programs for the Los Angeles County Sheriff's Department.

June Kizu holds an EdD from University of California, Los Angeles. She is currently an instructor at California State University at Dominguez Hills and volunteers tutoring young adults at Homeboy Industries, a gang intervention program. June is retired after 32 years of teaching elementary and middle schools in Los Angeles Unified School District. She is coauthor of "Mentoring for Alternative Certification Teachers: Perceptions from the Field," featured in the *Online Journal for the National Association of Alternative Certification* (Spring 2006).

Selene Kurland is currently coordinator of adult basic education (literacy) and teaches academic subjects for Harbor Community Adult School, Los Angeles Unified School District. Ms Kurland has developed and implemented curriculum and educational programs for more than 20 years. Additionally, she is a consultant, specializing in training, adult literacy, and program/curriculum development, whose clients include universities, school districts, governmental agencies, nonprofit organizations, and private industry. Selene has been a featured presenter at conferences for both vocational and adult educators and the recipient of numerous awards, fellowships, grants, and recently a published author in the *Journal of Educational Administration*. She graduated summa cum laude, with honors and distinction, in English and history from CSU, Dominguez Hills, where she also earned an MA in education administration.

Brian A. Mattson holds a PhD in sociology emphasizing studies in criminology at the University of Colorado and a master's degree in criminology from the University of Maryland. Dr. Mattson is currently the president of Northpointe Institute for Public Management, a nationally recognized correctional research, consulting, training, and software development firm that provides services to advance practices in federal, state, and local criminal justice systems. Dr. Mattson has consulted for the National Institute of Corrections, the National Alliance for Drug Endangered Children, the Child Welfare League of America and a wide variety of state and local justice agencies. Prior to his consulting work, he held a variety of posts in Jefferson County, Colorado where he was the director of the Children, Youth, & Families Division, director of the Criminal Justice Planning Division, and was the principal investigator on two federally funded system integration efforts.

Jeff Mulhaussen is the director of strategy and business development for Discovery Education, the education business unit of the Discovery Channel and its sister companies. In his capacity, Mr. Mulhausen works globally with ministries of education, publishers, leading technology companies, and other education focused entities to leverage digital solutions to improve student achievement. Mr. Mulhausen graduated with highest honors from Pennsylvania State University in accounting.

Anthony H. Normore holds a PhD from OISE/University of Toronto. He is associate professor and program development coordinator of the Doctorate Degree in Educational Leadership program at California State University Dominguez Hills in Los Angeles. Dr. Normore's research focuses on leadership development, preparation, and socialization of urban school leaders in the context of ethics and social justice. His most recent books include *Global Perspectives on Educational Leadership Reform: The Development and Preparation of Leaders of Learning and Learners of Leadership* (2010, Emerald Group Publishing); *Educational Leadership Preparation: Innovation and Interdisciplinary Approaches to the Ed.D. and Graduate Education* (2010, Palgrave MacMillan, and coauthored with Gaetane Jean-Marie, 2010); *Leadership for Social Justice: Promoting Equity and Excellence Through Inquiry and Reflective Practice* (2008, Information Age Publishing); *Leadership and Intercultural Dynamics* (2009, Information Age Publishing and coauthored with John Collard). Dr. Normore's research has appeared in various journals including *Journal of School Leadership, Journal of Educational Administration, Values and Ethics in Educational Administration, Leadership and Organizational Development Journal, Canadian Journal of Education Administration and Policy, International Journal of Urban Educational Leadership, Educational Policy, International Electronic Journal for Leadership in Learning, International Journal of the Humanities,* and *Journal of Research on Leadership Education.*

Sylvester Pues has an MA in education and supervision, with specialization in special education. He has over 45 years experience working in education, especially focused on special populations. Mr. Pues has worked as a classroom teacher, a special education teacher and administrator, a college/university instructor, as well as in staff development, teacher and tutor training, correctional education consultation and training, grants writing and administration, and private tutoring. Mr. Pues is a sought-after speaker for conferences, workshops, and staff development at local, state, and national levels, and is a member of a variety of local, state, and national education focused research and policy-changing committees. For the past several years he has focused strongly on adults with severe reading problems such as dyslexia and ADD/ADHD, by providing screening, assessment and tutoring of individuals with severe learning and reading problems.

Sara A. Millman Silva has been a teacher at Harbor Community Adult School, part of the adult division of Los Angeles Unified School District, since 2003. She works with at-risk students, ages 15 to 65, in the high school diploma program and prepares adults to take the General Education Development test. Prior to becoming a teacher, she was a psychiatric social worker specializing in psychosocial mental health rehabilitation. Her areas of research include incarcerated-based education, charter school best practices, and the special educational needs of pregnant and parenting teens. Sara has conducted in-service workshops, presented at local, state and international conferences, and recently published in *Journal of Educational Administration*.

Raquel Warley, PhD, LCSW, is a member of the faculty at the School of Social Work at California State University, Los Angeles, and a former lecturer at Hunter College School of Social Work in New York City. Dr. Warley has over 15 years of clinical and research experience with people as violent offenders. She received a bachelor of arts degree in forensic psychology from John Jay College School of Criminal Justice in 1993. Following her undergraduate education she obtained three graduate degrees: a master of arts in criminal justice (John Jay College, 1995), a master of social work (Hunter, 2002), and a master of philosophy (City University of New York, Graduate Center, 2006). In May 2009, she completed her doctorate degree at the City University of New York. Her publications include "Trauma, Drugs, and Violence Among Juvenile Offenders" (*Journal of Psychoactive Drugs*, 2000), "Prior Involvement With Drugs, Illegal Activities, Groups, & Guns Among a Sample of Young Homicide Offenders" (*The Varities of Homicide and Its Research: Proceedings of the 1999 Meeting of the Homicide Research Working Group*, 2000), and "Male Honor Contest Violence: Implications for Forensic Mental Health Practice With Juvenile Offenders" (*Forensic Mental Health Newsletter*, 2010). Her first book, entitled *Juvenile Homicide: Fatal Assault or Lethal Intent?* (LFB Scholarly Publishing), will be distributed in the fall of 2011.

David Werner has been teaching in and administering prison education programs since 1976. He is the author of *Correctional Education: Theory and Practice* (1990, 2003, 2011), the national sourcebook for people teaching in prison and jail settings. He has written over two dozen articles on prison education and has spoken widely and internationally on prison postsecondary education. He also gives presentations on prison fiction and on maturation issues facing men. His book on that subject is *In The Shadow of the Hunter: What it Means to Be a Man* (1997). A recent chapter of his is "What I Learned in Prison," in *In the Borderlands: Learning to Teach in Prisons and Alternative Settings* (2008). Currently, he is the chair of the Department of English at the University of La Verne and director, since 1982 of the University's Educational Programs in Corrections.

Amy Widestrom holds an MA and PhD in political science from the Maxwell School at Syracuse University. Her main area of research interest is political disenfranchisement and disaffection in the United States. She spends much of her time researching political behavior, social and urban policy, economic inequality, and the political effects of incarceration. Dr. Widestrom is a contributing author to two forthcoming edited volumes, one on the Tea Party and the 2010 midterm elections and the second on cities in American history, and has presented at numerous conferences. She has also received many awards, including a Brookings Institution Research Fellowship, and an American Political Science Association Congressional Fellowship, during which time she worked for the Senate Committee on Banking, Housing, and Urban Affairs.Currently, Dr. Widestrom is an assistant professor of political science at California State University, Long Beach.